RISK MANAGEMENT FOR FINANCIAL PLANNERS

EDITION

CHANDLER
HILLMAN
MASSMANN
REITZ
RICHARDSON
THAMANN

The
National
Underwriter
Company

A Unit of Highline Media LLC

5081 Olympic Boulevard • Erlanger, KY 41018 • www.NUCO.com

Library of Congress Control Number: 2004109631

ISBN 0-87218-655-5

THE NATIONAL UNDERWRITER COMPANY

Copyright © 2004

The National Underwriter Company
P.O. Box 14367
Cincinnati, Ohio 45250-0367

First Edition

Second Printing

Printed in the United States of America

DEDICATION

Darlene K. Chandler

*To my husband, Bobby, with love and thanks
for his support and encouragement*

Bruce Hillman

For Dawn, Chelsea and Jacob

Diane W. Richardson

To Joe

ABOUT THE AUTHORS

Darlene K. Chandler

Darlene K. Chandler is Director of Advanced Markets Administration Support at Farm Bureau Financial Services in West Des Moines, Iowa where she works with annuities and qualified retirement plans in addition to other advanced markets concepts. Prior to joining Farm Bureau, Ms. Chandler was an editor with the National Underwriter Company contributing to *Tax Facts 1*, the *Advanced Sales Reference Service*, and the *Taxline* newsletter. She has written several other books on life insurance and advanced market topics, including *The Annuity Handbook*. Additionally, for the past 15 years, Ms. Chandler has served as an associate editor for the *Journal of Financial Service Professionals*. An honors graduate of Ball State University in Indiana where she majored in English, Ms. Chandler received her law degree from the University of Cincinnati. She holds the insurance industry designations of Chartered Life Underwriter (CLU) and Chartered Financial Consultant (ChFC) and maintains a registered principal license. Ms. Chandler lives in West Des Moines, Iowa, with her husband, Bob Schneider, and their son, James.

Bruce Hillman

Bruce Hillman, J.D., is editorial director of P&C publications for the Professional Publishing Division of The National Underwriter Company. During his National Underwriter career he has been staff writer, assistant editor, associate editor, and managing editor of the *FC&S Bulletins*. His columns on insurance coverage interpretation appear regularly in the Property and Casualty/Risk & Benefits Management Edition of the *National Underwriter* weekly magazine and in the *Claims* magazine. He is co-author of The National Underwriter Company's *Commercial Property Coverage Guide*. He has a Masters of mass communication degree from the University of South Carolina and a Law degree from Salmon P. Chase College of Law.

Susan Massmann

Susan Massmann is a staff writer for The National Underwriter Company's *FC&S Bulletins*. She earned a Bachelor of Arts degree in English in 1991 and obtained a paralegal certificate in 1995. Ms. Massmann contributes to a column entitled "Decisions of Note," which appears regularly in the National Underwriter Company's *Claims* magazine. She also contributes to the "FC&S Onlines" column in the Property and Casualty/Risk & Benefits Management Edition of the *National Underwriter* weekly magazine and co-wrote a 2002 publication on business income insurance.

Diana B. Reitz

Diana B. Reitz, CPCU, AAI, is editor of *The Risk Funding & Self-Insurance Bulletins (RF&S)* and associate editor with the Risk and Insurance Markets division of the National Underwriter Company, publisher of *The FC&S Bulletins*. She specializes in analytical articles and books in risk management, alternative financing arrangements, commercial insurance coverage interpretation, and insurance business topics. A graduate of the University of Maryland, Ms. Reitz earned a Masters degree in human resource management from St. Francis College, Loretto, Pennsylvania. She completed the Council of Agents and Brokers (CIAB) Agency Management program at The Wharton School, University of Pennsylvania. She is a member of the Risk and Insurance Management Society (RIMS).

Diane W. Richardson

Diane W. Richardson, CPCU, joined The National Underwriter Company in April 1994 as an assistant editor and was promoted to associate editor in 1996. She regularly researches, writes, and edits material for *The FC&S Bulletins*. She is a regular contributor to the Property and Casualty/Risk & Benefits Management Edition of the *National Underwriter* weekly magazine. In addition to editing *Service First!*, a National Underwriter Company book on customer service, Ms. Richardson has written books entitled *Insuring to Value* (with Marshall & Swift), *Homeowners Coverage Guide*, *Personal Umbrella Coverage Guide*, and *Home-Based Business Coverage Guide*. Before joining The National Underwriter Company, Ms. Richardson worked as a personal lines underwriter, state filing supervisor, and agent. She earned a Bachelor of Arts degree from the University of Vermont and a Masters degree in education from Harvard University.

David D. Thamann

David D. Thamann, J.D., ARM, CPCU, has been an FC&S editor since 1987. Before joining The National Underwriter Company, he was a claims supervisor and senior underwriter for American Druggists Insurance Company, a commercial property lead underwriter for Transamerica Insurance, and a commercial package underwriter for CNA and Safeco Insurance companies. Mr. Thamann graduated from Salmon P. Chase College of Law and Xavier University. The publications he wrote or contributed to include *Business Auto Coverage Guide*, *Personal Auto Coverage Guide*, *Workers Compensation Guide*, and *Commercial General Liability Supplement*. Mr. Thamann contributes to "FC&S Onlines," which is published monthly in the Property and Casualty/Risk & Benefits Management Edition of the *National Underwriter* weekly magazine and wrote an article on "Employee Mental Disability Claims and Insurance" for the *Northern Kentucky Law Review*.

PREFACE

One of the great facets of my job as Acquisitions Editor with The National Underwriter Company is visiting college and university campuses and meeting directly with professors, program directors, and students. In the course of my travels, as well as in countless email and phone conversations, two key topics emerge when discussing the usefulness and convenience of college textbooks for financial planners. The first is the level of treatment a textbook allows its subject matter, how thoroughly the authors cover the material at hand in order to provide students with enough analysis for academic and future, practical use. The second topic, frankly, is whether or not the textbooks cover all the topics contained within the CFP® Certification Examination Topic List in sufficient detail. With a pass rate percentage at or near the mid-fifties, and the high number of students still sitting for the exam, the need has never been greater for textbooks that cover all aspects of the CFP® Certification Examination.

Risk Management for Financial Planners has been written to provide students with the most comprehensive information available as relates to the CFP® Certification Examination. In combination with the *Tools & Techniques of Life Insurance Planning*, 100% of the CFP® Certification Examination Topics List is covered, bringing the most thorough and complete coverage of risk management and insurance to the classroom to date. For professors, *Risk Management for Financial Planners* provides all the classroom aides and materials you need – including an Instructor Manual, Test Bank, PowerPoint Slides, Correlation Table, and much more.

Risk Management for Financial Planners is the first book to present the fundamentals of risk management as a means to complement, benefit, and promote all areas of financial planning. With its focus on the basics of risk management, students will learn how the art of financial planning involves more than the core activities of making and growing a client's money, but also involves uncovering the means to protect their wealth, including:

- Insurance company and policy selection

- Overviews of business liability and health-related insurance

- End of Chapter questions to reinforce key concepts

- Appendices that provide an explanation of insurance company ratings and an insurance directory, as well as an extensive glossary of key Risk Management terms

In short, *Risk Management for Financial Planners* covers all areas of risk management, including all non-life insurance aspects of the insurance discipline. Given The National Underwriter Company's vast experience in life insurance areas, our authors and editors provided a comprehensive treatment of life insurance in its own textbook, and included the topics of risk management and insurance in a second. Together, these texts provide the authoritative resource for students – undergraduates, graduates, and professionals – in the familiar and user-friendly Q&A format of our **Tools & Techniques** series.

As a premier publisher of market-tested materials, NUCO stands in a unique position among publishers serving the academic community – to leverage our professional content in a way that students gain first-hand knowledge of the careers and fields they prepare to enter. In other words, when you adopt a National Underwriter textbook for your course, students not only receive the authoritative content in a given subject, but they are also exposed to information and materials they will need for future success in the workforce.

Daniel S. Jones
Acquisitions Editor

CONTENTS

Part 1:

GENERAL PRINCIPLES OF INSURANCE

Chapter 1

GENERAL PRINCIPLES OF RISK AND INSURANCE

DEFINITIONS AND CONCEPTS

What is *insurance?* The insurance transaction is a purchase of a contract (called the insurance policy) that on behalf of the purchaser pledges the payment of a sum-certain amount (the "premium") in exchange for a promise on behalf of the other party (the insurance company or "insurer") to provide restitution or indemnity arising from the occurrence of a loss. That is, the insurance transaction guards against the financial or economic repercussions arising from that occurrence.

Some say that in purchasing insurance on a piece of real property (such as a home or business premises) or against the happening of some liability-producing event (such as physicians' or attorneys' malpractice), the purchaser is buying "peace of mind"; i.e., the knowledge that the economic hardship of a loss will be transferred to another party – the insurance company selling the coverage.

One classic definition of insurance is "a device for reducing risk by combining a sufficient number of exposure units to make their individual losses collectively predictable." In other words, the losses of the few are shared among the premiums of the many.

This is an illustration of the "law of large numbers," which is the primary underpinning to the insurance mechanism. This is the principle that allows insurance to operate. The rule says that the more exposure units in the mix, the easier it becomes to predict the group's losses. Flip a coin three times and it might turn up heads each time. Flip a coin one million times and it will be more nearly evenly split between heads and tails. Take thousands and thousands and thousands of similarly situated units (like homeowners, for instance) and you will be able to predict the losses that will occur in the group – and create a pool of financial resources (payment of premiums) that allows for payment of the individual members of the group's losses – and allows the insurer to turn a profit on the transaction.

This highlights the risk-transfer aspect of insurance. Another aspect of the definition of insurance says that insurance is a risk management technique – a means of budgeting a relatively small, known amount up-front (the premium) in place of a large – and possibly catastrophic – unknown future event (a possible loss).

Therefore, an adequate definition must include *the transfer of risk to a third party* (the insurer); the accumulation of a fund to pay the losses; and a large enough number of similar exposure units (the insureds).

Another element to introduce into the insurance mix is the idea of fortuitousness. Non-fortuitous loss (those losses that are certain to occur) may not be insured. It is the concept of fortuitous acts that are insurable – a loss may or may not occur, so it may be insured; if the loss is certain to happen, it generally may not be the subject of an insurance policy.

Therefore, in sum, insurance promises to indemnify the customer for accidental losses caused by certain perils. In exchange, the customer promises to pay the premium.

The insurance company agrees to take on the insured's risk of loss. In exchange, the insured promises to pay the premium. The insurer takes the premiums of the many people who buy insurance and pools them. It invests those premiums to earn more money, to pay its employees, to pay losses, and to earn a profit.

PERIL, HAZARD AND RISK

Before proceeding, the terms *peril, hazard,* and *risk* should be defined. Although these three terms are often used synonymously by practitioners in the field, they do have differing technical meanings.

Risk may refer to uncertainty as to the outcome of an event when two or more possibilities exist; i.e., a building may stand or it may burn down. There is a risk. In property insurance, risk may also mean the physical units of property insured or the physical units of property at risk. For example, some might say, "the only risk the underwriter wants to take is fire on pig iron under water," or "that fireproof concrete block building is a good fire risk."

A *peril*, in property & casualty insurance terms, is a *cause of a possible loss*. For example, fire is a peril in property insurance, as is water damage, mold, earth movement, etc. A peril may be a covered peril (coverage is included under the policy) or an excluded peril (coverage is specifically excluded under the policy).

A *hazard* is a specific situation that increases the probability of the occurrence of loss arising from a peril or that may influence the extent of the loss. For example, fire, flood, and explosion are property perils – and liability itself is a peril under liability policies. Slippery floors, congested aisles, and oily rags in the open are hazards.

THE CONCEPT OF "INDEMNITY"

"Indemnify" is an important part of the insurance definition. It means, "to make whole again." In other words, insurance puts the person back in the same position he or she was in prior to the loss – no better, no worse.

Example. Joe's 1995 car (worth about $7,000) is damaged in an accident. The body shop estimates that it will cost $10,000 to fix it. If the insurer spends the $10,000 to repair the car, the insured will be better off after the loss than prior to it. When the insurer pays Joe the $7,000 he is "indemnified" for his loss – he is paid an amount equal to what he lost. It's a fair general statement that an item of property cannot be insured for more than it's worth.

INSURANCE VERSUS GAMBLING

Insurance is not wagering. So how does insurance differ from gambling? When you gamble, you take a chance of losing money. That is correct, but when you gamble you also may break even or come out ahead. There are three possible outcomes: a loss, no loss, or a profit.

With insurance, on the other hand, there are only two possible outcomes: a loss or no loss. When you insure a home, it will either burn down or it won't burn down. If you have insurance on it and there is a fire, the insurance will put you back in the same position you were in prior to the fire.

REVIEW OF DEFINITIONS

Let's conclude this first section with a review of some important terms:

Risk is the chance of economic loss – a chance of a fire to a home.

Insurance is a way to reduce risk by combining similar units and sharing the losses of the few among the premiums of the many. The chance of loss of a group of homeowners is pooled and the premiums paid by all of them are used to pay for the losses of the few.

Insured is the person buying the insurance – for example, the homeowner.

Premium is the consideration paid by the insured in exchange for the insurer's promise to indemnify.

Indemnify is what an insurance policy does – it puts the insured back in the position he or she was in prior to the loss – no better off, no worse.

Losses are financial – losses of money or things worth money.

Perils are causes of loss – such as fire, wind, theft, injury, etc.

Hazards are things that increase the chance of loss from a peril, such as the storage of flammable liquids.

OTHER NON-INSURANCE RESPONSES TO RISK

People buy insurance to help them manage the risks in their lives. However, insurance is only one way to handle those risks. Some other methods of risk management are:

Retention – when one does not purchase insurance and decides to assume the risk on his or her own. If a loss does not happen, the person saves the money that he or she would have spent on insurance.

A good example of retention is the decision not to purchase collision insurance on an older car. Retention requires that the insured do a careful analysis of what he or she can afford to lose. Some corporations use large retentions as a financial risk management strategy. For example, insurance coverage does not "kick in" until a loss has exceeded $25,000 or more. The insured saves on premium but has coverage for disastrous losses.

Avoidance – this involves either not doing something at all or getting rid of it and not doing it any more. By relying on public transportation, one avoids the physical damage and liability risks of car ownership. By selling off a dangerous operation, a company is avoiding future losses from that operation.

Control – is the minimizing of hazards, the things that increase the chance of loss. By putting a burglar alarm in the car, the owner is using the technique of control.

Non-insurance transfer – is the transfer of risk to someone other than an insurer.

Example. When renting tools, the customer signs a form promising to bring them back in the same condition. If he or she does not, the storeowner will charge the customer for those tools. The storeowner has used a non-insurance transfer to protect his property.

VOLUNTARY AND SOCIAL INSURANCE

In today's market, there are two broad types of insurers – social and voluntary.

Social insurers are government agencies that provide "social insurance" – protection against loss from unemployment, injuries, sickness, old age, and premature death.

The three major types of social insurance are:

1. Old Age, Survivors, and Disability (commonly known as "Social Security");

2. Workers Compensation; and

3. Unemployment Compensation.

What distinguishes social insurance from voluntary insurance is that participation is mandatory. The premiums paid are required by law and are typically collected via payroll deduction. Employees and employers must pay into the social security fund. Employers must purchase both workers compensation insurance and unemployment compensation insurance.

END OF CHAPTER REVIEW

1. "Peril," "hazard," and "risk" are interchangeable terms.

   True   False ✓

2. Social insurance is distinguished from voluntary insurance due to its mandatory participation.

   True ✓   False

3. Retention, avoidance, and control are risk management techniques that fall under the insurance transfer device.

   True ✗   False ✓

4. The Law of Large Numbers states that the larger the number of units in a mix, the less predictable the outcome of an event will be.

   True   False ✓

5. Three major types of social insurance are homeowners insurance, workers compensation insurance, and unemployment insurance.

   True   False ✓

6. Avoidance is a risk management technique that involves not doing a certain thing in order to lessen the chance of loss from that activity.

   True ✓   False

Chapter 2

LEGAL ASPECTS OF INSURANCE AND RISK MANAGEMENT

THE NATURE OF THE INSURANCE POLICY

Insurance is a different kind of animal, contractually speaking. Whereas, at law generally parties are free to bargain at will with no restrictions, even about illegal transactions (although a contract pertaining to an illegal act will be held unenforceable as the court will not involve itself with illegal matters), such is not the case with the insurance policy. This is because the public policy or social aspect of insurance has been held to be so important to the efficient operation of society that certain principles operate in insurance policy interpretation that are not so with other types of contracts.

THE PRINCIPLE OF INDEMNITY

The insurance contract relies on the principle of indemnity. Its purpose is to "indemnify" the policyholder in the event of a covered loss. Indemnify means "to make whole" or "to reimburse." Ideally, after a loss an insured should not be in a worse or a better position than he or she was prior to the loss.

Example. ABC manufactures widgets in a factory that is ten years old. A tornado takes off the roof. With a 20-year lifespan, the roof has lost one-half of its use. Instead of putting on a ten-year old roof, the insurer will put on a new roof, but reduce its payment by 50%. ABC is indemnified for its loss.

One concept that seems contrary to the principle of indemnity is "replacement cost." Some property policies, the homeowners form, for example, pay to replace damaged property with property of "like kind and quality" regardless of actual cash value or worth.

Example. A homeowner loses his 15-year old roof to a tornado. His homeowners insurer doesn't go out and try to find 15-year old shingles to make the repairs. Rather, they put back new shingles and whatever else is needed to "replace" the damaged roof.

While the concept may seem off kilter with the principle of indemnity, it is statistically calculable under the Law of Large Numbers and developed to deal with a number of problems that arise under a purely actual cash value (actual worth) adjustment of a loss.

INSURABLE INTEREST

Another important aspect of the insurance transaction is that a party must have an *insurable interest* in property in order to enter into an insurance contract or policy regarding that property. To allow otherwise would encourage speculation (for instance, buying life insurance coverage on a complete stranger) or even encourage wrongful acts (the ability to buy fire insurance coverage on a building where the policy is written for a party with no financial or economic interest in that property might increase the *morale* risk of arson).

An insured must have a legitimate financial interest in the property to be insured. While the interest does not have to rise to the level of ownership, its loss must cost the insured money.

For example, a person can insure a lease interest or property in his care for which he is legally liable. Therefore, renters, leaseholders, and bailees have an insurable interest in nonowned property in their possession or care, and may therefore insure that property.

OTHER INSURANCE CONTRACT CHARACTERISTICS

An insurance contract is a personal contract between the insurer and the insured. While all contracts require "good faith" dealings between the parties, insurance requires more. It requires "utmost good faith."

Because of the importance of insurance to the financial security of people, and of society itself, insurance contracts have a public interest component that other types of private contracts do not. It is of interest to the general public good to hold insurers to higher standards of good faith and fair dealing than in other types of private contracts.

Insurance contracts differ from other types of private contracts between people or businesses because of this public interest. Insurance contracts are aleatory and are contracts of adhesion.

There is disparate bargaining power between the parties – on the one hand, a large and legally sophisticated insurance company, on the other, a small and legally unsophisticated consumer. Because of these things, courts have allowed extra-contractual damages for the breach of an insurance contract by an insurer – including punitive damages. This is something not available in the general contract law area.

As mentioned above, insurance contracts are aleatory. This is because the dollar amount to be exchanged is unequal.

Black's Law Dictionary says that an aleatory contract is one "in which promise by one party is conditioned on a fortuitous [unexpected or accidental] event." In other words, before an insurance contract performs, a fortuitous event must happen to the insured.

As an example, a policy covering a $200,000 home may cost $700 per year. But, if that home burns to the ground, the insurer will pay $200,000 for the home. It will also pay for any lost personal property and for the homeowner to live elsewhere while a new home is being built.

On the one hand, a party to the contract (the insured) may get nothing for his $700 but peace of mind. On the other hand, her $700 might buy $200,000 or more of worth, in the event of a catastrophe to the insured. Insurance is not a quid-pro-quo, dollar-for-dollar contract.

Most contracts are bargained – both parties have input as to the final contents. An insurance contract, however, is different. It is written and drawn by the insurer and offered to the customer on a "take it or leave it" basis. This is what is meant by a contract of adhesion

Since insurance contracts are written this way, courts interpret any ambiguity in the language strictly against the insurer. The insured gets the benefit of any unclearness of the phrasing. If the insurer wanted a specific meaning of a contract provision, it had the opportunity to write it that way. Where the policy does not clearly say what the insurer wants, the benefit of the doubt goes to the insured.

INSURANCE REGULATION AND CONTRACT REQUIREMENTS

Early in the 20th century, there were court and legislative attempts to bring insurance (as interstate commerce) under the purview of the federal government. This resulted in the 1945 McCarran-Ferguson Act, which allowed the individual states to regulate insurance and insurance companies within their borders. Although there have been movements to federalize insurance regulation, to date, McCarran-Ferguson still holds.

Up until 1887, no standard fire (or property) policy existed. In that year, the New York legislature drafted a form for use in that state. It was quickly adopted by insurers in New York and by other states. This was the beginning of insurance policy regulation, wherein the states set various statutory requirements that all property policies written within the state must adhere.

The New York policy was updated in 1918 and again in 1943. It is that version, "The 1943 New York Standard Fire Policy" that was adopted by nearly all the states, with only minor variations. It was more flexible than its predecessors, as it allowed for the addition of endorsements to modify the coverage.

The "1943 Policy" was the basis for all property insurance until the 1976 "simplified language" homeowners policy and the simplified commercial policies of the 1980's.

Even though the "1943 Policy" has been replaced by modular policies, many of its basic provisions may still be found in the policies in use today. In fact, some states still use the 1943 New York policy as the base requirement for property policies. Until recently, some states even required it to be attached to a "simplified language" homeowners policy.

INSURANCE POLICY CHARACTERISTICS

All property and casualty insurance policies contain the following: the declarations page, the insuring agreement, exclusions, conditions, and endorsements, if any.

The first page of an insurance policy is the declarations or the "dec page." It contains basic information about the policy, such as: name of the insurer and agent, name and address of the insured, policy period, limits of liability, forms applicable, and premium. This is who is being insured, for how long, and at what price.

The insuring agreement is the heart of the policy. This is the coverage pledge. It states what the insurer will do – indemnify the insured for covered losses – in exchange for the insured's payment of the premium.

The insuring agreement from a typical homeowners policy reads: "We will provide the insurance described in this policy in return for the premium and compliance with all applicable provisions of this policy."

It is important to know and understand what an insurance policy covers. It is also just as important to know what the policy does not cover. The exclusions section states what losses are not covered by a particular policy.

There are several reasons for insurance policy exclusions:

- The loss is not commercially insurable – such as flood or war.

- The exposure is more appropriately covered in another type of policy – such as automobile, aircraft, or workers compensation.

- The loss is wholly or partially in the control of the insured – such as the exclusion of marring and scratching damage to certain types of personal property.

- The loss is more appropriately covered by an endorsement to the basic policy – such as a jewelry floater endorsed to a homeowners policy.

- Small, predictable losses that are relatively expensive for the insurer to process – such as damage to a home or its contents done by a pet.

The conditions section lays out the rules and procedures that must be followed by both the insurer and the insured. These include:

- How to file a claim;

- How and when each party may cancel the contract;

- What each party must do after a loss; and

- How disagreements between the parties are handled.

While most insurance policies are rather "generic" in nature, a "generic" policy may not meet the needs of all insureds. "Endorsements" provide a way to tailor a basic policy to better meet the needs of a particular insured. Coverages can be added or deleted.

Example. One homeowner may have a valuable stamp collection; another may need liability coverage for a boat; a third needs liability coverage for a summer home on the beach. Each of these special situations can be handled on a homeowners policy with the use of special endorsements.

INSURANCE POLICY ANALYSIS

When analyzing any property and casualty insurance policy, the following eight questions are useful:

1. Who is insured?

2. What property or activity is insured?

3. What locations are insured?

4. What is the time period of the coverage?

5. What are the perils insured against?

6. Are direct losses, indirect losses, or both types insured?

7. What are the coverage limits?

8. Are there any miscellaneous clauses?

Each of these items are matched against the particular provisions and phrasing of the insurance policy to determine coverage.

END OF CHAPTER REVIEW

1. An insurance policy is "aleatory" in nature, meaning that the parties had disparate bargaining power in its formation.

    True ·   False ✓

2. Parties to insurance contracts are free to bargain for the conditions and provisions in the policy in an unrestricted fashion.

    True   False ✓

3. In order to enter into a contract of insurance for a piece of real property, the insurable interest requires an ownership interest by the insured in that property.

    True   False ✓

4. The insurance industry is regulated on a state-by-state basis.

    True ✓   False

5. A homeowners insurance policy is a contract of adhesion, meaning that it is offered by an insurer to a consumer on a "take it or leave it basis."

    True ✓   False

6. Provisions in a contract of adhesion are construed against the contract's drafter.

    True ✓   False

7. The indemnity principle states that an insured must be returned to a position of betterment in the event of a covered loss.

    True   False ✓

8. The declaration page of the insurance policy is where the insurer declares what perils are excluded under the contract.

    True   False ✓

Chapter 3

INSURANCE POLICY SELECTION

WHAT IS IT?

Insurance policies are contracts that are used to transfer the consequences of risk from one party, the insured, to another party, the insurer. The insurer may be an insurance company, a risk retention group, or another type of alternative risk transfer mechanism. For the purposes of this book, we confine the discussion to insurance policies that are provided by traditional insurance companies.

Insurance policies are used as a means of budgeting a relatively small, known amount up-front (the premium) in place of funding a much greater amount at the time of a large – and possibly catastrophic – unknown future event (a possible loss). Individuals and businesses may use insurance to protect their own property – homes, commercial buildings, autos, and other property. This is called first-party coverage. They also may purchase insurance to protect themselves against legal liability for injuring other people or damaging their property. This is called third-party coverage.

Many insurance companies provide both first- and third-party coverage in the same policy. For example, a typical homeowners insurance policy provides first-party protection on the insured's house as well as providing third-party personal liability coverage for injury or damage to visitors for which the homeowner is legally liable. For example, if a visitor falls on an icy sidewalk that the homeowner failed to clear, the homeowners policy will pay damages assessed because of the homeowner's negligence in maintaining a safe sidewalk. Likewise, auto policies can provide both first-party coverage on the insured's own vehicles as well as third-party coverage for injury or damage the insured causes others through the use of the insured's vehicle.

Insurance is based on the law of large numbers. Insurers must be certain that they have enough similar exposure units insured so that they can accurately predict these losses. The law of large numbers is based on the regularity of events. An insurer collects premiums from the many, pools those premiums, and out of that pool pays its insureds' losses and company expenses. Anything left is profit to be reinvested or distributed to shareholders.

Length of Time Required

Individuals may be able to purchase personal insurance policies in a relatively short period of time. They typically complete an application for coverage, sign it, and submit it through a licensed agent to apply for coverage with an insurance company. Insurance is regulated by individual states, and insurance agents or brokers must meet licensing requirements that are established by those states. Independent agents represent a number of insurance companies, so they may submit the application to several insurers in order to obtain the broadest coverage at the best available premium. Some agents work as exclusive agents or direct writers. Exclusive agents represent only one insurance company. Direct writers are employees of insurance companies and, as such, sell only that particular company's policies. When exclusive agents or direct writers are used, the application will be sent only to the company that is represented.

Small, less complicated businesses also may be able to obtain insurance coverage in a relatively short period of time. The process for them is similar to that for individuals. Large, complex businesses typically require much more time to obtain coverage. This is because the number of options available to them – in regard to coverage, premium, interested insurance companies, and premium payment options – increases as the size of the business increases. In other words, the larger the business, the higher the premium and the more options available. Because of this, it may take several months to design, quote, and bind a complex commercial insurance program for a large business.

Most agents have binding authorities with the companies they represent. As such, they may accept the application and bind the coverage at the same time. Coverage will remain in force – under binder – until either a policy is issued or the insurer declines to write the policy. During this time, coverage is available under the binder just the same as if the policy had already been issued.

Risk Tolerance

Risk tolerance typically refers to the amount of risk that an individual or a corporation wants to bear on its own, without transferring it to another party, such as an insurance company. For example, a homeowner with a small tolerance for risk may purchase a homeowners policy with only a $250 deductible on first-party damage to her home. She will purchase high limits of personal liability insurance and may purchase an umbrella liability policy, which provides additional personal liability coverage above and beyond that provided by her homeowners policy.

An individual with a high risk tolerance may elect a $2,000 deductible on damage to his home in order to save premium dollars. He is willing to risk paying up to $2,000 if his home is damaged.

In like fashion, corporations need to decide how much risk they want to retain and how much they want to transfer to the insurance company. Corporations retain risk through high deductibles, self-insuring a portion of their exposures, and even deciding not to insure an exposure at all. Some may be forced into a position of retaining a high degree of risk on exposures that are very difficult or expensive to insure. For example, a business may not insure a product it manufactures because insurance is too expensive. Instead, it may set up a self-insured program to fund liabilities it may incur because of the product.

BUSINESS USES

Insurance policies are used by property owners to protect the items they own. If a home or office building is destroyed by fire, for example, the insurance policy that covers the structure is called upon to pay to rebuild it. Banks and finance companies that issue mortgages and property loans often require that the property being financed be covered by insurance. This serves as a guarantee that the property being used to back up, or collateralize, the loan will be replaced if it is destroyed by a cause of loss that is covered by the policy.

Insurance also is used to protect the financial integrity of individuals and companies that may be held legally liable for injuring others or damaging property that is owned by others. Insurance policies that cover an individual's personal liability exposures or a company's general liability exposures provide coverage for both defense costs and damages. So, if a business is sued by an individual who slips and falls on the business premises, the company's general liability insurance policy typically will pay to defend the lawsuit. If damages are assessed, the policy also pays them, absent policy exclusions that preclude coverage.

Insurance provides a vital link in the financial stability of both individuals and businesses. Without it, money might not be available to repair damaged property and get businesses back into operation. Other insureds may be forced into bankruptcy if they are sued, found legally liable, and do not have sufficient financial means to pay the damages.

ADVANTAGES

1. Insurance presents an individual or business with the opportunity to incur a known, up-front cost (the premium) in exchange for the insurer's taking on the large, possibly catastrophic unknown (the potential for a large loss).

2. Securing an insurance policy may satisfy a contractual requirement. If a retail customer leases a building, the lease will probably require that he carry insurance that will cover any damage done to the building. The vast majority of all types of contracts include insurance requirements.

3. Banks and other financial institutions usually require that insurance be purchased to protect their interest in the buildings on which they hold mortgages. Loans on other types of property, such as cars, furnishings, and equipment, often are conditional on evidence that insurance on the items is in place.

4. Most insurance policies provide that the insurance company adjust and pay claims on behalf of the insured business. This takes a burden off company managers, who probably are not experts in claim-management procedures.

5. Insurance may be used to satisfy certain statutory or regulatory requirements. For example, state laws in all but Texas require that insurance be purchased to cover workers compensation exposures, unless the business is a qualified workers compensation self-insurer.

DISADVANTAGES

1. Spending money for insurance means that the insured has that much less to invest elsewhere – whether for home improvement, vacations, or retirement savings in the case of individuals or in new plant and equipment, new personnel, new training methods, or the acquisition of other businesses in the case of business owners. If the individual can

measure that loss, perhaps a trade-off can be made between less insurance and an aggressive investment policy.

2. Unfortunately, even the broadest of insurance policies will not cover every loss. Some individuals may be under the false impression that all claims will be covered by their insurance policies, but that is not possible. The selection of a good intermediary (see below) will help ease this situation.

3. The way in which most intermediaries are compensated – through commissions on the insurance they sell – has given rise to concern among some insureds about possible conflict of interest. An alternative is to compensate the agent on a fee basis.

4. Despite the advent of simplified insurance policies, with language that is designed to be more easily understood, insurance policies are difficult to read and understand. It is easy to assume coverage is broader and more complete than it actually is.

DESIGN FEATURES

Types of Insurance Intermediaries

As noted previously, property and casualty insurance is regulated by the states, which license intermediaries to sell and service insurance policies. These intermediaries typically are called agents or brokers. There are several types of agents and brokers:

- Independent agents
- Exclusive agents
- Employee agents
- Direct-writing agents
- Brokers
- Surplus lines brokers

Independent Agents

A producer who is an *independent agent* is an independent businessperson who represents the insurer. In fact, he typically is the agent of several insurers. The independent agent is appointed by insurers to represent them in a given state (although an insurance agent may hold licenses to transact insurance business in multiple states). Independent agents usually are compensated with commissions that insurance companies pay.

The advantage of working with an independent agent is that with the availability of several markets, the agent should be able to find a good match for the customer – both in terms of coverage and price. Examples of insurers who market their products through independent agents are the Cincinnati Insurance Companies, Fireman's Fund Insurance Co., and The Hartford.

Exclusive Agents

The exclusive agent is also an independent businessperson. However, exclusive agents represent only one insurance company. Unlike the independent agent, the exclusive agent may or may not own policy expirations (i.e., renewal rights), depending on the company. Either party may terminate the arrangement at any time. State Farm Insurance® is an example of an insurer that markets its products through exclusive agents. Exclusive agents usually are compensated with commissions that their company pays.

Employee Agents

Employee agents are licensed as insurance agents (producers) but are employees of the insurer. They do not own their expirations and are usually employed at will by the insurer. Liberty Mutual insurance is an example of an insurer that markets its products through employee agents. Employee agents usually are compensated through a salary paid by the company for which they work.

Direct–Writing Agents

A direct-writing agent is an employee agent that only does business over the telephone or Internet. Insurers that use direct-writing agents often are referred to as *direct writers*. GEICO is an example of a direct writer. Direct writers usually are compensated with salary.

Brokers

A broker is considered an agent of the insured. In general, there is no agency contract between the insurer and the broker. There may or may not be a formal service agreement between the broker and the insured. The broker has permission to place coverage with certain insurers. When a customer goes to a broker, the broker will try to place the customer with one of the companies with whom he has a relationship. However, the broker usually may not bind coverage for that customer without the express permission of the insurer.

In larger commercial settings, brokers have the advantage of finding the best match for the applicant, without being tied to any company or system. Brokers may be compensated by insurance policy commissions or by fees paid by the businesses they represent.

Surplus Lines Brokers

A surplus lines broker is a specialized insurance producer. A surplus lines broker has relationships with *nonadmitted insurers*. Nonadmitted insurers are not subject to rate and form regulation by the various states. An insured cannot approach a surplus lines broker directly. Rather, a licensed intermediary must approach the surplus lines broker.

Premiums paid to a surplus lines company are not protected by state guaranty funds. So, if a surplus lines insurer becomes insolvent and not able to pay claims, the insured has no way of recovering premium that it may have paid. The insured also may have to assume responsibility for any outstanding claims.

Surplus lines brokers usually are compensated with insurance company commissions.

Design Features

The insurance policy is a contract that spells out the terms and conditions of coverage. Insurance differs from other contracts in that it typically is not negotiated by parties that are on equal footing. Most insureds, other than very large businesses, have little, if any, say in the content or language of the policy. Most insurance contracts are written by the insurance company, filed for approval in the states in which the policies are being used, and then offered to potential customers on a take-it-or-leave-it basis. Large businesses may negotiate for specific coverage wording, or they may seek out a nonadmitted insurance company that may be able to offer customized coverage language.

Thus, an insurance policy is a *contract of adhesion* – the insurer has drafted the contract and the insured must adhere to it. Although this may not seem advantageous to the insured, it is important to remember that, because

> ### General Rule
> The insurance departments in most states do review policy language and approve or disapprove wording. But most insureds have little or no input into the policy language.

of this, courts typically interpret insurance policies in the light most favorable to the insured. If the insurer was not clear about the intent, the benefit of the doubt must be given to the insured. Coverage grants will be interpreted broadly and exclusions narrowly. Also, any undefined words will be given their ordinary meaning.

It is also a generally true statement that the states have established minimum coverage requirements that insurance policies must meet. Most of these statutes are based on the coverage that was statutorily mandated in the 1943 New York Standard Fire Policy. States have adjusted their requirements in the intervening years but still set minimum requirements. These requirements involve such items as minimum notices of cancellation and nonrenewal, allowable exclusions, and policy terms.

States set minimum standards because of the so-called public policy aspect of the insurance transaction. The importance of the insurance contract to the general welfare of the public-at-large requires that insurance transactions meet a high standard of review. In addition to the adhesion contract aspects of the insurance policy, there are also other differences between the insurance policy and other contracts. One of the most important differences is that breach of a contract in a usual business situation does not allow the breached party to recover punitive damages awards. However, the issue of bad faith in insurance transactions has developed at law such that insureds that can prove breach of an insurance contract by an insurer can, in some circumstances, sue for and recover punitive damages or bad faith dealing awards.

PARTS OF THE INSURANCE POLICY

Insureds should review their policies when they are issued. The various parts of a property and casualty insurance policy are discussed in the following section of this chapter.

Declarations Page

The first section of the policy is the *declarations page*. This section of the policy contains much important information – it is a guide to the rest of the policy. Items that are included on either the common policy declarations or the declarations page of a specific coverage part include:

1. *Named insured* – In most insurance policies the named insured has special rights and responsibilities above and beyond those of an *insured*. One responsibility is the payment of the premium. One right is the right to be notified of policy cancellation. Some policies automatically confer insured status on all family members or all subsidiaries of a company. However, the best advice is, of course, to read the policy.

2. *Address* – This is the mailing address to which premium notices, policy changes, and cancellation notices should be sent.

3. *Address of insured location* – Coverage, especially property insurance, may apply to only certain locations or properties of the insured. Those locations are listed here.

4. *Forms and endorsements that apply* – This section lists the coverage forms and endorsements that apply. For example, the property coverage part, auto part, or liability part form numbers would be listed. In general, the coverage *form* provides the basic insuring language. *Endorsements* modify the contract by broadening or limiting coverage and must be read in context with the coverage part. For example, one endorsement may exclude coverage for certain activities or locations of an insured. Another type of endorsement may add coverage for an additional insured, loss payee, or mortgage company that has a financial interest in the insured business or property.

5. *Policy period* – This states when coverage begins and when it ends. Most policies begin at 12:01 a.m. on the inception date of the policy and end at 12:01 a.m. on the expiration date. The exact time is important when determining which insurance policy applies to claims that may happen near the expiration date of a policy.

6. *Agent's name and address* – This is the information on the intermediary used to secure coverage. This is where the insured should turn with any questions.

7. *Name of insurance company* – This denotes the insurer. The insured needs to verify that it is the same as on any binder or the same name discussed with the intermediary. The financial rating should be checked again, as well.

8. *Premium* – This is the amount the customer pays for coverage. If it differs from what was agreed upon, clarification should be obtained. The premium section may also show a breakdown into a payment plan.

Coverage Parts

If all of the items on the declarations page are correct, then move to the policy itself. Does the policy presented to the insured match the binder and insurance specifications?

In general, an insurance policy is made up of an insuring agreement that describes the property or liability risk covered, a definitions section, exclusions, and policy conditions. Any applicable endorsements are also attached to the policy. Each section should be reviewed with the agent or broker delivering the policy to see that it matches the specifications. The insured should become familiar with the policy exclusions, particularly as it is this section of the form that is frequently misunderstood and troublesome.

Use of Deductibles

One way to keep the premium down is through the use of higher *deductibles*. A deductible is the amount for which the insured is responsible on any property loss before the insurance pays. If the property deductible is $1,000 and the loss is $10,000, the insured would pay $1,000 and the insurer, $9,000.

A higher deductible shows the insurer that the insured is willing to share in a greater portion of any loss, and the insurer rewards this willingness with a reduced rate. However, the individual or business must be certain that in case of a loss, it can quickly and easily come up with the amount of the deductible. The important thing is how much premium is being saved for choosing the higher deductible. In some cases, insurers may insist that an insured assume a higher deductible or it will decline to write the business.

WHERE CAN I FIND OUT MORE ABOUT IT?

1. Many insurers that specialize in particular industries or groups may have developed checklists. Other sources include coverage applications, which ask many of the questions that are necessary to determine what exposures need to be addressed.

2. Council of Insurance Agents and Brokers (CIAB), http://www.ciab.com/index.jsp.

3. Independent Insurance Agents and Brokers of America (IIABA), www.iiaa.org.

4. Professional Insurance Agents association, http://www.piaonline.org/.

5. *The FC&S Bulletins* (Cincinnati, OH: The National Underwriter Company, updated monthly), www.nationalunderwriter.com.

END OF CHAPTER REVIEW

1. Insurance is based on the law of large numbers, which means that an insurance company must insure a large number of similar types of exposures in order to accurately predict future losses.

   True ✓   False

2. An independent insurance agent represents only one insurance company and is an employee of that company.

   True   False ✓

3. Surplus lines brokers must be used when risk managers want to place their business with an admitted insurance carrier.

   True   False ✓

4. Choosing a higher deductible will result in a lower premium if all other factors remain consistent.

   True ✓   False

5. An insurance binder represents the insurance coverage that is purchased until the actual insurance policy is issued.

   True ✓   False

6. First-party coverage is used to protect insured businesses against the legal liability they may incur for injuring other people or damaging their property.

   True   False ✓

7. Exclusive agents represent a number of insurance companies but may not solicit quotations for insurance coverage from more than one company at a time.

   True   False ✓

8. One of the difficulties in trying to use insurance to transfer risk is that insurance policies often are difficult to read and understand, so often policyholders misunderstand the extent of coverage.

   True ✓   False

9. A broker is considered an agent of the insurance company.

   True   False ✓

Chapter 4

INSURANCE COMPANY SELECTION

Insurance is one of the principal means by which individuals and businesses transfer the financial uncertainty of losses resulting from risks such as damage to property, employee dishonesty, or risk of liability arising out of the insured's operations. Insurance policies transfer risk to the insurance company for financial consideration – the premium.

WHAT IS IT?

Insurance is a risk-transfer mechanism. Property and casualty insurance companies can be grouped into four types:

- stock insurance companies;

- mutual insurance companies;

- reciprocal exchanges; and

- Lloyd's associations.

Stock and Mutual Companies

Stock and mutual companies are the most prevalent type of traditional insurance mechanism.

Stock insurance companies are owned by the stockholders and are organized as for-profit corporations. Capital is derived from stockholders, and any profits or losses from operations are enjoyed by or borne by the stockholders.

Mutual insurance companies are owned by their policyholders. Profits in excess of the premiums charged are returned to the policyholders in the form of lower rates or as *dividends*. Mutual insurance companies cannot sell shares of stock through the capital markets, as stock companies can, so it is more difficult for mutual companies to raise capital than for stock insurers. There are two basic methods available to overcome this disadvantage – *demutualization* and merger. Demutualization is the conversion of a mutual insurance operation to a stock insurance structure. Merger is the consolidation of two or more companies into a single company.

Reciprocal Exchanges

In concept, *reciprocal exchanges*, which also are described as interinsurance exchanges, are unincorporated arrangements in which one policyholder agrees to participate in insuring all other policyholders. In exchange, the other policyholders insure that policyholder.

Lloyd's Associations

Lloyd's associations are yet another approach to providing insurance. Lloyd's of London is the most famous Lloyd's association. It is not an insurance company. It provides facilities where insurance can be transacted with its members. Originally, insurance was transacted by individuals known as *names* that would underwrite small portions of others' risks.

Risk Retention Groups

Risk retention groups (RRGs) are organizations formed to spread the liability risks of groups of similar businesses. In 1981, Congress gave businesses the right to form RRGs to provide products and completed operations liability coverage to members of groups. In 1986, the Product Liability Risk Retention Act of 1981 was substantially expanded when Congress permitted risk retention and purchasing groups to delve into a broader range of liability coverages, including liability arising from a business's premises and operations in addition to products and completed operations. *Purchasing groups* are similar to RRGs, but they do not actually provide insurance. They are simply groups that form with a main purpose of purchasing insurance on a group basis.

REGULATION: FEDERAL AND STATE LAW

Insurance companies are regulated on a state-by-state basis. Each state has an insurance department, which is headed by an insurance commissioner. The primary responsibility of the insurance departments is to protect consumers by regulating insurance coverage and monitoring the solvency of insurance companies. State insurance departments regulate the coverage wording and insurance policy structure of insurers that are admitted to do business in their jurisdictions. The insurance departments also monitor insurers that do business in their states, even if they are not fully licensed there.

State insurance commissioners formed the National Association of Insurance Commissioners (NAIC) to coordinate the regulation of multistate insurers. The NAIC supports the development of uniform practices and policies when appropriate.

The state-regulation of property and casualty insurance differs from the federal oversight of employee benefits. The Employee Retirement Income and Security Act (ERISA) typically governs the provision of employee benefits coverage. ERISA is a federal law.

Although NAIC helps to coordinate the state regulation of property and casualty insurers, there are differences from state to state on various matters. There has been a great deal of discussion in recent years about changing from a state to a federal system of insurance company regulation. There also has been interest in offering optional federal charters for insurance companies, as well as retaining the current state-based system.

DESIGN FEATURES

Types of Insurance Arrangements

The four types of organizational structure of insurance coverage were discussed previously. In addition to organization structure, insureds should consider the following when selecting an insurance company:

- status as an admitted or nonadmitted company;

- financial strength;

- size;

- claims-paying philosophy; and

- ability to provide support services.

Admitted and Nonadmitted Insurers

Insurance companies are either *admitted* or *nonadmitted* on a state-by-state basis.

Admitted companies are licensed to conduct business within a given state and are subject to state regula-

tion and *guaranty funds*. (Guaranty funds assume the liabilities of insolvent insurers and handle the payment of claims that may be filed or come due after insolvency. They do not guarantee that all claims will be paid but, rather, attempt to uniformly manage the remaining claim-paying responsibilities of insolvent insurance companies.) Nonadmitted companies are not licensed in particular states or territories and are not directly regulated by the states in which they are not admitted.

Financial Strength

It is critical to carefully evaluate the financial strength of any insurance company that is being considered for coverage. In fact, financial strength is perhaps the most important aspect of selection. A number of companies publish financial strength ratings. Each of them employs a proprietary rating scale and publishes detailed reports in areas such as management, the use of reinsurance, the states in which the insurers are licensed to transact insurance, and the nature of the insurers' operations. Among the main rating agencies are A.M. Best, Fitch Ratings, Moody's, Standard & Poor's, and Weiss Ratings. Each of these companies monitor the financial stability of insurance companies and offer guidance on their ability to adequately handle the accounts the insurers write. The five publish their own rating grades, which many agents and brokers use when selecting an insurer.

There are other methods to gauge financial strength. Among them are trade publications, networks and associations of agents, and insurance buyer organizations.

Despite the fact that insurance carrier financial strength is monitored by multiple rating organizations, some insurance company failures have not been anticipated. When insurance companies become insolvent, the claims that are the subject of their coverage policies often are not paid or, if paid, may not be paid in full, depending upon the amount of capital available.

Risk–Based Capital

The NAIC has developed a *Risk-Based Capital (RBC) system* for analyzing the financial strength of both property and casualty and life insurance companies. This approach is designed to determine if an insurer has an adequate amount of capital, which is called *policyholders' surplus*. Policyholders' surplus is similar to owners' equity for noninsurance companies. It is the difference between the insurance company's admitted assets and its liabilities or the amount that may be used to meet the insurance company's contractual obligations in the event of insolvency.

Before the RBC system was adopted, adequacy of capital was determined by comparing the ratio of written premium to surplus (owners' equity) method. Under the *written premium ratio system*, sometimes called the *Kenny Rule*, an insurer was assumed to have adequate capital if the ratio of its written premium to surplus was below some target, such as 3 to 1. However, the RBC system was developed because of concerns that the use of one standard ratio was not appropriate to determine the surplus needs of all insurers.

The purpose of the RBC system is not to provide ratings for companies, but rather to provide benchmarks. The system determines a desirable capital level that is based on the risk generated by each insurer's investment philosophy, book of business, and cash flow pattern. If the company fails to meet the target, it is given closer scrutiny.

There are two RBC formulas. One applies to life insurers and the other to property and casualty insurers. The risks examined for property and casualty insurers include:

1. asset risk;

2. credit risk;

3. underwriting risk; and

4. all other business risk.

Asset risk is the likelihood that the value of the insurer's investment portfolio will decline. Property and casualty credit risk is the chance that the insurer will not collect premiums, reinsurance, and other receivables. Underwriting risk is that premium rates and/or loss reserves will be inadequate to cover losses as they reach maturity. All other business risk includes items such as an unusually large guaranty fund assessment. Off-balance-sheet risks, such as excessive premium growth, guarantees of parents, and affiliate obligations also are examined.

The temptation to use only RBC to rate and rank companies should be avoided. It is only one of several techniques that may be used to judge financial strength and prospective solvency on respective insurance companies.[1]

Insurance Regulatory Information System (IRIS)

The NAIC Insurance Regulatory Information System (IRIS) represents a strengthening of the insurance regulatory process. It is part of a system designed to provide state insurance departments with an integrated approach to screening and analyzing the financial condition of insurance companies. IRIS was developed by a committee of state insurance regulators and is intended to assist state insurance departments allocate resources to the insurers in greatest need of regulatory attention. IRIS, however, is not intended to replace the in-depth financial analysis and examinations that state insurance departments conduct.[2] The IRIS ratios are a series of calculations that are used to develop and gauge the acceptability of various financial measures. The adequacy of policyholders' surplus is a key indicator of an insurer's ability to absorb above-average losses, and IRIS ratios help to gauge the adequacy of policyholders' surplus.

Figure 4.1 outlines the ratio formulas and range of acceptable values. Additional information on IRIS measurements is available from the NAIC (www.naic.org).

Size

Information published by the various rating organizations includes details on the size of individual insurance companies. Size is important because it reflects the assets that are available to back the liabilities of insurance companies.

Claims–Paying Philosophy

Some insurance companies are well known for erring in favor of their policyholders when coverage is not clear-cut. Other insurers have a reputation for contesting claim payments whenever possible. An insurance company's claims-paying philosophy can only be measured subjectively.

Support Services

One of the key factors in the choice of insurers is how well they can support their policyholders by offering loss control and other services. Loss control is an effort to prevent claims from happening and to manage those claims that do occur. Insurance is a service business in addition to being a financial safety net. Therefore, policyholders often investigate the level of services that are included when selecting a particular insurance company.

Figure 4.1

PROPERTY AND LIABILITY INSURANCE REGULATORY INFORMATION SYSTEM (IRIS) RATIOS		
Ratio	Description	Acceptable Values
#1 Gross Premium to = Surplus Ratio	(Gross Premium Written) ÷ (Policyholders Surplus)	Less than or equal to 900%
#1A Net Premium to = Surplus Ratio	(Net Premium Written) ÷ (Policyholders Surplus)	Less than or equal to 300%
#2 Change in Net = Writings Ratio	(Change in Net Writings) ÷ (Net Premium Written [Prior Year])	Greater than -33% and less than +33%
Note: Changes in writings is equal to net premium written for current year minus the net premium written for the prior year.		
#3 Surplus Aid to = Surplus Ratio	(Surplus Aid) ÷ (Policyholders' Surplus)	Less than 15%
Note: Surplus aid is equal to the ceding commissions ratio multiplied by ceded reinsurance unearned premium for nonaffiliates. The ceding commissions ratio is determined by dividing reinsurance ceded commissions by reinsurance ceded premium. Estimated surplus aid is calculated as a percentage of policyholders' surplus in order to obtain the ratio result.		
#4 Two-Year Overall = Operating Ratio	(Two-year Loss Ratio) + (Two-year Expense Ratio) - (Two-year Investment Income Ratio)	Less than 100%
Note: The two-year loss ratio is determined by adding together the total of losses, loss adjustment expenses, and policyholder dividends and dividing by net premiums earned. The expense ratio is equal to other underwriting expenses less other income divided by net premiums written. The investment income ratio is net investment income divided by net premiums earned. A two-year overall operating ratio of less than 100 percent shows an operating profit; more than 100 percent shows an operating loss.		
#5 Investment Yield = Ratio	(Net Investment Income) ÷ (Average Cash and Invested Assets [Current and Prior Year])	Greater than 4.5% and less than 10%
#6 Change in Surplus = Ratio	(Change in Surplus) ÷ (Adjusted Surplus Prior Year)	Greater than -10% and less than +50%
Note: Change in surplus is equal to adjusted surplus for the current year minus adjusted surplus for the prior year. Adjusted surplus is the total of policyholders' surplus plus deferred acquisition expense for either the current or		

Figure 4.1 (cont'd)

Ratio	Description	Acceptable Values
prior year. Deferred acquisition expense is determined by multiplying unearned premiums reserve by the ratio of acquisition expenses to net premiums written. Acquisition expenses include commissions, taxes, licenses and fees, and half of all other underwriting expenses.		
#7 Liabilities to Liquid Assets Ratio =	(Liabilities) ÷ (Liquid Assets)	Less than 105%
Note: Liquid assets are equal to (1) installment premiums booked but deferred and not yet due plus (2) cash and invested assets plus accrued investment income minus (3) investments in affiliated companies minus (4) excess of real estate over 5 % of liabilities.		
#8 Ratio of Agents' Balances to Surplus =	(Agents' Balances in Course of Collection) ÷ (Policyholders Surplus)	Less than 40%
#9 One-Year Reserve Development to Prior Year's Surplus Ratio =	(One Year Reserve Development) ÷ (Prior Year's Policyholders Surplus)	Less than 20%
Note: One-year reserve development is equal to incurred losses for all years except current accident year minus incurred losses for all years as reported in prior year.		
#10 Two-Year Reserve Development to Policyholders Surplus =	(Two-year Reserve Development) ÷ (Second Prior Year's Policyholders Surplus)	Less than 20%
Note: Two-year reserve development is equal to incurred losses for all years except two prior accident years minus reserves set for those losses for all years as reported in second prior year.		
#11 Estimated Current Reserve Deficiency to Surplus =	(Estimated Reserve Deficiency [redundancy]) ÷ Policyholders Surplus	Less than 25%
Note: Estimated reserve deficiency (redundancy) is equal to estimated reserves required minus stated reserves for the current year. The estimated reserves required are equal to net premium earned for current year times average ratio of developed reserves to premium.[3]		

Investments and Insurance Companies

Insurance companies collect premiums and invest those premiums until claims must be paid. Insurance companies are required by law to establish financial reserves (as liabilities) when claims are filed but before they are paid.

These reserves are estimates of what these claims ultimately will cost. The money set aside as claim reserves is invested and it, along with invested premiums, earns investment income that accounts for a substantial portion of an insurance company's income. The types of investments that insurance companies may use are regulated with the goal of protecting an insurer's financial stability. However, investment income does fluctuate with general economic conditions – just as such economic conditions affect noninsurance company investment income.

REINSURANCE

Reinsurance is a concept under which one insurer transfers part or all of certain risks that it has agreed to insure to one or more other insurers. Reinsurance is used by insurance companies for many reasons, including:

- stabilizing loss ratios and underwriting results;

- protecting against overwhelming financial impact from catastrophes;

- increasing policyholders' surplus;

- increasing capacity; and

- exiting a line of business.

The insurer that purchases reinsurance is called the *ceding insurer* or *ceding company*. The ceding insurer also may be called the *primary insurer*, the *direct insurer*, the *cedant*, or the *reinsured*. The insurance company that accepts the transfer of risk is called the *reinsurer*, *assuming insurer*, or *assuming company*.

There are two basic types of reinsurance:

- treaty reinsurance; and

- facultative reinsurance.

A *treaty* is a contract governing what portion and types of risks are ceded (transferred by contract) to the reinsurer. It is negotiated between the ceding company (primary insurer) and the reinsurance company. Under a treaty, the reinsurer automatically assumes part of each risk that meets the criteria of the treaty. The reinsurance coverage becomes effective at the time that direct insurance covered by the treaty is written.

Facultative reinsurance is negotiated separately as direct insurers underwrite risks. The direct insurer is not obligated to cede any risks, and the reinsurer is not obligated to accept any risk. Facultative reinsurance may be used to permit writing a risk that is larger than the direct insurer wants to assume, even after taking the carrier's treaty reinsurance into account; to protect a treaty; to obtain more competitive pricing; or to obtain coverage for a special exposure that the primary insurer cannot cover.

Treaty Reinsurance

The automatic nature of treaty reinsurance tends to eliminate some of the reinsurer's exposure to adverse selection that may occur in connection with facultative reinsurance. This is because treaty reinsurance is automatic and does not offer the opportunity to cede only unusually difficult risks. All risks that fall within the dictates of the treaty must be ceded and accepted.

There are many types of reinsurance treaties. The general and subcategories of traditional treaty reinsurance are

1. Pro Rata (proportional)

    - Quota share

    - Surplus share

2. Excess of Loss (nonproportional)

    - Per risk

    - Per occurrence (or catastrophe)

    - Aggregate (or stop loss)

Pro Rata Treaties

The ceding insurer and reinsurer share the amount of insurance, premium, and covered losses in the same proportion. If the reinsurer assumed one-third of the amount of insurance, it gets one-third of the premium and pays one-third of each covered loss.

Quota Share Treaties

Under a quota share treaty, the reinsurer participates in a fixed percentage of the premiums and losses of the ceding company. If the quota share to the reinsurer were 30%, the reinsurer would receive 30% of premiums and losses. In the case of a $25,000 loss, the reinsurer would pay 30% or $7,500.

Surplus Share Treaties

A surplus share treaty allows the primary insurer to underwrite the full amount of insurance it has established as a retention limit and reinsure only those amounts above the retention limit. The retention limit is called its *line*. The amount of the reinsurance available in the treaty is set as a multiple of the primary insurer's line. The primary insurer's retention is stated as a dollar amount under a surplus share treaty, rather than as a percentage.

Excess of Loss Treaties

Excess of loss treaties do not come into play until the amount of loss exceeds the retention. In other words, they do not contribute to losses that are below the retention or line. In addition, the methods to calculate excess reinsurance premiums are much more complex than the simple proportionate percentage basis used in pro rata treaties. Reinsurers customarily do not pay ceding commissions to direct insurers under excess of loss reinsurance treaties.

Per Risk Treaties

Per risk or per loss excess reinsurance treaties protect the direct insurer against the financial effects of individual large losses. The reinsurer does not pay anything unless an individual claim exceeds the retention, and then it only pays the amount in excess of the retention. The premium for an excess of loss treaty is negotiated based upon the ceding company's entire book of reinsured policies.

Per Occurrence Treaties

Per occurrence treaties are also known as *catastrophe treaties* when used in property insurance. They are similar to per risk excess treaties except that both the retention and the treaty limit apply to all losses arising from a single event, such as a hurricane, tornado, riot, or earthquake. Rate making for catastrophe treaties depends heavily on judgment of the reinsurance underwriter.

Aggregate Excess Treaties

Aggregate excess treaties sometimes are called *stop loss treaties*. They come into play when the aggregate losses during a specified period of time exceed the retention of the treaty. The stated period usually is twelve months but not necessarily a calendar year. The retention under an aggregate excess treaty may be stated in dollars or as a loss ratio. *Loss ratio* is the ratio of incurred losses to earned premiums. For example, an aggregate excess treaty will pay when the ceding company's loss ratio exceeds the stated amount. Aggregate excess treaties are the most effective types of treaties in limiting the ceding company's loss ratio.

Facultative Reinsurance

Under facultative reinsurance, the reinsurer has no obligation to accept any offered business. Facultative reinsurance is used to reinsure specific policies rather than an entire book of business. The primary reasons that direct insurers use facultative reinsurance are:

1. To provide coverage for areas that are excluded in the company's treaty reinsurance;

2. To protect a treaty when a direct insurer wants to write an exposure that poses higher than average risk;

3. To provide coverage for limits that exceed treaty maximums;

4. To provide large line capacity on a single risk;

5. To provide additional stabilization of loss experience; or

6. To provide a pricing advantage.

Reinsurance Pools

Reinsurance pools have been used when the potential loss of a risk exceeds any one company's ability to underwrite the risk. Under this arrangement, a number of companies combine resources and assume a percentage of the risks submitted to the pool. For example, this arrangement might be used in aviation insurance where the loss of a single passenger jetliner could produce a multimillion-dollar loss.

Reinsurers can deal with adverse conditions by raising rates, restricting coverage, reducing the number of risks that they will write, and negotiating higher retentions with ceding companies. Factors such as these may sharply influence both pricing and availability of coverage in the direct market. When many of these factors deteriorate at the same time, the effect on policyholders can be dramatic.

UNDERWRITING

Underwriting is the process through which an insurance company analyzes the exposures that a prospective policyholder encompasses, decides whether and how much of those risks to accept, designs the insurance program the insurer will offer, and establishes a premium for the coverage. Underwriting can be simply defined as the selection process through which insurance companies choose the clients they wish to insure.

Often rates and coverage wording is established and filed with the applicable state insurance departments. Underwriters start with these filed coverage forms and rates. In some cases, the standard filed provisions are sufficient and are used to design the insurance program that is offered. However, underwriters who deal with larger and more complex accounts often must deviate from the filed provisions in order to adequately address client needs. Underwriting even of complex risks still must be done within the context of state regulation, however.

WHERE CAN I FIND OUT MORE ABOUT IT?

1. American Institute for Chartered Property Casualty Underwriters (AICPCU) and the Insurance Institute of America (IIA), http://www.aicpcu.org/.

2. *The Risk Funding & Self-insurance Bulletins* (Cincinnati, OH: The National Underwriter Company, updated quarterly).

CHAPTER ENDNOTES

1. "Excess Coverage and Deductibles," *The Risk Funding & Self-Insurance Bulletins (RF&S Bulletins)*, March 2001, Ec-13 to Ec-18.

2. NAIC, Insurance Regulatory Information System (IRIS), 2001 Property/Casualty Edition, 7.

3. "Property and Liability Insurance Regulatory Information System (IRIS) Ratios," *The Risk Funding & Self-Insurance Bulletins (RF&S Bulletins)*, June 2001, Eo-1 to Eo-3, compiled from information obtained from the NAIC.

END OF CHAPTER REVIEW

1. Property and casualty insurance companies are regulated on a federal basis, but there has been discussion in recent years to convert to a state-by-state system of regulation.

    True   False ✓

2. Lloyd's associations are a type of mutual insurance company.

    True   False ✓

3. The four types of property and casualty insurance companies are mutual insurance companies, reciprocal exchanges, risk retention groups, and stock insurance companies.

    True   False ✓

4. The Risk-Based Capital system was developed by the National Association of Insurance Commissioners as a method to analyze the financial strength of both life and property/casualty insurance companies.

    True ✓   False

5. Insurance is considered a risk-transfer mechanism.

    True ✓   False

6. The NAIC developed the Insurance Regulatory Information System (IRIS) to replace the in-depth financial analysis and examinations that state insurance departments traditionally conducted.

    True   False ✓

7. Underwriting risk for property and casualty insurance companies is the risk that the insurer will not be able to collect the reinsurance, premiums, and other receivables that it contemplates when issuing insurance policies.

    True   False ✓

8. Reinsurance is used by property and casualty insurance companies to transfer part or all of certain risks to other insurers.

    True ✓   False

9. Nonadmitted property and casualty insurance companies are not licensed or directly regulated by the states in which they are not admitted.

    True ✓   False

10. The two types of reinsurance are treaty reinsurance and facultative reinsurance.

    True ✓   False

11. Facultative reinsurance is used to reinsure specific risks or parts of risks on a case-by-case basis.

    True ✓   False

12. Underwriting is the process through which insurance companies develop coverage forms and file them with regulators.

    True   False ✓

Part 2:

PROPERTY & CASUALTY

Chapter 5

OVERVIEW OF PROPERTY INSURANCE

INSURANCE NEEDS AND RATIONALE ANALYSIS

Insurance is just one tool for managing risks. Some exposures may be more efficiently treated with risk management techniques other than insurance. The rationale for choosing to insure a loss exposure is that the risk is transferred to someone else. Insureds pay premiums and spread the cost of losses among all insureds. To determine if insurance is the best method of risk management, loss exposures should be identified and analyzed.

To obtain necessary information about the risk, a systematic approach must be taken. First, the loss exposures must be identified. There are several avenues for identifying exposures, including the following:

1. checklists or questionnaires that list or ask specific questions about conceivable property exposures;

2. an analysis of financial statements that may disclose exposures;

3. flowcharts depicting relationships between various operations; and

4. loss analysis that reveals exposures that have been encountered in the past.

Another valuable risk-identifying tool is an onsite inspection.

Once the exposures have been identified, analysis as to the insurability of the exposure should take place. The exposure should be analyzed for its frequency (how often it occurs) and severity (how much economic damage it will cause). If the exposure meets the characteristics that are desirable for an insurable risk, then insurance is a viable risk management tool to apply to the property risk exposure.

EVALUATION OF REAL AND PERSONAL PROPERTY EXPOSURES

Real property includes buildings (such as manufacturing plants, office buildings, apartments, condominiums, and houses); structures (such as swimming pools and fences); and the land on which the buildings and structures are located. Personal property refers to items that are not included in the real property category, such as the furniture or clothing found in a home or business personal property like fax machines, office furniture, and finished stock. More information about real and personal property insurance can be found in Chapter 6, "Commercial Property Insurance" and Chapter 9, "Personal Property Insurance."

To evaluate potential risk exposures for real property, many factors should be examined. The identification of property exposures that need to be considered can be summarized by the acronym COPE, which stands for construction, occupancy, protection, and exposures.

1. *Construction* – Types of construction, such as frame or masonry, as well as the materials used for flooring, roofs, and partitions should be considered.

2. *Occupancy* – How will the property be used? A building that houses fireworks will certainly have different loss exposures than the dentist office next door.

3. *Protection* – Protection refers to the kind and quality of protection, both public and private, available to the property. Protection includes fire extinguishers, sprinkler systems, and the training, equipment, and proximity of the public fire department.

4. *Exposures* – Exposures are outside sources that create the chance for losses. Exposures may be vehicles or aircraft that could crash into buildings or structures, or occupants of a building whose business activities pose a risk to the building's other occupants.

EVALUATION OF AUTO RISK EXPOSURES

Automobiles fall into two categories: personal and business. Personal auto insurance may be written to cover private passenger autos, pickup trucks, vans and trailers. A business auto policy may be used to insure vehicles used in the course of business, whether owned, leased, or hired by the organization.

For personal auto insurance, several criteria should be reviewed. The following factors help determine the frequency and severity of hazards to which the auto will be exposed:

- age;
- sex;
- marital status;
- how the car will be used;
- the type of car; and
- the occupation of the insured.

Another important issue to consider is where the vehicle is garaged. If the area is densely populated, more cars are on the road and the potential for accidents increases.

For commercial autos, the following factors should be examined:

- whether the organization leases vehicles;
- how many vehicles are in an organization's fleet;
- if individuals' vehicles will be used for business purposes;
- if customers' vehicles are driven by employees (e.g., valet service); or
- if the vehicles are used for public transportation.

Both personal and commercial auto policies provide coverage for property damage and liability. For more information on auto insurance, see Chapter 7, "Automobile and Recreational Vehicle Insurance."

QUESTIONS AND ANSWERS

Question – What are some means for identifying loss exposures?

Answer – Checklists, questionnaires, analysis of financial statements, flowcharts, and onsite inspections.

Question – What types of property are considered real property?

Answer – Buildings, structures, and land.

Question – What are the four criteria used for identifying property exposures?

Answer – Construction, occupancy, protection, and exposure.

Question – What are some factors that should be reviewed in identifying personal auto exposures?

Answer – The age, sex, marital status, and occupation of the insured; the type of vehicle and how it will be used; and where the vehicle will be garaged.

Question – What areas should be considered when identifying business auto exposures?

Answer – If the vehicles are leased, hired, or owned by the organization; the number of vehicles; and whose vehicle will be used and for what purpose.

END OF CHAPTER REVIEW

1. Insurance is the only tool for managing risks.

    True   False

2. The next step after identifying the exposures is to purchase insurance.

    True   False

3. Manufacturing plants, office buildings, houses, and condominiums are all examples of real property.

    True   False

4. COPE is an acronym – which stands for construction, occupancy, protection, and exposures – that is used identify property exposures.

   True   False

5. Auto insurance consists of three types: commercial, personal, and leisure.

   True   False

Chapter 6

COMMERCIAL PROPERTY INSURANCE

WHAT IS IT?

The term *commercial property insurance* refers to the many types of policy forms that businesses or not-for-profit organizations may use. The most common forms cover buildings and personal property used in the business, boiler and machinery equipment, business income (loss of income because of a property loss), and crime exposures. At times there is a need for a coverage called *inland marine insurance*, which may cover such items as a contractor's heavy equipment or goods while they are being transported. Additional types of commercial property insurance include coverage for condominium associations, buildings under construction, and flood damage.

BUSINESS USES

Commercial property insurance will pay to repair or replace damaged property. If the property is not replaced, the policy usually will pay for its *actual cash value*. (In insurance terms, actual cash value connotes the replacement cost of property less depreciation.) Property insurance is considered *first-party* insurance coverage because it normally benefits the party who owns the property that has been damaged or destroyed. It can be a valuable source of recovery after, for example, a fire damages or destroys a covered building and its contents. If the insured business had to rebuild the property without the benefit of insurance, the cost could seriously constrain the business's cash flow.

In addition, many lenders require that insurance be carried on property that is used as collateral for a mortgage or loan. In these transactions, the mortgage holder or lender often requires that the property be insured. This protects the lender's financial interest in it. In many cases, the financing of high-valued properties is not completed until evidence of satisfactory property insurance is provided.

ADVANTAGES

1. Peace of mind and a sense of security that money will be available to repair or replace damaged property.

2. Loss control services (many insurers provide these) that may decrease the chance of loss.

3. Standardized coverage forms, which have been interpreted in the courts.

4. The opportunity to pay small dollar amounts for possible large recoveries.

5. The opportunity to take advantage of the greater financial resources of insurers.

6. The ability to eliminate potential loss of revenue.

7. Eliminating a reduction in property value because of unrepaired damage.

8. The fact that commercial property insurance is provided by an industry that is regulated by state departments of insurance.

DISADVANTAGES

1. The insurance coverage costs money, and the premium spent on insurance is money that the insured business does not have for any of its business plans.

2. The desired coverage may not be available.

3. It may be difficult to identify exposures.

4. It may be difficult to establish the appropriate amount of insurance.

5. The amount of loss may exceed the insurance that is in place.

6. An insurer may become insolvent and unable to pay claims.

7. Loss may not be covered because of policy exclusions or limitations.

8. An insurance policy might be cancelled or nonrenewed for a number of reasons.

DESIGN FEATURES

The design features of the most common commercial property coverage forms are discussed in this chapter, beginning with the commercial building and personal property coverage form.

Building and Personal Property Coverage

The common coverage forms in use are those from the *Insurance Services Office* (ISO) and *American Association of Insurance Services* (AAIS). These organizations provide forms, collect information on claims, and provide many other services to the insurance industry. Both the ISO and AAIS forms cover buildings and contents; other structures that are not buildings, such as outdoor fixtures; and personal business property that may not, strictly speaking, be *contents* of the building. For example, business personal property in the open (or in a vehicle) within one hundred feet of the described premises is covered on both.

For larger commercial risks, the selected form may be combined with a commercial general liability form (CGL), business auto form, workers compensation and employers liability form, boiler and machinery form, crime coverage, and perhaps inland marine coverage to make a complete insurance package. For smaller risks – a mom-and-pop grocery, perhaps – a businessowners form, which provides some of these coverages in one policy, may be all that is necessary. Very large properties with high values may be insured on stand-alone property forms that are endorsed (amended) to provide specialized coverage enhancements.

Methods of Insuring Commercial Property

There are two methods of insuring commercial property. The first is to assign a separate limit to each building or each class of property that is to be insured. This is called *specific insurance*. For example, an insured might have a limit of $200,000 on a building at 100 Canal Street and a limit of $50,000 on its contents.

The other method is to *blanket* insure the same property. Under this method, one limit of $250,000 will apply to building and contents located at 100 Canal Street. Or, the insured business might own three buildings at different locations. It might elect to purchase $1,000,000 of insurance that would apply to the three buildings, exclusive of their contents. Under blanket insurance, there is no per-building limit. The advantage of blanket insurance is that, in general, there should be enough insurance to cover a

loss at any one building. If a loss to the building at 100 Canal Street exceeded $200,000, the entire $1,000,000 of coverage typically would be available to settle the claim.

Policy Structure

The commercial property policy is formed by attaching a *causes of loss form* and the *commercial property conditions* to the *coverage form*.

- The coverage form tells what is covered (buildings, contents, other structures).

- The causes of loss form lists the *perils* (potential causes of loss, such as fire or windstorm) that will apply; and

- The conditions form provides information on the insurer's right to cancel, who pays the premium, and what will happen if the named insured dies.

What's Covered?

Buildings

The building and personal property form covers the building or structure described in the policy declarations. (The declarations page usually is the first page of an insurance policy, which identifies the insurance company, the effective period of coverage or policy term, forms and endorsements that are attached, the named insured, and the limits of coverage.) Included are completed additions and, under certain conditions, additions in the course of construction, and fixtures – such as bookcases or partitions attached to the walls – and outdoor fixtures – which could include signs or even a metal tent frame attached to a concrete patio. Also included within the meaning of building are permanently installed machinery and equipment, which could include a furnace or central air conditioning system mounted on the roof. Personal property that the insured owns and uses to maintain or service the building or premises is also covered as part of the building. This property could include appliances such as refrigerators and stoves, floor coverings, and fire extinguishing equipment.

Business Personal Property

The next category of covered property is business personal property. Many items are included in this category; among them furniture and (once again) fixtures, machinery, leased property the insured has a contractual responsibility to insure, other personal property used in the business, and labor and materials the insured uses to perform work on personal property of others. For example, the insured's business may be processing jams and jellies for another company. The insured's business personal property will therefore be the jars, lids, and labels, while the contents that come from the other company would belong to the other company.

The term fixtures as used in the context of personal property is generally held to mean property that may be removed by a tenant, such as shelving or counters. This is different from improvements and betterments, which also are covered as business personal property. Improvements and betterments are items installed by the tenant that become part of the realty and are not removable, such as a storefront plate glass window. Here, the policy responds to a covered loss by paying the insured's use interest in the property; that is, the policy either pays the value of the items if the insured replaces them or the value of the items prorated over the remaining time of the lease.

Business personal property includes the insured's *stock*, which means merchandise held in storage or for sale, raw materials and in-process or finished products, and any packing or shipping materials. The final category of covered property is for personal property of others.

Property Not Covered

Although the coverage forms appear to be quite broad, there are many types of property that have limited coverage or no coverage at all. Some types of property are better insured elsewhere, such as autos or vehicles licensed for use on public roads; others are considered uninsurable, such as land and contraband. Other examples of property that is not covered are: bills and currency; bridges, roadways, and other paved surfaces; personal property while air- or waterborne; and underground pipes and foundations below the lowest basement floor. This is not an all-inclusive list, however. Property coverage forms must be consulted on a regular basis for a complete listing.

Additional Coverages

The commercial property forms contain additional coverages, which are in addition to that discussed previously. These coverages may include:

1. expense to remove debris of covered property that has been damaged or destroyed by a covered peril;

2. fire department service charge;

3. limited expense to clean up pollutants from land or water at the described premises;

4. additional cost to repair or replace a damaged building because of an ordinance or law (if the insured has purchased replacement cost coverage on buildings, discussed below); and

5. limited coverage to restore lost or damaged electronic data.

All of these have dollar caps on what will be paid, but they are in addition to the limits of liability shown on the declarations page.

Coverage Extensions

The coverage forms also contain coverage extensions. These extensions provide additional amounts of insurance for the designated property. But, in order to make a claim under any of these, the declarations page must show a coinsurance percentage of at least 80% or more or a value reporting symbol.

Coinsurance is a means of enforcing insurance to value, which means purchasing enough insurance to match the value of the covered property. Because the majority of property losses are partial (only part of a structure is damaged), many persons may be enticed to purchase only minimum limits of coverage, believing that they would never need more. An insurer would therefore be in the position of paying many small claims yet never recouping enough premium dollars to pay all losses and expenses. The coinsurance clause on a property policy requires that the insured purchase an amount of insurance equal to a specified percentage of the value of the insured property. The insured gets a reduced rate, and the insurer collects enough premium. Common coinsurance percentages are 80, 90, or 100% of the property value. If the insured does not maintain the required percentage of insurance, claim payments are reduced, and the insured is penalized for not carrying enough insurance.

Value reporting is used with business personal property. It means that a limit of insurance is set high enough to cover the maximum value of property the insured expects to have on hand at any time during the policy period. Actual values of this property are reported on a periodic basis, such as monthly or quarterly. If values are accurately reported, then the insurer will pay the full amount of a covered loss – subject to the limit selected – even if the amount of the loss is greater than the value last reported. Value reporting is particularly useful when amounts of merchandise or product on hand fluctuate. Think, for example, of the amount of merchandise in a toy store before the holidays as opposed to in January.

How Losses Are Settled

Limit of Insurance

A commercial property policy will pay up to the limit of insurance that is shown in the declarations for any one occurrence. In general, an occurrence is an event that triggers coverage under a policy, such as a fire, windstorm, or hail storm. Additional limits of insurance may be paid for ancillary property, such as signs and the property covered under the extensions and additional coverages.

Deductibles

This policy section tells how a deductible is applied to a loss. A deductible is the amount of a loss that the insured agrees to assume. Although deductibles typically are stated as dollar amounts, they may be percentages. For example, in earthquake coverage, a percentage is applied to the amount of loss. Insureds may select different deductibles to apply to different property covered on the same policy. A policy might cover three apartment buildings at the same location, with a different deductible applying to each one and another deductible applying to business personal property.

Valuation

Valuation means how a property is financially valued at the time of loss. Commercial property policies typically offer a choice of three valuation systems:

1. *Replacement cost* typically means the cost to repair or replace damaged property.

2. *Agreed value* means that the insured and insurer agree, before a loss occurs, that the value shown for a covered item is its insured value for loss settlement purposes.

3. *Actual cash value* is commonly defined as replacement cost minus depreciation.

Perils Insured Against

The business and personal property forms tell what kinds of property are covered and how losses will be settled. These forms alone will not provide coverage. Causes of loss forms must be attached. These forms list the perils (causes of loss such as fire or hail) that the property will be protected against. All of the causes of loss forms state that they cover direct physical loss. That is, physical, rather than consequential, loss is covered by the forms. Consequential losses are those that may result from a property loss. For example, because a warehouse is destroyed, a business grinds to a halt and loses income. The loss of income is a consequential loss. Or, two of an insured's fleet of seven tractor-trailers burn. The loss of the trucks is a physical loss; the loss of their use is a consequential loss.

There are three causes of loss forms: basic, broad, and special. The basic and broad forms are structured to state which causes of loss are covered. The number of covered causes of loss in the basic form is eleven—fire, lightning, explosion, windstorm and hail, smoke, aircraft or vehicles, riot or civil commotion, vandalism, sprinkler leakage, sinkhole collapse, and volcanic action. The broad contains fourteen—the eleven previously listed plus falling objects, weight of snow, ice or sleet, and water damage from a plumbing device. The special form covers any cause of loss that is not specifically excluded and does not list all of the causes of loss like the basic and broad forms. In addition, the broad and special forms provide coverages not found in the basic form.

The broad form provides two additional coverages. The first of these is for direct physical loss or damage to covered property caused by collapse of an insured building or part of an insured building. Therefore, the coverage applies to the building or to the property contained within it

Coverage for collapse may be limited. It may be covered only if caused by one of the perils listed on either the basic or broad forms; by hidden decay or insect or vermin damage; by weight of people, personal property, or rain collected on a roof; or by defective materials or construction methods if the collapse occurs during construction, remodeling, or renovation. There are also restrictions on certain types of property. Coverage for collapse is included within the limit applying to the property.

The current broad form also provides limited coverage for clean up of fungus, which includes all forms of mold, wet or dry rot, and bacteria. The event triggering the coverage must be one of the causes of loss listed for the broad form other than fire or lightning. If the insured has purchased flood coverage, the mold remediation coverage will also respond. However, this coverage is included within the limit of liability applying to the insured property. This is the most that will be paid no matter what causes the mold damage.

The current special form provides collapse and mold remediation, and adds three coverage extensions. These are for property in transit; water damage, other liquids, powder or molten material damage; and glass. The details of these coverages are described in the special form.

Coverage Limitations and Exclusions

All policies of insurance contain limitations and exclusions. That is, coverage for some types of property is limited, and there is no coverage at all for other types of property. There are reasons for this. For one, many insureds do not need and would not be willing to pay for extensive coverage on property such as heavy equipment, for example. Then, some exposures are uninsurable (such as war) or that are better insured elsewhere (such as flood, which is often insured through the federal government).

All of the causes of loss forms contain exclusions. However, because the special form covers anything not otherwise excluded, it actually contains more exclusions than do the other forms. All of the standard forms exclude the following:

- *Ordinance or law* – This exclusion precludes coverage for increased costs incurred to comply with any ordinance or law when damaged property is being rebuilt or replaced. (However, the ISO coverage form gives $10,000 additional coverage for ordinance or law provided the insured has selected replacement cost.)

- *Earth movement* – There is no coverage for landslide, mine subsidence, or earth shifting. However, if the earth movement results in fire or explosion, that resulting damage is covered.

- *Governmental action* – There is no coverage for seizure or destruction of property by order of a governmental authority, but there is coverage if the property is destroyed to prevent a fire from spreading.

- *Nuclear hazard* – Although closely allied with the *war* exclusion, it need not be the same. Remember Three Mile Island and the nuclear damage that arose because of the reactor's malfunction.

- *Utility services* – If a power or other utility failure occurs off the insured premises, there is no coverage for the resulting loss unless the failure results in a covered cause of loss on the insured premises.

- *War and military action* – Although not included in the exclusions, acts of terrorism, including biological or nuclear action, are now frequently excluded by endorsement. Some terrorism exclusions give limited coverage (fire resulting from the act is covered) but many are absolute (no coverage whatsoever).

- *Water* – Although some water damage is covered, most is excluded.

Doctrine of Concurrent Causation

All of the above exclusions are preceded by language intended to prevent operation of the *doctrine of concurrent causation*. This doctrine holds that if any covered cause of loss contributes to an otherwise excluded loss, the entire loss must be covered. For example, if human negligence (not specifically excluded) causes a utility failure, the doctrine of concurrent causation would operate to provide coverage. The exclusions just discussed are prefaced with language stating that there is no coverage – no matter what other cause or event contributes "concurrently or in any sequence" (ISO's language) to the loss. Therefore, these exclusions apply no matter what other factors are involved.

Coverage for some of these exposures may be purchased – notably earthquake, flood, ordinance and law, and failure of utility service.

Other Exclusions

The next list of exclusions contains many that are not absolute. For example, a loss that is confined to the subject of the exclusion may not be covered, but resulting damage to other property may well be covered. They appear in all the causes of loss forms.

- *Artificially generated electric current* – But if the current results in a fire, the fire damage is covered.

- *Explosion of steam boilers, pipes, or engines owned by, leased by, or under the control of the insured* – But if the explosion results in fire or combustion explosion, the resulting damage is covered.

- *Mechanical breakdown* – But if a covered cause of loss results (such as a fire or sprinkler leakage) that damage is covered.

- *Neglect* – If the insured does not use all reasonable means to preserve or protect covered property from further damage at the time of a loss, the resulting damage is not covered.

In the special form, no perils are named, only the applicable exclusions. The special form, therefore, excludes loss caused by such things as wear and tear, rust, smog, smudging, or smoke from industrial operations, settling, nesting or infestation of insects, birds, rodents or other animals, and delay or loss of use or market – as well as a number of causes of loss that are either uninsurable or better insured on another coverage form.

Like most lines of insurance, commercial property coverage can be tailored to suit the insured's needs. A variety of endorsements may be used to provide coverage for perils that are excluded in the policy.

Business Income Coverage

The business income forms provide coverage for the net profit or loss before income taxes that would have been earned had there been no loss, plus continuing normal operating expenses, including payroll. A covered cause of loss must be the cause of the loss of income. For example, flood is excluded on standard policies, so if a flood damages the insured premises, forcing the business to stop operations, there is no coverage for business income. It is possible for an insured to sustain a business income loss without direct loss to his own insured property. For example, if the insured leases part of a building, and a fire occurs in another part of the building that forces the insured to temporarily close, the loss is covered even though there is no direct physical damage to the insured's property.

Values of buildings – including what it would cost to replace them as well as increased costs of construction because of ordinance or law – and the cost to replace personal business property must be determined. Additional equipment that might be necessary to operate on an emergency basis should also be considered. Bottom line, the amount of business income coverage pur-

chased should be enough to allow the business to reestablish itself on a preloss basis.

Rental value may be included in the coverage. Rental value, as the name implies, is net profit or loss the insured would earn as rental income from property he owns or rents to others, and the fair rental value of any part of that premises the insured occupies himself.

Additional coverages and extensions may also be available. These include the following:

- *Civil authority* – If access to the premises is prohibited by civil authority because of a direct physical loss of property by a covered cause of loss at other than the insured premises, coverage is provided for loss of business income for up to three weeks.

- *Alterations and new buildings* – Loss or damage to new buildings or structures caused by a covered cause of loss resulting in business interruption triggers coverage.

- *Extended business income* – When a business cannot operate for a time and then resumes operations, there is a gap between when production begins and market share is recaptured. This coverage gives the insured time to get operations back up to speed.

- *Interruption of computer operations* – The forms provide a specific amount for all loss because of interruption of computer operations when caused by a covered cause of loss.

- *Newly acquired locations* – A specific amount is available for covered business interruption at a newly acquired location.

- *Expenses to reduce loss* – This coverage is found only on the business income (without extra expense) form. This coverage extension responds to necessary expenses incurred – but only to the extent they reduce the total business income loss. For example, a business income loss is $250,000. The insured rents other equipment for $25,000 and reduces the business income loss to $100,000. He collects $125,000. But if the equipment costs $125,000 and he reduces the loss only to $200,000, he only can collect $250,000 and will be out $75,000. This coverage is sometimes confused with extra expense coverage.

Extra expense coverage, distinguished from expenses to reduce loss, will pay costs the insured incurs that would not have been necessary had there not been a covered loss. It may be included on the business income coverage form, or it may be purchased as a separate type of coverage. Extra expense coverage could be used for renting replacement equipment, hiring extra workers, or paying the expense of relocating the business to another premises. It also might include the cost to subcontract work to complete a project that the insured, because of the loss, cannot. The coverage also may pay to repair or replace property to the extent it reduces the business income loss.

There are a few more things to note about business income coverage. A time deductible usually applies. Coverage for business income will not begin until seventy-two hours after the time of the direct physical loss, and it ends on the earlier of the date when the property should be (*should be*, not *is*) restored, repaired, or rebuilt at the described premises or the date business resumes at a new permanent location. A coinsurance percentage, if the insured has chosen one, applies. Finally, various exclusions do apply.

It is frequently necessary to tailor business income coverage, and several coverage endorsements are available to do that.

Boiler and Machinery

Manufacturing operations rely on machinery to process goods. Even businesses not engaged in manufacturing have some kinds of equipment, such as furnaces, air conditioners, or computers that can break down. Coverage for these exposures is limited under the building and personal property forms, so special coverage is needed.

The current coverage forms can include coverage for loss or damage to the covered equipment as well as consequential losses, such as for spoilage or loss of business income. For example, if the insured leases the premises, she will not own the boiler but might still be legally liable for damages arising out of an explosion.

Although computer breakdown is a part of the coverage, loss caused by a computer error or virus is not covered. There are specialty lines of insurance that provide coverage for loss arising from hacking, denial of service, or misuse of data, among others.

As is typical in property insurance, there are exclusions that affect coverage. Therefore, coverage forms should be reviewed with care.

Builders Risk

Buildings under construction present unique exposures in that, as buildings go up, their values change. Owners, contractors, and subcontractors may all have insurable interests to protect. Coverage is necessary to protect not only the building itself, but also the materials and supplies used in construction.

There are two common types of forms used. The first, which is the standard commercial property form, is often adequate for smaller projects. Because collapse during the course of construction is a very real possibility, coverage should be added by endorsement. The form provides limited coverage for materials and supplies that are owned by others; located in, on, or within one hundred feet of the premises, in the care of the insured; and intended to become a permanent part of the building.

The other form falls into the category of inland marine insurance. Coverage under this type of form is generally much broader than that of the standard forms. For example, these forms generally cover collapse of a building while in the course of construction, while the standard forms do not. The forms often cover property in transit to the building site, boiler explosion, and property of others. Coverage for flood, earthquake, and soft costs may usually be added. Soft costs are those that arise when a covered loss occurs. They may include additional cost to refinance a lease on leased equipment, additional interest on a new loan necessitated by a loss, or additional architect fees.

Condominium Association

Condominium buildings are owned in common by those persons owning units within the building. The coverage form for this type of structure is similar to the business and personal property form. A causes of loss form and the commercial property conditions forms are then attached along with any endorsements.

The condominium form adds another category of covered property, for property contained in the individual units. Covered property consists of appliances, such as dishwashers and refrigerators, and fixtures, improvements, and alterations that are a part of the building or structures if the condominium association agreement requires it.

Flood Insurance

The federal government reinsures most flood coverage. Flood insurance is available either directly from the government or through private insurers who participate in the "Write Your Own" program. Larger commercial risks may be able to purchase flood insurance as a part of their property coverage programs. This approach probably will result in broader coverage than that available from the National Flood Insurance Program (NFIP).

There are three forms in use through the federal program: the dwelling form, the general property form, and the residential condominium building association policy. The general property form is the one used for nonresidential risks, including commercial condos. The form may be used to cover both building and personal property, which, under this form, includes stock.

The forms cover direct physical loss caused by flood as defined in the policy. Flood can include run-off of surface waters, mudflow (also defined in the form), and collapse or subsidence of land along the shore of a lake or similar body of water if the result of a flood. Consequential losses, such as loss of use of the property or business income, are not covered. The exclusions and the types of property not covered vary substantially from the building and personal property forms.

Federal flood coverage is not unlimited. Maximum per building and contents limits apply. Flood coverage forms do not cover much property in a basement, which includes any sunken room or portion of a room having its floor below ground level on all sides. Because many manufacturing operations have heavy equipment on a ground floor or in a basement, a flood could cause great harm. And, because flood is an excluded cause of loss on many property forms, business income coverage, which is triggered by a covered cause of loss, would not be available unless specifically endorsed.

The residential condominium building association policy is used for, as the name implies, condominium buildings in which at least 75% of the floor area is occupied for residential purposes. (Either the dwelling or the general property form is used to insure a unit within the condo building.) The form covers the building and contents owned in common.

Inland Marine

Most inland marine forms provide coverage for property in transit. Broad coverage is common, although some forms provide more limited coverage. Lost or damaged property may be valued on an actual cash value basis, replacement cost basis, or, in the case of property in transit between buyer and seller, on an invoice basis.

Commonly used forms are those for musical instruments, cameras, signs, film (used for commercial film production), mail, physicians and dentists' equipment, and jewelry (coverage for a commercial jewelry establishment is referred to as a jeweler's block policy). When these forms are used, they are attached to a general commercial conditions form, an inland marine conditions form, and a declarations page.

Although the coverage is extremely broad (for example, flood is not excluded), loss resulting from war, governmental action, and nuclear hazard are not covered.

Businessowners

Businessowners insurance is generally used for a smaller business for which the commercial property form would be too costly. The eligibility requirements include a cap on annual gross sales and a limit on the business's total floor area. Examples of the classes of business suited to the program are apartment buildings, office buildings, wholesale or mercantile operations, and small contractors. Restaurants meeting eligibility requirements may be written.

Unlike the building and personal property form, the businessowners form automatically includes coverage for loss of business income and accounts receivable. The insured may also include, for additional premium, coverage for money and securities, employee dishonesty, and mechanical breakdown (boiler and machinery coverage).

Under the current program, liability coverage is included. The liability coverage is similar in nature to that of the commercial general liability form, discussed elsewhere.

WHERE CAN I FIND OUT MORE ABOUT IT?

1. Federal Emergency Management Agency (FEMA) (http://www.fema.gov/nfip/).

2. *The FC&S Bulletins* (Cincinnati, OH: The National Underwriter Company, updated monthly) (http://www.nationalunderwriter.com/nucatalog/).

3. Bruce Hillman and Michael K. McCracken, *Commercial Property Coverage Guide*, 2nd ed. (Cincinnati, OH: The National Underwriter Company, 2001).

4. American Institute for Chartered Property Casualty Underwriters and the Insurance Institute of America, including courses in the Associate in Claims (AIC) and Chartered Property Casualty Underwriter (CPCU) courses of study (http://www.aicpcu.org/programs/index.htm).

QUESTIONS AND ANSWERS

Question – What types of property may typically be covered under a standard commercial property form?

Answer – Most commonly, commercial property forms cover buildings and contents; other structures that are not buildings, such as outdoor fixtures; and personal business property that may not, strictly speaking, be contents of the building.

Question – What are two methods for insuring commercial property?

Answer – The first is to assign a separate limit to each building or each class of property that is to be insured. This is called specific insurance. The other method is to blanket insure the same property, which means that more than one building or structure at the same location or several buildings at different locations are given one limit to cover all buildings at all locations.

Question – What types of property are not generally covered under a commercial property policy and why?

Answer – Property such as autos and vehicles licensed for use on public roads are not covered because they are better insured elsewhere. Land and contraband are not covered because they are considered uninsurable.

Question – What are the three types of causes of loss forms and the differences among them?

Answer – The three causes of loss forms are basic, broad, and special. The basic and broad forms state which causes of loss are covered, such as fire, lightning, or windstorm and hail. The broad form lists more causes of loss than the basic. The special form covers any cause of loss that is not specifically excluded and does not list all of the causes of loss like the basic and broad forms.

Question – Would a loss resulting from war typically be covered under a standard commercial property policy?

Answer – No. The standard forms contain exclusions that preclude coverage, including a war and military action exclusion.

Question – What does business income coverage generally insure?

Answer – The net profit or loss before income taxes that would have been earned had there been no loss, plus continuing normal operating expenses, including payroll.

END OF CHAPTER REVIEW

1. The actual cash value of property is its replacement cost plus depreciation.

   True   False

2. One advantage of commercial property insurance is the opportunity to pay small dollar amounts for possible large recoveries.

   True   False

3. The ISO and AAIS forms do not cover structures that are not buildings, such as outdoor fixtures.

   True   False

4. There are three methods for insuring commercial property: specific insurance, blanket insurance, and first-party insurance.

   True   False

5. The commercial property policy is formed by attaching a causes of loss form and commercial property conditions to the coverage form.

   True   False

6. Business personal property that is covered under the commercial property policy includes autos, land, bills and currency, and roadways.

   True   False

7. Coinsurance means that a limit of insurance is set high enough to cover the maximum value of property the insured expects to have on hand at any time during the policy period.

   True   False

8. While deductibles are generally stated as dollar amounts, they may also be percentages.

   True   False

9. The basic and broad causes of loss forms state which causes of loss are covered, and the special causes of loss form covers any cause of loss that is not specifically excluded.

   True   False

10. Business income forms provide coverage for profit or loss after income taxes, minus continuing expenses.

    True   False

Chapter 7

AUTOMOBILE AND RECREATIONAL VEHICLE INSURANCE

─────── ■ ───────

WHAT IS IT?

Many clients can elect to self-insure a variety of items. For example, a client can choose not to insure a diamond ring because the ring is always kept in a safe deposit box. Automobile insurance – liability, in particular – is not one of those things. In this chapter, we discuss the coverages in the personal auto policy and the importance of them to your clients. We will look at business auto coverages in Chapter 8. We touch on additional, but often necessary, coverages. Does the client frequently rent a car? Own a classic car? We conclude the chapter with a discussion of insurance for recreational vehicles.

Personal auto insurance is written on a specified auto basis (that is, each vehicle is described by make, model, and serial number) for qualifying vehicles owned by an individual or by husband and wife. Autos owned by individuals, other than husband and wife, residing together, may be insured by endorsement. Autos leased under a long-term arrangement are considered owned and are eligible. A personal auto policy may even be written for someone who owns no autos, called a named nonowner policy.

Qualifying vehicles are those having no fewer than four wheels of the private passenger type. Pickups and vans also qualify, but they can have a gross vehicle weight of less than 10,000 pounds and cannot be used for delivery or transportation of goods and materials. Pickups or vans used for farming or ranching may be insured, though, as may vehicles such as a plumber's van used to transport his or her equipment.

Persons insured on the auto policy are: the person shown in the declarations, or named insured, his or her spouse if a resident of the same household, and family members of either, who reside in the same household as the named insured. Family members are those related by marriage, blood, or adoption. Wards or foster children are included.

Auto policies typically cover an insured's liability for bodily injury or property damage, medical payments coverage, uninsured and underinsured motorist coverage, and physical damages.

Insurance for recreational vehicles is structured much the same way as an auto policy. Many times, however, coverage for these vehicles may be endorsed onto an auto or homeowners policy. Watercraft are frequently written on an individual policy, although some coverage is available on a standard homeowners policy, depending upon the watercraft.

THE AUTO POLICY

Commonly, an auto policy contains coverage parts: liability, medical payments coverage, uninsured and underinsured motorist coverage, and physical damage coverage. If these parts were to be ranked in order of their importance, it would likely be: liability; uninsured and underinsured motorist; medical payments; and physical damage coverage. The reason for ranking the coverages in this order was touched on earlier. Many people, although they might not like the possibility, could walk away from a total loss to a vehicle. Few, however, could walk away from a million-dollar suit claiming bodily injury. Often people will complain about a $250 deductible for comprehensive coverage, but not stop to think of the risk they run by carrying minimal liability limits.

Liability

Although it is not the purpose of this text to recommend limits of insurance, an adequate limit of liability is the first line of defense in protecting a client's assets.

The liability section of an auto policy states that the insurer will pay damages (that is, money) for bodily injury or property damage for which any insured becomes legally responsible because of an auto accident. The insurer will also settle or defend any claim or suit asking for these damages. The insurer pays defense costs in addition to the limit of liability. So, for example, an insured may carry bodily injury liability limits of $100,000 per person, $300,000 per accident, and a property damage liability limit of $100,000. This means that the most that will be paid in event of an accident for which the insured is legally responsible is $100,000 per person, but not more than $300,000 for all bodily injury claims arising out of that accident, even if five persons are injured and each sues for $100,000. No matter how many vehicles are damaged in the accident (a Hummer and a Lincoln Navigator), the most available for property damage claims is $100,000. Defense costs are in addition to the total amount of the limits – in this scenario, $400,000.

Besides settling or defending any claims or suits, the company agrees to pay on behalf of an insured certain supplementary payments. These payments are in addition to the limit of liability and do not reduce that limit as they are paid out by the company. These are currently: up to $250 for the cost of bail bonds required because of an accident; premiums on appeal bonds and bonds to release attachments; interest accruing after a judgment is entered; up to $200 per day for the insured's loss of earnings because of attendance at a trial or hearing; and other reasonable expenses incurred by the insured at the insurer's request.

As is common in all policies of insurance, there are exclusions applying to the liability coverage. Intentionally-caused bodily injury or property damage and liability coverage for the ownership, maintenance, or use of a vehicle regularly furnished to the named insured other than an insured auto are but two.

Uninsured and Underinsured Motorist Coverage

The insurer promises to pay compensatory damages that an insured is legally entitled to recover from the owner or operator of an uninsured motor vehicle because of bodily injury sustained by an insured and caused by an auto accident. The owner's or operator's liability for these damages must arise out of the ownership, maintenance or use of the uninsured motor vehicle. An example of this coverage is if A is injured by a negligent driver, B, who has no insurance on his auto, A's uninsured motorists coverage will pay the damages to A that he, by rights, should have recovered from B.

A key element of the uninsured motorists coverage insuring agreement is that the operator or owner of the uninsured motor vehicle must be legally responsible to pay for the insured's damages. The insurance company has no obligation to pay for an insured's injuries unless the elements of legal liability are present. That is one of the reasons uninsured motorists coverage has been described as reverse liability insurance. Think of uninsured motorists insurance in this way: the insurance

company becomes, in a sense, the liability insurer of any uninsured motorist that injures its insured.

The named insured – "you" as stated in the policy – or any family member is an insured. Also, an insured is any other person *occupying* (which means in, upon, getting in, on, out or off) the named insured's covered auto. A third type of insured person is the person who may not be involved physically in an accident, but who is entitled to damages from the person or organization responsible for having caused bodily injury to an insured of either kind described previously. This type of covered person, often called a derivative insured, might be the husband of an injured wife claiming damages for loss of consortium, or the father of an injured child claiming damages for medical expenses. Uninsured motorists coverage, like the medical payments coverage of the personal auto policy, is available to persons *other than the named insured or a family member* only while occupying the named insured's covered auto.

Even if a named insured chooses to buy uninsured motorists insurance, a possible gap in coverage can arise. For example, suppose that A is an insured under a personal auto policy with an uninsured motorist limit of $100,000 and A is injured by a negligent driver, B, whose $15/30,000 bodily injury limits satisfy the applicable state financial responsibility law. A's policy, therefore, does not consider B's car as an uninsured motor vehicle. Even if A's expenses exceed B's liability limits, A cannot collect uninsured motorists insurance. To remedy this potential area of disappointment, the *underinsured* motorists coverage endorsement may be attached to the personal auto policy. This is a general version of the underinsured motorists coverage endorsement; many states have state-specific endorsements that offer the underinsured motorists coverage but with due deference to the specific state's laws and regulations.

The insuring agreement of the underinsured motorist endorsement is similar to that of the uninsured motorist agreement, except that it promises compensatory damages because of bodily injury sustained by an insured and caused by an accident arising out of the ownership, maintenance, or use of an *underinsured* motor vehicle. It should be noted that the insurer pays *only after* the limits of liability under any applicable bodily injury bonds or policies have been exhausted by payment of judgments or settlements, or a tentative settlement has been made between an injured insured and the insurer of the underinsured motor vehicle. In this latter instance, the insurer of the injured claimant must have been given prompt written notice of the tentative settlement and must have advanced payment to its injured insured in an amount equal to the tentative settlement within thirty days after receipt of the notification.

"Underinsured motor vehicle" is defined as "a land motor vehicle or trailer of any type to which a bodily injury liability bond or policy applies at the time of the accident buts its limit for bodily injury liability is less than the limit of liability for this coverage." This, in effect, allows an insured to recover, up to the limit of liability scheduled for underinsured motorists coverage, the difference between his or her actual damages for bodily injury and the amount of the liability insurance carried by the at-fault driver. Returning to the example above, if A's actual damages for bodily injury are $50,000, his underinsured motorists coverage will pay $35,000, the difference between A's damages and B's limit of liability.

The importance of uninsured and underinsured motorist protection cannot be emphasized too strongly. All too often another driver is legally responsible for an insured's' bodily injury, but when the other driver's insurance coverage is depleted, securing a judgment might well be futile.

Medical Payments Coverage

The insurer promises to pay reasonable expenses incurred for necessary medical and funeral services because of bodily injury that is caused by accident, and sustained by an insured. In this coverage, an *insured* is: the named insured or any family member injured while occupying, or as a pedestrian when struck by a motor vehicle designed for use mainly on public roads or a trailer of any type. Included as well is any person occupying a covered vehicle. As used in this coverage, "pedestrian" is intended to include a bicyclist.

The insurer will pay only those expenses incurred for services rendered within three years from the date of the accident.

As is the case with the other coverages, exclusions apply. For example, there is no coverage for any insured for injury incurred while riding a vehicle having fewer than four wheels. There is no coverage for bodily injury occurring during the course of employment if workers compensation benefits are required or available.

Sometimes, in an attempt to save money, insureds will select the minimum limit available (usually $1,000) or drop the coverage altogether, particularly if they have medical insurance. This cost saving should be

offset against the peace of mind in knowing that the coverage will apply to any non-family passengers in an insured auto. Having this "first dollar" coverage can often prevent a time-consuming lawsuit for a small amount of money.

Personal Injury Protection

Many states have gone to a system of "no-fault" auto insurance. This is a system under which a person injured in an auto accident receives compensation for his or her economic loss from his or her own insurer, regardless of fault. Some states have an unrestricted right to sue; others have a monetary or verbal threshold. Some states allow insureds to reject this coverage. Clients should discuss this option and any questions about the coverage with their agents.

Physical Damage Coverage

Under the terms of the insuring agreement, the insurer will pay for direct and accidental loss to covered autos or any nonowned auto (see below), including the equipment. Any applicable deductible that is shown in the declarations is subtracted from the loss payment. Also, if there is a loss to a nonowned auto, the insurer will provide the broadest coverage that is applicable to any covered auto shown in the declarations. If, for example, a policy insures one owned auto for collision and comprehensive and another owned auto for comprehensive only, a nonowned auto will be covered for both comprehensive and collision if a loss occurs. And, with reference to the deductible, if there is a loss to more than one covered auto or nonowned auto resulting from the same collision, only the highest applicable deductible will apply.

The term "nonowned auto" includes any private passenger auto, pickup, van, or trailer not owned by, or furnished, or available for the regular use of the named insured or any family member, while in the custody of or being operated by the named insured or any family member. There is no requirement that the insured be legally liable for damage to the auto; the insured must only have been operating the auto or had it in his custody at the time of loss. The term also includes any nonowned auto or trailer used as a temporary substitute for a covered auto that is out of normal use because of its breakdown, repair, servicing, loss, or destruction.

The traditional division of automobile physical damage insurance into collision and comprehensive is maintained in the personal auto policy, but without any mention of the word "comprehensive." If "other than collision loss" coverage is indicated in the declarations of a personal auto policy, any damage to the covered auto besides collision is covered on an open perils basis – subject to any deductible listed in the declarations, to the insuring agreement's stipulation that damage be "direct and accidental" and, of course, to any applicable exclusions.

The policy defines collision as the upset of the named insured's covered auto or a nonowned auto or the impact with another vehicle or object. Listed as not being collision – and thus constituting "other than collision" – is loss caused by missiles, falling objects, fire, theft or larceny, explosion, earthquake, windstorm, hail, water, flood, malicious mischief or vandalism, riot or civil commotion, contact with a bird or an animal, or the breakage of glass. Although breakage of glass is listed as not being loss by collision, the policy states that if glass breakage is caused by collision, the named insured may elect to have it considered loss by collision. Without this qualification, a named insured whose car has deductibles on both collision and comprehensive coverage would become responsible, technically, for paying both deductibles after a collision involving body damage and glass breakage to the car. So, basically, the insured can claim glass breakage as either collision or other than collision, depending on which is more advantageous to the insured.

It should be noted that the list of items that are not to be considered "other than collision" is not intended to imply that these and only these are "other than collision." Without the list, it might be possible to say that a falling boulder damaging a car was really a collision loss and subject to a higher deductible.

As noted earlier, if an insured were to rank coverages in order of importance, this would be the least. Would the loss of a new SUV be a hardship? Of course. Would a suit claiming damages of $1,000,000 be catastrophic?

RECREATIONAL VEHICLE COVERAGE

Many persons mistakenly think that motorcycles are automatically covered by their auto policy, just as many think that homeowners insurance will cover an all-terrain vehicle (ATV). Clients should be aware that, as noted above, an auto policy will not respond to liability arising out of use of a vehicle having fewer than four wheels. Homeowners policies provide limited liability for use of a snowmobile or ATV, but no physical damage coverage at all. Motorized vehicles from motor homes to

golf carts, therefore, often require special coverage. The method for insuring these vehicles is either to attach an endorsement to the auto policy, or, in some cases, to the homeowners policy.

If the auto policy is modified, it is through use of endorsement PP 03 23 miscellaneous type vehicle, which may be used to insure motor homes, travel trailers, motorcycles (including motor scooters, motorbikes, and go-carts), snowmobiles and ATVs, golf carts, dune buggies, antique and classic vehicles, and electric autos. The endorsement allows the vehicle to be described, and liability, uninsured and underinsured motorist, physical damage, and medical payments coverages to be indicated. Because motorcyclists, snowmobilers, and ATV riders frequently carry passengers, one of the most important coverages with these vehicles is to make sure that the "passenger hazard" exclusion is deleted – that is, that there *will* be liability coverage for your clients in event of an injury to a passenger.

Boatowners Coverage

Homeowners policies provide limited liability and physical damage coverage for watercraft. For any client owning more than a canoe or rowboat, an insurance agent should review and discuss additional coverage as necessary. Boatowners policies are similar in format to auto policies.

WHERE CAN I FIND OUT MORE ABOUT IT?

1. *The FC&S Bulletins* (Cincinnati, OH: The National Underwriter Company, updated monthly).

2. David Thamann, *Personal Auto Coverage Guide: Interpretation and Coverage Guide* (Cincinnati, OH: The National Underwriter Company, 1999).

QUESTIONS AND ANSWERS

Question – What is the difference between *liability protection* and *physical damage protection* as it applies to the Personal Auto Policy (PAP)?

Answer – Liability protection generally pays for damages that the insured becomes legally obligated to pay to a third party because of property damage or bodily injury that he causes. Physical damage protection covers the actual damage to the covered auto.

Question – What is no-fault auto insurance?

Answer – No-fault insurance is a system under which a person injured in an auto accident receives compensation for economic loss from his or her own carrier.

Question – Why should special coverage be arranged for recreational vehicles, such as an ATV or motorcycle?

Answer – Common auto and homeowners policies will not respond to accidents involving these vehicles under most circumstances. The auto policy, for example, states that it does not provide liability protection for vehicles having fewer than four wheels, or that are designed mainly for use off public roads. The homeowners policy will not provide physical damage coverage for any motorized vehicle other than one used to service the insured's residence, and will only provide limited liability coverage.

END OF CHAPTER REVIEW

1. Clients incur little risk in carrying minimal liability limits, and can save money as well.

   True   False

2. Any motorized vehicle can qualify for a private passenger auto policy.

   True   False

3. The coverage parts of an auto policy are: liability, uninsured and underinsured motorist coverage, medical payments, and physical damage.

   True   False

4. Defense costs are in addition to the limit of liability for bodily injury and property damage.

   True   False

5. "Underinsured motor vehicle" coverage means that an insured, injured by an uninsured party, collects from that driver's insurer an amount equal to the insured driver's liability limits.

   True   False

6. An important provision in medical payments coverage is that it will respond to passengers occupying a covered auto.

   True   False

7. A "nonowned auto" means an auto the insured leases.

   True   False

8. A large rock bounces down a hill and hits the insured's vehicle. The loss is covered under "other than collision," even though the rock collided with the vehicle.

   True   False

9. An auto policy will automatically cover a motorcycle.

   True   False

Chapter 8

BUSINESS AND BUSINESS ACTIVITY INSURANCE

WHAT IS IT?

Many persons engage in business activities without really thinking that is what they are doing. For example, a woman with two small preschoolers might decide that she could earn some extra income by watching two other neighbor children on a regular basis. Or, a man with a woodworking hobby could make and sell rocking chairs at county fairs or flea markets. Even something as simple as maintaining a home office could have liability repercussions that should be addressed. In this chapter, we examine coverage for personal business activities, that is, those that can be insured through personal, rather than commercial, insurance. We will not discuss coverages that fall within specialty insurance, such as malpractice for physicians, surgeons, or dentists, errors and omissions for insurance agents, or directors and officers liability for paid directors of corporations, etc. These are discussed elsewhere in this text.

First, what is a "business?" The homeowners forms generally define a *business* as including a "trade, occupation, or profession." The definition can be extended to include farming and services performed for others for a fee (such as housecleaning or home day care). Often, a *business* does not include part-time activities carried out by minors, like lawn care or baby-sitting. Much confusion (and litigation) has arisen, though, around exactly what connotes a business activity, because homeowners forms do not provide liability coverage for bodily injury or property damage arising out of or in connection with a business engaged in by an insured.

Courts have generally found that a *business* involves two elements: continuity or recurrent character of the activity, and a profit motive. Thus, even an adult's part-time activity (snow-plowing for money) can be construed as a business and therefore not covered by the homeowners policy.

One homeowners form now states that certain activities are *not* to be considered "business" if no insured receives more than $2,000 in total compensation for the twelve months preceding the beginning of the policy period. (Home day care, for other than a relative or for mutual exchange of services, is not covered unless coverage is specifically arranged.) This form also declares that volunteer activities, for which no compensation is received other than payment for expenses, are not to be considered a "business."

THE PERSONAL AUTO POLICY AND BUSINESS USE

It is common for people to use their own autos in the course of business. A salesperson, for instance, making calls within his territory near his home, might well use his or her own auto. The personal auto policy rules allow for this, although insurers will generally set a higher rate on this usage than simply driving to and from work. Rules also allow plumbers, electricians, or carpenters (not an inclusive list) to use a personally owned pick-up or panel van in the course of a business. What the personal auto policy does *not* allow is for the personal vehicle to be used as a "livery conveyance" – that is, the vehicle is held out to the public for hire. (Some insurers now specifically exclude liability for any delivery use, specifically targeting pizza delivery.)

The personal auto policy provides liability coverage for an insured for bodily injury to a domestic employee while that employee is in the course of employment, unless workers compensation benefits are required or available.

Although the personal auto policy excludes liability coverage for any vehicle that is regularly furnished to an insured, it does not preclude coverage if the insured occasionally drives a company car or rents a car for business. The business auto policy, as opposed to the personal auto policy, excludes coverage if, while in the course of employment, one employee negligently injures another. This is the fellow-employee exclusion. For example, say two employees, one the insured, are making a business call together in the insured's personal vehicle. The insured has an at-fault accident, and the co-worker, who is also injured, sues the insured. A commercial auto policy, even assuming one is in place, will not respond, but the insured's personal auto policy will.

THE HOMEOWNERS POLICY AND BUSINESS ACTIVITIES

Homeowners forms are not designed to cover business activities or business property. Having said that, there are some coverages available that will meet many insureds' needs.

In regards to business property, some homeowners forms limit coverage for property "used at any time or in any manner" for any business purpose to $2,500 while the property is on the insured's premises, and $250 while the property is away from the insured's premises (amounts may vary by insurer). Others state that the limited coverage is for property "used primarily" for business. This allows leeway for an insured who, say, has a laptop used both for business and personal activities. Many policies will not cover any other structure on the insured's premises that is used for any business purpose, even, say, a garage used to store unsold Tupperware products.

Some business activities and property can be covered by endorsement to the homeowners policy. Rules allow "permitted incidental occupancies" – that is, incidental to the use of the dwelling as a residence. Coverage can be added for another structure used for business purposes (office, studio, or private school are the exposures contemplated), for an incidental office in the home, and for increased amounts applying to business property. Also covered is the insured's liability for bodily injury or property damage arising out of the incidental use of the premises. It is important to note, though, that there is no liability coverage for anything *other than* bodily injury or property damage. For example, if an insured, working for a realtor, had an office in her home and a client visited, tripped over a step and was injured, the endorsed policy would respond. But if the client sued for negligent misrepresentation of a piece of property, there would be no coverage.

Some incidental farming exposures can be endorsed onto a standard homeowners policy, but often it is better to purchase a farmowners policy.

HOME–BASED BUSINESSES

It is increasingly common for persons to own and run a business from their homes. When this is the case, there are endorsements available that provide insurance that meets most needs. These endorsements effectively function as complete policies. Although they do not provide certain specialty coverages, such as for errors and omissions, or violation of intellectual property laws, they are adequate for many purposes.

There are eligibility requirements. The business must be owned by a person insured on the homeowners policy to which the endorsement is attached. Generally, the forms are designed to cover office, service, sale of tangible products, or sale of crafts operations. Some forms also allow coverage for food, including making and selling consumable products, and for bed-and-breakfasts. Some insurers cap the gross annual receipts and the number of employees.

Property coverage on the home-based business forms includes coverage for business property on the premises, other structures on the premises used in connection with the covered business, property of others in the insured's care for business purposes (such as a sofa being reupholstered), and for valuable papers and records.

Liability coverage for bodily injury or property damage arising out of the insured's or his employee's "acts within the course of employment" is included. Personal and advertising injury coverage is included. There is coverage for slander, libel, or unintentional use of another's advertising idea or copyright infringement.

When coverage is endorsed onto a homeowners policy with a home-based business coverage form, coverage for loss of income arising out of a covered loss is included. Say, for example, there is a fire at the insured's home so that he is faced not only with losing income during the time the home is being repaired, but also must find another place to carry on the business. These forms will respond to those needs. But if a flood forces the business to suspend its operations, there is no coverage. "Flood" is an excluded cause of loss under the underlying homeowners forms. (See Chapter 9, "Personal Property Coverage.")

Although, as noted, these forms provide considerable coverage, they do not provide professional liability coverage, nor do they provide workers compensation. And, as noted above, they are intended for use when the business is incidental to the use of the home as a residence. If the business expands so that the home is no longer an insured's residence, or if the business relocates to another location, commercial insurance (perhaps a businessowners policy) should be contemplated.

WHERE CAN I FIND OUT MORE ABOUT IT?

1. *The FC&S Bulletins* (Cincinnati, OH: The National Underwriter Company, updated monthly).

2. Diane Richardson, *Home-Based Business Coverage Guide: Interpretation and Analysis* (Cincinnati, OH: The National Underwriter Company, 2002).

QUESTIONS AND ANSWERS

Question – What elements must be present for an activity to constitute a "business"? Are part-time activities exempt?

Answer – Generally, two elements must be present: continuity or recurrent character, and a profit motive. Therefore, a part-time occupation if done on a regular basis for profit is considered a business activity.

Question – My client, a pediatrician, has an office in her home as well as a main office with other doctors. What should I look for in regards to insurance protection?

Answer – Although a standard homeowners form can be endorsed to cover an incidental office exposure, liability coverage is for bodily injury or property damage arising out of, say, a patient's visit to the premises. In other words, there is no coverage for any bodily injury resulting from the doctor's practice of medicine. She should have medical malpractice coverage through a specialty insurer. She might well have this with the other doctors in the practice. She might also need a special floater for physicians and surgeons equipment, which would cover this type of property away from the main office. By adding the incidental occupancy endorsement to the homeowners, coverage for property used in business is increased. This could apply to a computer, copier, or other supplies used in the home office.

Question – I have a client who acts as a foster parent. Surely this isn't a business activity – or is it?

Answer – At least one court[1], while agreeing that the amount received might not constitute financial gain, nonetheless remanded the suit for trial as to whether a profit motive existed. Any person contemplating this activity should make sure that any bodily injury or property damage liability will be covered by the foster agency. And, should the foster child make a claim against the insureds for bodily injury, the personal homeowners and auto policy will not necessarily respond, since foster children are, by definition, insureds. The homeowners policy specifically excludes coverage; the auto policy varies by jurisdiction.

CHAPTER ENDNOTES

1. Stuart v. American States Insurance Co, 953 P.2d 463 (Wash. 1998).

END OF CHAPTER REVIEW

1. The courts have generally found that a "business" as defined in the standard homeowners policy is comprised of two elements: continuity and a profit motive.

   True   False

2. A child cuts grass for neighbors during the summer. Because there is continuity and a profit motive, this is considered a "business" activity.

   True   False

3. A person should not use his or her personal auto for any business use, because the personal auto policy excludes liability coverage.

   True   False

4. A homeowners policy may be endorsed to include some incidental business activities.

   True   False

5. Homeowners policies may be endorsed to include professional liability coverage for, say, an attorney or physician.

   True   False

6. When an insured runs a business from his or her home, the best course is to add a home-based business coverage form.

   True   False

7. An advantage to a home-based business coverage form is that the insured will have loss of income coverage.

   True   False

8. Most home-based business coverage forms cover workers compensation.

   True   False

Chapter 9

PERSONAL PROPERTY INSURANCE

WHAT IS IT?

In this chapter, we discuss coverages for personal property – that is, property owned by one or more individuals. (We discuss some business coverage in Chapter 8, and other business exposures in Chapters 6 and 11 through 14.) The property can be *real*; that is, land and the buildings or other structures affixed to it. It can also be *personal* in the sense that household furnishings, clothing, or a fine art collection are all *personal property*. Autos and boats can be personal property as well; these were discussed in Chapter 7. In this chapter we limit ourselves to residences, contents, and other miscellaneous property.

THE HOMEOWNERS POLICY

The common way to insure a residence and its contents is by means of a homeowners policy. Whereas in the past insureds had to purchase separate fire and liability policies, today these are combined so that homeowners policies cover the residence, property contained within, and liability for bodily injury or property damage caused by an insured. The forms that can be used to cover dwellings and personal property are often designated the HO-2, HO-3, and HO-5. These forms provide varying degrees of coverage. Those used primarily to cover personal property are the HO-4 (for tenants) and HO-6 (for condominium owners).

Any of these policies that include coverage on the dwelling structures – Forms 2, 3, and 5 – may be issued to owner-occupants of one- to four-family dwellings that are used primarily for residential purposes. Some incidental occupancies are permitted (see the discussion in Chapter 8). A homeowners form may be used for the purchaser-occupant(s) of a dwelling, who enters into a long-term installment contract. In these instances, the seller maintains title to the property until the terms of the contract are completed, but does not function as a mortgagee.

A homeowners form can be used when the occupant(s) of a dwelling has a life estate arrangement. The intended owner-occupants of dwellings that are under construction may be insured on a homeowners form so long as the policy is written in the name of the intended owner-occupant(s). Seasonal or secondary residences can be insured on a homeowners form.

A recent development, but one that has certainly become more common, is the arrangement whereby a residence is put into a trust. The grantor (or the grantor and spouse) retains the right to live in the residence for a period of years. At the end of the trust term, the residence passes to the beneficiaries. Transfer taxes are minimized through this arrangement.

Property held by a trust was previously subject to insurer and underwriting discretion. The definition of "named insured," as in the auto policy, refers to the spouse, but a trust cannot have a spouse. Some insurers, however, have adopted endorsements that tailor coverage. If your client is subject to this arrangement, his or her agent should review coverage, and contact the insurer if questions arise.

The eligibility requirements for the HO-4, contents broad form, contain the same stipulations as to residential use of the premises and incidental occupancies. Up to one additional family or two boarders or roomers is allowed per dwelling or unit. Tenants of apartments, including cooperative units, single-family dwellings, or mobile homes are most commonly insured by the HO-4. And, as noted earlier, condominium owners (and cooperative apartment owners) are insured on an HO-6.

Dwellings with incidental business occupancy are eligible for homeowners coverage if two conditions are met. First, the premises must be occupied principally as a dwelling. Second, except for the incidental occupancy, no other business may be conducted on the premises. Permitted incidental occupancies include, but are not limited to, business or professional offices, and private schools or studios that provide instruction in music, dance, or photography. Because of the limitations and exclusions of coverage for certain property if a business is conducted on the premises, coverage should be carefully reviewed and arranged to protect the insured.

Who Is an Insured?

As was the case with the auto policy, the words "you" and "your" refer to the named insured – that is, the person whose name appears on the declarations page – and that person's spouse, if residing in the same household. Insureds are also relatives by blood, marriage (including common law), or adoption who reside in the named insured's household. Also included are wards or foster children under the age of 21, but not "significant others." Some insurers, in response to alternative living arrangements, utilize an endorsement that essentially extends "insured" status for both property and liability to the person named in the endorsement. Generally, persons who are "insureds" are covered for personal property and liability for bodily injury or property damage. There is an exception, which will be noted later.

Homeowners Section I Coverages

Insurance provided under Section I of the homeowners policy is divided into five coverage parts:

1. *Coverage A: Dwelling* – Includes structures attached to the dwelling, such as a deck or carport, on-premises construction materials and supplies (and, in form HO-6, building additions and alterations and certain items of real property used by the insured or which the insured is responsible for insuring). Coverage A is not included in tenants' coverage form HO-4, but a limited amount for additions and alterations is included in the additional coverages.

2. *Coverage B: Other structures* – Covers other structures located on the premises that are not connected to the dwelling. This coverage is not included in forms HO-4 or HO-6, but coverage A of form HO-6 applies to items of real property or structures on the residence premises.

3. *Coverage C: Personal property* – Generally applies anywhere in the world to property owned or used by an insured. At the insured's request, also covers property of others while it is located on the part of the residence premises occupied by an insured, and property of a guest or residence employee while in any residence occupied by an insured.

4. *Coverage D: Loss of use* – Consists of three loss-of-use coverages: (a) additional living expense, (b) fair rental value, and (c) prohibited use (that is, when a civil authority prevents access). This coverage applies when a covered loss makes the insured premises unfit to live in.

5. *Additional coverages* – The policy contains additional coverages for incidental exposures: among them debris removal; trees, shrubs, other plants; loss assessment; and credit card, fund transfer card, forgery and counterfeit money. These coverages are usually limited to low dollar amounts, although larger limits may be purchased.

Section I also contains a list of property for which limited or no coverage is provided. Recovery for theft of jewelry, watches, and furs, for example, is limited, although the amount varies by insurer. Coverage for watercraft is limited. Coverage for property on or away from the residence premises and primarily used in a business is limited. There is no coverage for motorized vehicles other than those used to service the premises (a riding lawnmower) or assist the handicapped. The homeowners policy is not designed to insure all types of personal property. Autos, for example, should be insured on an auto policy. Even watercraft, particularly motorized watercraft, are better insured on a boatowners policy.

Named and Special Perils Coverage

Many homeowners policies are written on a named perils basis. For an insured, this means that for a loss to be covered, it must have been caused by an identifiable peril, such as fire, lightning, windstorm, explosion, or vandalism, for example. (This is not a complete list.) Homeowners forms HO-2, HO-4, HO-6, and HO-3 (for contents only) cover property on this basis. The insuring agreement states that the carrier insures against direct physical loss caused by one of the enumerated perils. The disadvantage of this coverage is that the insured must be able to point to the peril that caused the loss.

The other option is special perils coverage. The advantage is that after the insured declares he has had a loss, it is then up to the insurer to discover whether or not an exclusion applies. Indeed, the policy will usually state that the carrier insures against direct physical loss to the property described. Unless an exclusion applies, the loss is covered. Form HO-3 (for the dwelling) and the HO-5 (for dwelling and contents) cover property on this basis. Special perils coverage for contents can be added to the HO-3 by endorsement.

Exclusions

Insurance premiums for personal property are based on the law of large numbers – that is, in any given time frame X number of losses will occur. Insurers also base rates on the principle that losses are fortuitous – that is, a loss might or might not occur to any one insured. If a loss were certain to occur (as to a house built ten feet from the bank of the Mississippi River), insurers would find few persons willing to pay the premium to cover the loss. For this reason, although homeowners policies can be arranged to cover a broad range of personal property, they also contain exclusions.

Loss caused by flood, war, or earthquake is excluded (although insurance for flood and earthquake can be purchased). Loss caused intentionally or by failing to protect property at the time of a loss is not covered. Some losses are excluded, but if they result in an ensuing loss that is not excluded, that loss is covered. For example, there is an exclusion for loss caused by birds. Dents in siding caused by a determined woodpecker are not covered. But if birds build a next in the insured's chimney, with the result that when the first fire of the fall season is lit in the fireplace the house is seriously damaged by fire, that loss is covered. Fire is the ensuing covered cause of loss. This list is not exhaustive. If clients have questions or concerns about their policies, they should discuss them with their agents.

Loss Settlement Provisions

Homeowners forms that are written on a replacement cost basis (HO-2, HO-3 and HO-5) promise to settle a loss to the dwelling by paying not more than the least of: (1) the limit for the dwelling as shown on the declarations; (2) the replacement cost, with like kind and materials, of the damaged building; or (3) the amount necessarily spent to repair or replace the dwelling. This is predicated on the insured's carrying at least 80% of the replacement cost of the dwelling immediately before the loss. Many insurers allow adding an endorsement which provides "guaranteed replacement," as long as the insured maintains full insurance to value, and notifies the insurer in event of an addition or remodeling that adds more than a certain percentage (often 5%) to the value of the dwelling. Some insurers, however, are backing away from guaranteed rebuilding. Other insurers add an endorsement promising to increase coverage by a certain percentage in event the limit is insufficient. This is not the same as guaranteed rebuilding, but it is better than nothing. The advantage is that if the replacement value of the insured's dwelling has increased more than the policy limits indicate, the insured will not face having insufficient insurance to replace his or her dwelling. Clients should discuss these options with their agents.

Contents losses are settled on an actual cash value, which is usually defined as replacement cost new minus depreciation. Insureds have the option of adding "replacement cost coverage" for this property. When this coverage is chosen, and a covered loss occurs, the insured receives an actual cash settlement, which can be amended to replacement cost within 180 days.

Homeowners Section II Coverages

Personal liability insurance is liability protection that applies to activities and conditions at the insured premises, and to the personal (non-business) activities of the named insured and members of the insured's household anywhere in the world. Most commonly the coverage is written as mandatory section II of the homeowners policy. As was noted earlier, there is an exception as to who qualifies as an insured. Persons having legal responsibility for an animal or watercraft to which the insurance applies are insureds, unless they have custody of the animal or watercraft in the course of a business. Also counted as "insureds" are those using a motor vehicle (as used in the homeowners policy, a self-propelled vehicle designed for recreational use off public roads) on an insured location and with the consent of an insured. These individuals are "insured" only for this liability; they have no property coverage under the policy.

The liability coverage of the homeowners forms consists of two principal elements. Coverage E (some insurers use different letters) is personal liability insurance, which protects insureds against liability for negligently caused bodily injury or property damage. Coverage F is medical payments insurance. Both coverages are automatically included; neither one is optional. Homeowners section II coverage also contains four additional coverages: (1) claim expenses; (2) first aid expense; (3) damage to property of others; and (4) loss assessment.

In order for section II coverage to apply, the injury or damage must be caused by an "occurrence." An "occurrence" is defined as "an accident, including continuous or repeated exposure to substantially the same general harmful conditions, which results, during the policy period" in bodily injury or property damage.

"Bodily injury" is defined as "bodily harm, sickness, or disease, including required care, loss of services, and death that results." "Property damage" is defined as "physical injury to, destruction of, or loss of use of tangible property." Note that the loss of use coverage does not require actual *physical injury* to property of others; covered damage can arise if the owner is deprived of the property's use. A common example is negligent blocking of access to property of others, with no actual physical damage. Since the definition includes the words *physical injury* to tangible property, claims for damages arising from, say, economic loss, are not covered. For example, if a homeowner erects a fence so that a neighbor's panoramic view of the ocean is obstructed, the policy will not respond to a claim for damages because there has been no physical injury to the neighbor's property.

Coverage F of the homeowners policies provides medical payments coverage for accidents to persons other than insureds on the insured location with the permission of any insured or, under certain circumstances only, away from the insured location. The insurer agrees to pay the "necessary medical expenses that are incurred or medically ascertained[1] within three years from the date of an accident causing bodily injury." The provision for covering expenses that are "ascertained" within the three-year period addresses the problems associated with claims that involve treatment beyond one year after the time of accident. Dental injuries to children, for example, often cannot be fully treated until the child is older.

Medical expense is defined in the insuring agreement as "reasonable charges for medical, surgical, x-ray, dental, ambulance, hospital, professional nursing, prosthetic devices and funeral services." Unlike the auto medical payments insurance that covers the insured and family members, and other passengers or users of an insured automobile, but not outsiders, the homeowners medical payments coverage applies to outsiders and residence employees, but not to the insured or other residents of the insured's household.

Another unique feature of this coverage is that it does *not* apply to persons on the insured premises without permission of an insured; in other words, trespassers. But the permission need not be specific to the occasion for there to be coverage. A neighbor, for instance, making an uninvited but presumably welcome social call, a mail carrier, or other delivery person all have *implied* permission to be on the premises even though not specifically invited.

There are numerous exclusions applying to the liability and medical payments coverages. The following list is not inclusive. Clients' agents can review exclusions and arrange for coverage to fill any gaps. There is no coverage for bodily injury or property damage arising out of:

1. *A business engaged in by an insured* – Some homeowners forms do not count as "business" activities those which generate a limited amount of money, such as a boy's summer lawn-mowing service, or an insured's making and selling ceramic items at the occasional county show.

2. *The ownership, maintenance, or use of motor vehicles, or the entrustment by an insured of a motor vehicle, or vicarious liability for the actions of a child or minor using a motor vehicle* – There are some exceptions (such as the use of a golf cart to play golf), but for the most part these activities are best insured elsewhere. Likewise, liability arising out of the use of many watercraft is excluded.

3. *Bodily injury or property damage that is expected or intended by an insured* – Many forms add that the exclusion applies even if the bodily injury or property damage is of a different kind or quality, or to another person, than was intended. This exclusion also, in many jurisdictions, serves to preclude coverage for *any other insured* under the policy; for example, if the parents of a child intentionally injuring another are sued for negligent supervision.

MISCELLANEOUS PROPERTY COVERAGES

Many persons have property that merits special attention. Jewelry is the most obvious, since the coverage included in the homeowners for this property is extremely limited. A fine arts collection is another example. The advantage to scheduling this property is that coverage is on a *special perils* basis—that is, a loss is covered unless specifically excluded. The exclusions, however, when arranging coverage on this basis are few. Even loss by flood and earthquake is covered. And, coverage can frequently be arranged on an *agreed value* basis, that is, the amount of coverage on any particular item is agreed to be its value at the time of a loss. Otherwise, as is the case with unscheduled property (contents), loss settlement may be on an actual cash value basis. Another advantage to scheduling is that this provides an additional amount of insurance. Say, for example, an insured owns a $500,000 house (at replacement cost), contents valued at around $350,000, jewelry worth $50,000, and a fine arts collection valued at over $100,000. But his insurance policy indicates $500,000 on the dwelling, $300,000 contents, and no additional coverage for the jewelry or fine arts. In event of a total loss, the most he can collect is $500,000 to replace the dwelling and $300,000 to replace contents. Policy provisions and limits do not allow an insured to decide to replace the $500,000 home with a $75,000 home and collect the remaining $425,000 plus the $300,000 limit for contents to replace all the lost property. Had the jewelry and fine arts been scheduled, he could collect the total of $500,000 for the dwelling, $300,000 for the contents, $50,000 for the jewelry, and $100,000 for the fine arts.

Ownership of rental property and seasonal or secondary residences are other areas meriting special insurance coverage. The homeowners form on the insured's primary residence can extend liability coverage to a seasonal or secondary residence, or to dwellings which are rented to others. Some insurers allow two residences to be insured for both property and liability coverage on one form. If that is not the case, then another homeowners (or condo) policy should be used to insure the property. Rental property, however, should be insured separately on a form called a dwelling fire policy. This policy covers only damage to the property itself. If an insured wishes to obtain separate liability coverage (other than adding coverage to his homeowner's) this can be done.

WHERE CAN I FIND OUT MORE ABOUT IT?

1. *The FC&S Bulletins* (Cincinnati, OH: The National Underwriter Company, updated monthly).

2. Diane Richardson, *The Homeowners Coverage Guide: Interpretation and Analysis*, 2nd ed. (Cincinnati, OH: The National Underwriter Company, 2002).

QUESTIONS AND ANSWERS

Question – What is the difference between an HO-3 and an HO-4?

Answer – An HO-3 is used to insure a dwelling and its contents, while an HO-4 insures contents only.

Question – Who is considered an insured on a homeowners policy? Is there a difference from the auto policy?

Answer – Like the auto policy, the words "you" and "your" refer to the named insured and spouse, if residing in the same household. Resident relatives (that is, related by marriage, blood, or adoption) are insured. Wards or foster children under the age of 21 are insured. Unlike the auto policy, some insurers allow a non-related person to be given insured status through endorsement.

Question – A client has three all-terrain vehicles, a snowmobile, and motorcycle. Will homeowners insurance provide any coverage for bodily injury or property damage arising from the use of these vehicles?

Answer – The homeowners policy will cover liability arising out of the use of the all-terrain vehicles and the snowmobile, but only while they are used on an insured location. "Insured location" is a defined term, and so liability coverage is extremely limited. The homeowners policy will not cover any property damage or bodily injury arising out of the use of the motorcycle.

Question – How does coverage for medical payments differ between the auto policy and the homeowners?

Answer – Unlike the auto policy which covers the insured, family members, and others occupying the covered auto, the homeowners policy applies to residence employees and other than the insured, family members, or other residents of the insured's household.

CHAPTER ENDNOTES

1. See *Webster's Collegiate Dictionary, Tenth Edition*: "ascertain: to find out or learn with certainty."

END OF CHAPTER REVIEW

1. Homeowners policies, including those that cover contents only, include liability coverage for bodily injury and property damage.

    True   False

2. A residence held by a trust cannot be insured on a homeowners form.

    True   False

3. The homeowners section I coverages are: coverage A, dwelling, coverage B, other structures, coverage C, personal property, coverage D, loss of use, and the additional coverages.

    True   False

4. The term "insured" does not include foster children.

    True   False

5. The disadvantage of a "named peril" policy is that, in event of a loss, the insured must be able to identify the peril that caused the loss.

    True   False

6. Among the causes of loss that a standard homeowners policy will not cover are flood and earthquake.

    True   False

7. A person can insure a house with a replacement value of $150,000 for $50,000 and, as long as he has "guaranteed replacement," collect $150,000 in event of a total loss.

    True   False

8. Homeowners liability coverage responds to an accident that results during the policy period in bodily injury or property damage.

    True   False

9. The medical payments section of a homeowners policy will respond to any accident to an insured.

    True   False

10. "Agreed value" coverage means that the amount of coverage on an item is agreed to be the item's value at the time of a loss.

    True   False

Chapter 10

PERSONAL UMBRELLA COVERAGE

WHAT IS IT?

An umbrella policy provides worldwide liability coverage over and above that provided by underlying policies. For most persons, these underlying policies will be auto and homeowners. The liability coverage can be excess, or it can be "drop down." As excess liability, the umbrella provides coverage on top of that already in place. As "drop down," it provides broader coverage than that in the underlying policies. The minimum limit of liability coverage available on any umbrella is $1,000,000. Many insurers will write umbrella coverage for $10,000,000.

Why should someone purchase an umbrella policy? Umbrellas can help preserve an insured's assets by providing high limits of liability coverage. Who would be more likely to be sued in event of an accident, Bill Gates (yes, that Bill Gates) or Suzy Gates, who drives a '95 Chevy Cavalier? This is not to say only the wealthy are targets, as witnessed by the number of civil lawsuits. In 2002, the latest year for which statistics are available, the National Center for State Courts recorded 80,743,561 civil suits (http://www.ncsconline.org/).

WHAT DO UMBRELLAS HAVE IN COMMON?

Although both major policy forms drafters for property and casualty insurers – the Insurance Services Office (ISO) and the American Association of Insurance Services (AAIS) – have umbrella forms, these forms are of fairly recent development. Prior to that, many insurers, if they offered umbrella coverage, designed their own forms. Therefore, although there are some common elements throughout the forms, there are also many differences. For this reason, umbrella forms should be carefully reviewed to make sure there are no unlooked-for gaps in coverage. Ideally, an insured should purchase all policies – auto, homeowners, and umbrella – from the same insurer. An insurer is more likely to try to maintain a client's business if it writes the entire account, and there are less likely to be coverage gaps. Also, few insurers will write a personal umbrella unless they also write either the homeowners or the auto policy or, preferably, both.

There are only a few states that regulate personal umbrellas. Umbrellas are perceived as nonessential.

Every state requires auto insurance (or evidence of financial responsibility); every lending institution requires homeowners insurance. This is not the case with umbrella coverage.

However, umbrella policies do have some elements in common. For the insured, one of the most important is the duty to defend. This duty is in addition to the duty to indemnify, and appears in every umbrella policy.

All umbrella policies assume that an insured will maintain certain underlying limits of insurance. These vary from insurer to insurer. One many require auto limits of at least $100,000/$300,000/$100,000 (that is, bodily injury limits of $100,000 per person, $300,000 per accident, and $100,000 property damage), while another requires at least $500,000 combined single limits. (That is, the $500,000 applies to all bodily injury and property damage arising out of one accident.) Personal liability, usually provided by the underlying homeowners policy, must usually be $100,000. If there is a watercraft not covered by the homeowners, perhaps because it falls outside that form's limited coverage, then the insured must carry a boatowners policy. Motorized recreational vehicles used away from the insured's residence must be properly insured (see Chapter 7, "Automobile and Recreational Vehicle Insurance," and Chapter 9, "Personal Property Insurance.")

All umbrella policies have a deductible, which is called the *retained limit*. This is the part of the loss the insured is expected to assume before the umbrella insurer will step in. The retained limit is often $250, but higher limits are available for a premium credit.

We stress the importance of maintaining the underlying limits. An umbrella will not "drop down" in event an insured, say, allows an auto policy to lapse and then has an accident. If the insured is sued for damages of $100,000 and the auto policy has lapsed, the umbrella will not respond until the amount of damages claimed reaches the limit the insured should have had, plus the retained limit.

All umbrellas respond to a suit for damages alleging bodily injury or property damage arising out of a covered occurrence. Similarly to the auto and homeowners forms, bodily injury and property damage are defined terms. Ideally, an umbrella should also respond to a claim alleging personal injury, which usually means "injury arising out of: false arrest, detention or imprisonment, or malicious prosecution or humiliation; libel, slander, or defamation of character; or invasion of privacy, wrongful eviction or wrongful entry." Although personal injury coverage can be added to many homeowners by endorsement, the umbrella policy should automatically provide the coverage.

All umbrellas require that the bodily injury, property damage, or personal injury result from an accident. Because "malicious prosecution" could hardly be viewed as an accident, some insurers add that an "occurrence" means an "accident" which results in bodily injury or property damage, or "an offense" which results in personal injury.

All umbrellas define "insured" similarly to the definitions already discussed in Chapter 7, "Automobile and Recreational Vehicle Insurance," and Chapter 9, "Personal Property Insurance." That is, named insured and spouse if resident in the same household, resident relatives, and various other entities are insureds if covered in the underlying required policies.

Finally, umbrella policies respond to a covered occurrence that takes place anywhere in the world.

WHAT *DON'T* UMBRELLAS HAVE IN COMMON?

Unfortunately for insureds, the answer is "quite a lot." It is not the purpose of this chapter to investigate every nuance in the various umbrella forms in use. Insureds are well advised to review all possible exposures with their agents and design an insurance program to meet their needs. However, there are certain things to keep in mind. First, although a policy might be designated an *umbrella*, it might well be only an excess liability policy. As noted earlier, an excess liability policy only provides coverage over that of the underlying policies. It does not provide coverage for any exposure not already covered by the underlying form.

A true umbrella provides coverage where the underlying form does not. For example, both homeowners and auto policies exclude coverage for property in the insured's care, custody or control. The homeowners exclusion states the insurer will not cover "property damage to property rented to, occupied or used by or in the care of an insured," but excepts loss caused by fire,

smoke, or explosion. The auto policy excludes liability coverage for property damage to property rented to, used by, or in the care of the insured. But one umbrella form states that it will not cover "property damage to any property for which an insured is contractually obligated to provide insurance at the time of the occurrence." So, for example, if an insured negligently sets off the sprinkler system in a hotel room, the umbrella policy responds, since the insured was not contractually obligated to provide insurance. On the other hand, if an insured rents a car and is required to provide insurance (usually insurance *is* required) the umbrella does not respond. Another umbrella form states it will not cover "property damage to property rented to, occupied by or used by, or in the care, custody or control of the insured, to the extent that the insured is obligated by contract to provide insurance for such property." Again, loss by fire, smoke or explosion is excepted. The coverage in this second form operates like the coverage in the first form – giving coverage where none existed in the underlying homeowners form.

Another example, although this is much less common, is that the umbrella also covers auto accidents occurring anywhere in the world. The auto policy only applies to accidents within the United States and its territories, and Canada, but earlier umbrella forms provided primary coverage for overseas accidents. However, now that travel overseas is much more common, and many persons rent vehicles abroad, most umbrella insurers require that the insured purchase at least the limits he or she maintained in the United States, or the maximum available.

Some umbrella insurers will cover certain limited business exposures, although most will not. A very few include limited coverage for rented aircraft as long as the aircraft is rented with a crew. Coverage for watercraft varies significantly from insurer to insurer. For example, one umbrella form states the insurer will "cover any insured while operating a borrowed or rented watercraft regardless of size or horsepower, as long as it is with the owner's permission and used for the purpose intended." Now, most homeowners forms cover a borrowed sailboat over 26 feet, borrowed watercraft with inboard or inboard-outdrive over 50 horsepower, or borrowed watercraft with outboard engines over 25 horsepower. But for a rented vessel, coverage applies only to a sailboat under 26 feet, or an inboard or inboard-outdrive of less than 50 horsepower. (A rented or borrowed watercraft with outboard engines over 25 horsepower is covered.) Thus, the umbrella gives extremely broad coverage for a borrowed or rented watercraft, even if the underlying homeowners policy does not. But unlike the broad coverage grant in the umbrella just described, other forms follow the wording in the homeowners and will not provide any coverage in addition to that in the homeowners policy unless an underlying boatowners policy is in place.

UNDERWRITING AND UMBRELLAS

Umbrella policies are strictly underwritten. Insurers are "on the hook" for at least one million dollars, so the reason is obvious. Underwriting criteria is strict, and insurers do not consider that having an umbrella policy is a God-given right. Many insurers will not write umbrellas over, say, a youthful driver with several moving violations, or even an adult with one moving violation if that violation happens to be a DUI. Performance boats or performance cars (depending upon who drives them) can be flinch points.

As noted earlier, umbrella insurers require an insured to carry underlying auto and personal liability (often fulfilled by a homeowners policy) insurance. What happens if there are no personal vehicles? If an insured uses a regularly furnished company car, but also has personal vehicles, he or she should endorse extended nonowned coverage for named individuals onto the personal auto policy. If there are no personally owned vehicles at all, then the umbrella insurer might require a named nonowner policy, which provides the necessary underlying liability limits. An insured's agent can make the appropriate arrangements.

WHERE CAN I FIND OUT MORE ABOUT IT?

1. *The FC&S Bulletins* (Cincinnati, OH: The National Underwriter Company, updated monthly).

2. Diane Richardson, *Personal Umbrella Coverage Guide: Interpretation and Analysis* (Cincinnati, OH: The National Underwriter Company, 2000).

QUESTIONS AND ANSWERS

Question – What property does an umbrella cover?

Answer – An umbrella does not cover property at all. It only covers an insured's liability for bodily injury, property damage, or personal injury caused by an accident.

Question – How can I tell if an umbrella policy is really an umbrella, or simply an excess liability policy?

Answer – Unfortunately, few umbrella policies are actually entitled "Excess Liability Policy." The only way to be sure whether the coverage "follows form," that is, is excess, or provides "stand-alone" coverage is to read and compare what is covered (or excluded) in each policy.

Question – Why are there no standard umbrella forms?

Answer – Until recently, insurers developed their own umbrella forms. Insurance Services Office (ISO) and American Association of Insurance Services (AAIS) have each developed an umbrella form. Many insurers, even those who have their own forms, often incorporate material from either of these into their own policies. The reason for this is that much of the language, particularly that in the ISO homeowners and auto, that has been incorporated into the umbrella form has been tested in court.

Question – My client travels extensively to Mexico, where he rents a car. Won't this personal auto policy, and therefore his umbrella policy, cover any liability he might incur?

Answer – No as to the personal auto policy. The personal auto policy covers bodily injury or property damage in the United States, its territories and possessions, Puerto Rico, and Canada. Very limited coverage for Mexico is available by endorsement, but it only applies within twenty-five miles of the U.S.-Mexican border. As for the personal umbrella, generally coverage for auto liability follows form; that is, if there is no underlying applicable insurance, the personal umbrella will not respond either. The best thing for your client to do is obtain underlying coverage from the rental agency in Mexico for both bodily injury and property damage, as well as physical damage coverage for the rented vehicle.

END OF CHAPTER REVIEW

1. An umbrella policy provides worldwide liability coverage over and above that provided by underlying policies.

    True   False

2. A true statement would be that all personal umbrella policies are alike.

    True   False

3. Something all personal umbrella policies have in common is that the insurer has a duty to defend.

    True   False

4. Another word for a deductible with regard to an umbrella policy is "retained limit."

    True   False

5. Umbrella insurers typically require an insured to maintain certain underlying liability limits, such as $100,000 homeowners liability coverage for bodily injury and property damage.

    True   False

6. A person has an umbrella policy, and accidentally allows his auto policy to lapse. If he has an accident, the umbrella policy drops down to cover any resulting bodily injury or property damage.

    True   False

7. A common problem with umbrella forms is that there really are no standard forms.

    True   False

8. A true umbrella should provide coverage where the underlying form does not.

    True   False

Part 3:

GENERAL BUSINESS INSURANCE

Chapter 11

OVERVIEW OF BUSINESS LIABILITY

WHAT IS IT?

Business liability is the risk exposures that any business entity assumes in its dealings with the public. Among the exposures that a business faces are the following: premises and operations liability; products and completed operations liability. To survive as a going concern, a business must identify its liability exposures and decide how to deal with those exposures.

ADVANTAGES

1. Many (if not most) of the business entity's liability risk exposures have been transferred. The insured business does not have to worry about and plan for certain types of losses, and so, the time and money spent on responses to losses can be spent on other items designed to aid the profitability, continuing operations, and survivability of the company. And, should a loss occur, or a lawsuit be filed, the company resources won't be spent paying for the loss or defense costs.

2. The premium paid for the commerical general liability (CGL) form is a legitimate business expense that can be deducted from tax liabilities.

3. After a loss occurs or a lawsuit is filed, the insured can rely on the insurance company to handle most, if not all, of the legal work and other paper work. If the insurance company is competent, the liability claims against the insured will be disposed of or paid promptly so the insured need not spend time and resources addressing the problem.

4. Before a loss or lawsuit occurs, an insurance company could act as a loss control aid to the insured so that liability exposures can be discovered and analyzed and preventive measures put into place so as to prevent losses. For example, an insurer may send its loss control specialist to the insured's premises, the specialist finds something that could cause a future loss and recommends steps to prevent the loss, and the insured implements the recommendation, and no loss occurs thanks to the loss control inspection and efforts.

DISADVANTAGES

1. The insurance coverage costs money, and the premium spent on insurance is money that the insured business does not have for any of its business plans.

2. If the insurer is incompetent or not willing to settle a claim quickly, the insured business is the one getting the bad publicity, and it could end up becoming embroiled in a lawsuit with not only the claimant but also with its own insurer.

3. The insured, through the insurance contract, has agreed to give up any control over the management and settlement of the claim. The general liability insurer retains for itself the right to investigate and settle any claim or lawsuit without the insured having any right to either force a settlement or reject a settlement. This may or may not fit the management style of the company, but that is part of the CGL contract.

4. If the insurer becomes insolvent, the burden of management and settlement of the claim or lawsuit falls back on the insured. No court would allow an injured party to go without compensation just because the insurer of the entity at fault files for bankruptcy. The insured will be forced to pay the compensation because, after all, it is the party legally liable for the injuries to the claimant.

5. While the CGL form does provide financial protection for the insured, that protection is limited by the form's exclusions and set policy limits – not all the risk exposures of the insured will be covered by the CGL form – and the policy limits are of a finite character, so the final sum for which the insured is liable may exceed the policy limits, leaving the insured with the responsibility of paying that excess amount.

BUSINESS LIABILITY INSURANCE

One of the ways a business can handle its liability exposures is by purchasing insurance. The commercial general liability (CGL) coverage form, CG 00 01 or

CG 00 02, is an insurance policy that provides insurance coverage for most of the business liability exposures. CG 00 01 is an occurrence form and CG 00 02 is a claims-made form. An occurrence form simply means that for coverage to apply the injury or damage must occur during the policy period; a claim based on those injuries or damages can be made at any time during or after the policy period. A claims-made form also requires an occurrence to take place during the policy period, but in addition, the claim for damages has to be made during the policy period.

Both CGL forms have basically the same policy structure:

1. *Insuring agreements* – The insuring agreements are the contractual connection between the insured and the insurance company whereby, in consideration for the premium paid by the insured, the insurer agrees to pay those sums that the insured becomes legally obligated to pay as damages.

2. *Exclusions* – The exclusions on the CGL form are those exposures that the insurance policy will not cover.

3. *Supplementary payments* – Supplementary payments are amounts that the insurer promises to pay (in addition to the stated limits of insurance) for certain expenses incurred in handling and settling a claim or lawsuit against the insured.

4. *Who-is-an-insured clauses* – These clauses tell who is considered an insured under the terms of the policy.

5. *Limits of insurance section* – This section describes the amounts that the insurer will pay for a claim against the insured; these limits are stated on the declarations page of the policy.

6. *Conditions* – The conditions set guidelines for the insurer and the insured to follow; these are part of the insurance contract between the insured and the insurer and should be followed as legally binding on both parties.

7. *Definitions* – The definitions tell the insured and the insurer what certain terms used on the CGL form mean; these definitions are important in that the applicability of insuring agreements, exclusions, and conditions may depend on how a word or phrase is defined.

The CGL form is termed "general liability" because it provides coverage for the overall business risk exposures of the insured, that is, the premises and operations liability and the products and completed operations liability of the insured.

Example. The insured owns an office building. If a visitor trips and falls in the building lobby and is injured, a claim can be made against the building owner for the injuries. The insured as the owner of the building owes a duty to visitors to maintain the premises in such a way that no harm comes to them. If that duty is breached and harm results to an innocent victim, the building owner is held responsible and is liable to the injured person for the damages done to him. The CGL form would provide insurance coverage for the insured building owner's liability.

Example. The insured owns an apartment building and his employee is laying carpet in a hallway. While hammering the tacks into the carpet, the employee lets the hammer slip and it flies into the face of a deliveryman, breaking a cheekbone. The insured – through his employee's activity – is performing an operation in his building and this operation caused an injury. The CGL form would apply to a resultant claim.

Example. The insured manufactures chairs. A customer buys the product and when he sits on it, the chair collapses and the customer falls, breaking his arm. This is a product failure for which the insured is liable because he made the product and offered it for sale as a safe and useful product to the general public. The product failed and this was a breach of the insured's duty. The breach caused harm and the CGL form would apply to a claim due to this breach.

Example. The insured is a contractor and builds a retaining wall for a customer. One month after the job was completed, the wall falls on the customer's son and causes severe internal injuries. The insured's completed operations caused the injury to an innocent victim and the CGL form would respond to a claim made against the insured.

The key point throughout all these examples is that the insured was legally liable for the injuries. The CGL form will provide insurance coverage for the insured, but he must be legally liable, that is, obligated by law, to pay for the damages he caused to another. If the insured is not legally liable, there is no obligation on the insurer's part, through the CGL form, to pay for the injured person's damages. Of course, even though the CGL form will not pay damages if the insured is not legally liable, the form will pay defense costs for the insured if he is sued due to the damages. This duty to defend is a contractual obligation under the terms of the CGL form and is a broader duty than the duty to pay damages.

LIMITATIONS AND EXCLUSIONS

The CGL form does apply to the insured's general liability exposures. However, this coverage is not absolute. There are exclusions and limitations written into the CGL form that affect the scope of coverage.

One of the limitations is that the liability insurance provided by the CGL form is for bodily injury (BI), property damage (PD), or personal and advertising injury. These are all defined terms on the policy and if the injury or damage claim alleged against the insured does not match one of these definitions, the CGL form will not cover the claim. For example, bodily injury on the CGL form is defined as "bodily injury, sickness, or disease sustained by a person, including death resulting from any of these at any time." If the claim against the insured is one of discrimination or breach of contract, the CGL form will not respond because there was no BI or PD as defined on the form. As another example, personal injury is defined on the CGL form as including infringing upon another's copyright, but does not include patent infringement; so, a patent infringement claim against the insured will not be covered by the CGL form.

Another limitation is that the injury or damage has to take place in the coverage territory and during the policy period. Coverage territory is a defined term and "during the policy period" means that the injury or damage has to occur while the policy is in force. There usually is no problem in determining whether the injury or damage occurred in the coverage territory, but "during the policy period" is a period subject to differing interpretations by courts around the country.

Another limitation is on just how much the insurer will pay for a claim against the insured. When an insured chooses to buy an insurance policy, he has to decide the limits of insurance. These stated limits are the most that the insurer will pay for a claim regardless of the number of insureds, claims made or lawsuits brought, or persons or organizations making the claims or bringing the lawsuits. If the amount the insured is legally liable to pay an injured person exceeds the limits of insurance stated on the CGL form, that particular part of the risk will not fall to the insurer.

The exclusions on the CGL form are standardized and represent those types of risk exposures that an insurer either cannot or does not want to insure against. For example, coverage A (BI and PD) on the CGL form has an exclusion for BI or PD expected or intended from the standpoint of the insured. The coverage A insuring agreement is based on an occurrence – an accident – so if the insured intended to hurt someone or damage another's property, that would not be in accord with the intent of the insuring agreement. Other examples are the workers compensation and employers liability exclusions; these are better handled by a workers compensation policy in accordance with the workers compensation system established in the various states. Also, BI or PD arising from the escape or release of pollutants is largely excluded under a CGL form because of the specialty type nature of that exposure.

The coverage B (personal and advertising injury) insuring agreement on the CGL form does apply to intended acts of the insured, but this does not mean the coverage is without limitations. For example, coverage B will not apply to criminal acts committed by the insured. The same is true of a knowing violation of the rights of another by publishing material that the insured knows is false. And, if the insured is in the business of advertising, broadcasting, publishing, or telecasting, the personal and advertising liability coverage will not apply; these businesses need a specialty type liability policy that can specifically address their unique liability exposures.

Other exclusions are added to the CGL form through the use of endorsements. There are many situations when either an insured or an insurer will desire to exclude certain coverages that may otherwise be provided by or potentially within the coverage of the CGL form, so endorsements are added to the CGL form to prevent such coverage. For example, the standard CGL form does not exclude BI or PD arising out of the providing of professional health care services. Since this type of coverage is meant to be written through specialty type policies (such as hospital professional liability or physicians professional liability insurance), an insurer would normally add an endorsement like CG 21 16, Exclusion – Designated Professional Services, to the

CGL form to prevent the CGL form from applying to a claim based on medical malpractice. As another example, if the insured does not desire products-completed operations liability insurance for some reason, or the insurer is not willing to provide that coverage, endorsement CG 21 04, Exclusion – Products/Completed Operations Hazard, can be added to the CGL form to prevent such coverage.

Thus, while the scope of coverage under the CGL form may be very general, that coverage can be limited or excluded depending on the requirements and objectives of the insured and the insurer.

OTHER TYPES OF INSURANCE FOR BUSINESS LIABILITY RISKS

The business entity seeking to transfer its liability risk exposures through the use of a commercial general liability insurance form should analyze its exposures and decide if a CGL form is the appropriate tool with which to handle the exposures.

A CGL form will apply to liability exposures that a business entity faces arising out of the entity's premises, operations, products, and completed operations. A CGL form would be the appropriate tool to transfer risk exposures for businesses such as retail stores, offices, motels and hotels, service organizations, theaters, and clubs. These entities have no out-of-the-ordinary risk exposures and a commercial general liability policy should be adequate to protect the insured's interests.

However, for businesses that do have special exposures or that have risk exposures that the insurance company does not wish to insure, there are other liability policies that can fill the risk exposure gaps on the CGL form that exist. For example, there are pollution liability coverage forms that offer protection for this type of liability; there is an employment-related practices liability form that applies to injuries based on things like humiliation, discrimination, and sexual harassment; and there are various professional liability policies that more properly apply to professional liability exposures than does the CGL form (see Chapter 12, "Professional Liability Insurance").

And, speaking of policies that more properly apply than does the CGL form, there are certain risks that, while not always specifically excluded under a CGL form, should have a different liability form so that the insured's unique exposures are properly handled. For example, there is an owners and contractors protective liability coverage that applies to BI or PD arising out of operations performed for the named insured by a contractor or the named insured's acts or omissions in connection with the general supervision of those operations; an underground storage tank policy that applies to BI or PD arising out of a release of petroleum from an underground storage tank into water or subsurface soils; and a warehouseman's legal liability coverage policy that applies to the insured's legal liability for loss to property while in his care, custody, or control.

Whatever liability risk exposures an entity has, if the business decision is made to manage those exposures through insurance, the risk manager of the business entity must look at all the possible liability exposures, and decide what type of liability policy is best suited for the purpose. A CGL form will apply to most of the liability exposures, but other liability policies may be needed to complete the protective circle around the insured. One size does not fit all when it comes to buying insurance. So, the specific problems, exposures, goals, and financial situation of the individual have to be determined before an insurance buying decision is made.

As part of the decision making process, the entity should discuss its liability exposures with an experienced insurance agent so that, not only can all the risk exposures be identified, but also so that the proper types of liability policies can be purchased. One more thing for an insured and an agent to discuss – premium. The premium paid for the liability insurance should be within the capabilities of the insured to pay, and should be in line with what the insured has decided it can afford to pay and wants to pay to have its liability risks covered by an insurance policy.

Once the CGL form (and any other liability policies) has been purchased, the insured needs to monitor the results.

1. Have the liability policies been applicable to the losses and claims?

2. Are the limits of insurance adequate?

3. Is the amount paid in premium cost effective?

4. Are there any new exposures that have arisen or ceased to exist since the liability policies became effective?

5. Have any claims and lawsuits been properly and satisfactorily handled by the insurer?

If the results of this monitoring are satisfactory, the insured can rest assured that its decision to purchase liability insurance was a wise business decision. If the results are not as expected, changes have to be made.

WHERE CAN I FIND OUT MORE ABOUT IT?

1. *The FC&S Bulletins* (Cincinnati, OH: The National Underwriter Company, updated monthly).

2. Donald S. Malecki and Arthur l. Flitner, *Commercial General Liability*, 7th ed. (Cincinnati, OH: The National Underwriter Company, 2001).

QUESTIONS AND ANSWERS

Question – What are the two types of commercial general liability forms?

Answer – An occurrence type and a claims-made type.

Question – What are supplementary payments under the CGL form?

Answer – Amounts that the insurer promises to pay for certain expenses incurred in handling and settling a claim or lawsuit against the insured.

Question – How does the CGL form define "bodily injury"?

Answer – Bodily injury, sickness, or disease sustained by a person, including death resulting from any of these at any time.

Question – What is coverage B under the CGL form?

Answer – Coverage B is for personal and advertising injury liability.

Question – To what type of business risk exposures does the commercial general liability apply?

Answer – The CGL form provides coverage for the following business risk exposures: the premises and operations liability and the products and completed operations liability of the insured.

END OF CHAPTER REVIEW

1. Under an occurrence form, the injury or damage can occur at any time before or after the policy period.

    True   False

2. A claims-made form requires the claim for damages to be made during the policy period.

    True   False

3. Supplementary payments made under a general liability policy are in addition to the stated limits of insurance.

    True   False

4. The duty to defend the insured in case of a lawsuit against him is dependent on his being legally liable for the alleged injury or damage.

    True   False

5. The commercial general liability coverage form provides liability insurance for bodily injury, property damage, and personal and advertising injury.

    True   False

6. The definition of personal injury on the general liability policy includes patent infringement.

    True   False

7. A warehouseman's legal liability policy applies to the insured's legal liability for loss to property while in his care, custody, or control.

    True   False

8. A premium paid for general liability insurance is a legitimate business expense that can be deducted from tax liabilities.

    True   False

9. The general liability insurer retains for itself the right to settle any claim or lawsuit against the insured without seeking approval from the insured.

    True   False

Chapter 12

PROFESSIONAL LIABILITY INSURANCE

WHAT IS IT?

Virtually any business or firm can become liable for injury to others resulting from a condition on its premises or arising out of its operations in progress, products, completed work, and other exposures. Commercia general liability (CGL) insurance covers those exposures. General liability insurance is discussed in Chapter 11.

Individuals or organizations that render professional services face an additional liability exposure – their failure to use due care and the degree of skill expected of a person in a particular profession. This standard of care is higher than that of general liability exposures, which sets the bar at how a *reasonable* individual would act in the particular situation. Insurance for such professional exposures are known by various names and without complete consistency. Some of the typical names are professional liability insurance, malpractice insurance, or errors and omissions liability insurance.

The general subject of professional liability insurance is covered in this chapter. The discussion introduces the area of professional liability insurance and the standard coverage forms that are available.

BUSINESS USES

Professional liability insurance is available for a wide array of professional categories. Among them are the healthcare professions, including physicians, hospitals, clinics, nurses, and allied healthcare providers; business professionals, including accountants and actuaries; legal professionals, namely attorneys; and other professionals, such as insurance agents, veterinarians, architects, and optometrists.

What constitutes a professional? There are lengthy legal treatises that answer this question in detail. However, in general, professionals are considered to be individuals who:

- have a high degree of education and specialized training;

- are licensed by a governmental board or entity;

- operate under a code of ethics that is above that of the general services sector;

- emphasize social responsibility, which typically is recognized by a public law or regulation; and

- operate under a disciplinary system that sets licensing requirements.

Individuals who fall within a profession are subject to the higher standard of care and are eligible to purchase professional liability insurance. If a profession does not fall under one of the categories for which insurance companies have designed a specialized coverage form, they may be able to purchase Miscellaneous Professional Liability insurance, which can be modified to fit the needs of miscellaneous types of professions.

ADVANTAGES

1. Commercial general liability insurance specifically excludes coverage for certain types of professionals. In addition, underwriters often will attach a professional services exclusions on CGL policies that are offered to professional individuals and corporations. This creates a grave exposure for the professional because the standard of care under which they operate creates a heightened liability exposure. Professional liability insurance helps to fund this exposure.

2. CGL insurance responds only to bodily injury, property damage, or personal injury (libel, slander, invasion of privacy, etc.). Professional liability claims often involve financial damages, which are not covered by the CGL policy.

3. Another advantage of professional liability insurance is that it typically responds to claims alleging that the professional *failed to perform* as well as caused damages because of the way she performed. Failure to perform claims typically are not covered by the CGL insurance form.

4. Some insurance companies may offer specialized professional liability error prevention training and

guidance to their policyholders, which can provide valuable assistance in avoiding committing acts that are likely to result in claims.

5. In addition, some states require that professionals (such as doctors) carry professional liability insurance before they can be licensed.

DISADVANTAGES

1. Cost is a factor with professional liability insurance.

2. Professional liability insurance also may be difficult to obtain. For example, medical malpractice insurance was virtually unavailable – except for exorbitant prices – in a number of states during the first few years of the Twenty First Century. Lawsuits against physicians and hospitals were so prevalent, and damages claims were so high (according to the insurance industry) that many physicians effectively were shut out of the market. Some changed specialties because the insurance premiums for their chosen area of specialization had escalated beyond their ability to pay.

3. A great deal of professional liability insurance is issued through Lloyd's and other nonstandard carriers. Such forms differ from insurer to insurer, so each must be read individually to discover particular coverage nuances and pertinent exclusions of coverage.

DESIGN FEATURES

As for standard forms, the Insurance Services Office (ISO) maintains standard coverage parts for hospital professional; physicians, surgeons, and dentists professional; lawyers professional liability insurance; and a number of other related coverage forms and endorsements. Rules and rating procedures are contained within division seven of the commercial lines manual (CLM).

Occurrence or Claims–Made Forms

These standard forms include both an occurrence version and claims-made version. An occurrence typically is defined as an event that triggers coverage on an insurance policy. An occurrence-based policy covers injury or damage that occurs during the policy period even if the claim is not brought until months or even years after the event. In contrast, a claims-made policy responds only to claims for injury or damage that are made to the insurer during the policy period or a designated extended reporting period. Once a claims-made policy term expires, new claims that arise from events that occurred during that policy period must be filed on the claims-made policy that is in effect on the date that the claim is made.

Example. A healthcare professional insurance policy runs from July 1 to June 30 each year. On July 5, 2003, the professional performs surgery on a patient and leaves a sponge behind after closing the incision. The sponge does not cause the patient problems right away. However, on October 5, 2005, the patient is rushed to the hospital with serious pain. The sponge is found, and the patient files a malpractice claim against the surgeon who erred. If the surgeon carried an occurrence-based policy, the insurance policy that was in effect on July 5, 2003 – the date when the error occurred – would respond to the claim. However, if the surgeon carried claims-made coverage, the policy that was in effect on October 5, 2005, would respond – this policy, with a term of July 1, 2005, to June 30, 2006, was not purchased until two years after the occurrence. It applies to the claim, however, because the claim was made during its term of coverage.

Types of Injury and Damages

Unlike other liability coverage, professional liability insurance is not restricted to liability for injury caused by an occurrence (i.e., caused by an accident). In many cases, the professional person will do exactly what he or she intends to do, but, for example, a diagnosis will turn out to be faulty and the patient injured as a result. Injury of this type might not be caused by an occurrence, but it can be and often has been the basis of liability.

Another feature of professional liability coverage is that the insuring agreements are not framed in terms of "bodily injury" and "property damage." The hospital and physicians liability forms both apply to damages because of "injury" resulting from professional services. Since "injury" is not defined in either form, it is considered to encompass bodily injury and property damage as well as "personal injury" like humiliation, invasion of privacy, and slander if they arise out of professional services.

Lawyers liability insurance covers damages because of "any act or omission" in the rendering of professional services as a lawyer but flatly excludes both bodily injury and damage to *tangible* property. The principal exposure that lawyers liability insurance does cover is *monetary loss* attributable to the insured's malpractice. An example is a judgment entered against a client as a result of the insured's failure to provide such defense as the client was entitled to expect from a qualified attorney. Lawyers liability insurance is also broad enough to cover damages for certain types of personal injury such as libel, slander, and humiliation so long as the injury results from the rendering of or the failure to render professional services as a lawyer and is not reached by the policy's definition of "bodily injury" or by any other policy exclusions.

For much of their history, hospital liability and physicians liability insurance were issued subject to a per claim limit of liability and an aggregate limit of liability. The per claim limit applied to each claim made against the insured regardless of the number of claims arising from a single act or omission, and the aggregate limit was the most that would be paid as damages on behalf of the insured during any policy year. In 1977, a modified form was introduced in many territories that replaced the per claim limit with a per "medical incident" limit. The purpose of the change was to eliminate the availability of the full limit of liability for each of the several claims that might result from a single act or omission on the part of the insured. For example, a patient and his family might make separate claims against a physician for damages resulting from the same alleged instance of malpractice. Under the earlier forms, the per claim limit would apply separately for each claim. Under the later forms, the per "medical incident" limit is the most that can be collected for both claims.

By the same token, standard forms for professional liability insurance traditionally required that the insurance company obtain the insured's written consent before settling any claim, a point once considered so important that early malpractice policies were titled "physicians defense." The reputation of the professional person was regarded as such a critical asset that an insurer was not allowed to settle any claim until all legal remedies were exhausted and the professional agreed to the settlement. The consent-to-settle feature was not carried forward in the current editions of hospital liability and physicians liability insurance; it remained a feature of lawyers liability insurance until that form was revised in 1981. However, policies that are issued by individual carriers still may contain this feature.

Besides the lawyers liability forms introduced in 1981, revised editions of the hospital liability and physicians liability forms were introduced in that same year. Note that ISO has recently released a revised version of the physicians, surgeons, and dentists professional liability coverage form. Other ISO-filed forms include:

- hospital professional liability form;

- allied health care providers professional liability form;

- blood banks professional liability form;

- diagnostic testing laboratories professional form;

- optometrists form; and

- veterinarians form.

Most of these coverages were previously provided as endorsements, but now are stand-alone coverage forms.

The coverage forms are published in both the occurrence version and the claims-made version. Note that the claims-made lawyers liability form does not impose a retroactive date. Instead, it excludes any claim arising out of an act or omission occurring prior to the effective date of the policy – but only if the insured knew or could have reasonably foreseen before policy inception that the prior act or omission might result in a claim. Hence, the lawyers liability form covers prior acts or omissions that the insured could not have reasonably foreseen as leading to a claim. If the insured's prior acts pose an unacceptable risk, the insurer can impose a retroactive date on lawyers liability coverage.

A retroactive date defines the time period of events to which the policy applies. Claims resulting from occurrences prior to the policy's stated retroactive date are excluded.

WHERE CAN I FIND OUT MORE ABOUT IT?

1. *FC&S Bulletins* (Cincinnati, OH: The National Underwriter Company, updated monthly).

2. The Professional Liability Underwriting Society (PLUS), 4248 Park Glen Road, Minneapolis, MN 55416, Phone (952) 928-4644, http://plusweb.org/.

END OF CHAPTER REVIEW

1. Individuals who are considered professionals operate under a code of ethics that is higher than that of the general population.

   True   False

2. Commercial general liability insurance includes coverage for professional liability as a separate limit of insurance, which is called the general aggregate.

   True   False

3. Professional liability insurance typically responds to claims that allege a failure to perform, as well as to claims alleging injury caused by the way in which a person did perform.

   True   False

4. The standard of care that professionals owe is higher than that of general liability exposures, which are based on how a reasonable individual would act in a situation.

   True   False

5. Lawyers professional liability insurance typically provides coverage for monetary (or financial) loss that can be attributed to the insured lawyer's mistakes or malpractice.

   True   False

6. The ISO lawyers liability form is offered as either an occurrence-based or a claims-made form.

   True   False

7. Per claim limits of liability refer to the most that an insurance company will pay as damages for an insured during a specific policy period.

   True   False

8. Professional liability coverage is restricted to liability for injury caused by an accident.

   True   False

9. Retroactive dates on claims-made policies provide coverage for claims arising from accidents or occurrence that take place prior to the retroactive date that is stated on the policy.

   True   False

Chapter 13

DIRECTORS AND OFFICERS LIABILITY INSURANCE

WHAT IS IT?

Directors and officers (D&O) liability insurance is a coverage developed to protect individuals who serve as directors and officers of corporations. The policy responds primarily to financial loss arising from wrongful acts committed or alleged against these individuals. Its original scope has been expanded, however, beyond solely insuring such personal liabilities. Some D&O policies now offer coverage for certain types of loss arising from wrongful acts claimed against the entity itself. A debate has arisen in the insurance and risk management community about the wisdom of providing entity coverage on D&O policies because it can exhaust coverage limits that individual directors and officers may be counting on.

D&O policy forms differ from insurer to insurer. In fact, insurance companies may even offer different forms of coverage from within their own organizations. Because of this, D&O policies cannot be measured against a standard format, but, rather, must be compared one-to-one against each other. It can be said in general, however, that D&O policies are written to respond to financial loss, and not bodily injury or property damage claims, which are more appropriately insured by other types of liability policies.

There are certain attributes and coverage areas that are of particular importance when reviewing D&O coverage. This chapter highlights those in order to give financial services professionals a road map by which to evaluate a particular insurance company's D&O program – and whether it is appropriate for the exposures involved.

Types of Entities Needing D&O Coverage

Many types of organizations have boards of directors. These include

1. publicly traded corporations;

2. privately or closely held companies; and

3. not-for-profit organizations.

Publicly traded corporations are those whose shares are traded publicly on a stock exchange. *Privately held companies* are companies that are owned by one or a small group of individuals – or a family. These companies do not offer ownership of company shares to the general public. *Closely held companies* are typically owned by a small group of individuals. Members of the group may trade or sell shares among themselves or select individuals, but they do not offer ownership in the company to the general public. *Not-for-profit* organizations (which may be erroneously referred to as non-profit organizations) are organized for a purpose other than that of making a profit, although not-for-profit organizations are permitted to realize a profit from their operations. Such organizations usually are organized to serve a community, charitable, or fraternal purpose.[1] For the sake of simplicity in this chapter, the terms *entity, organization*, and *corporation* are used in their broadest generic sense. In general, the terms are used interchangeably to include publicly traded, private, and not-for-profit organizations. Chapter sections that deal with D&O insurance that is designed solely and specifically for one type of organization will clearly state how the discussion is limited.

Responsibilities of Directors and Officers

Directors are elected by an entity's shareholders or membership to govern the entity. Collectively, these individuals are referred to as the board of directors. Many directors are recruited from outside the entity and may be community leaders, experts in a particular area such as accounting, or officers of noncompetitor companies that are engaged in similar types of operations. A director may also be a corporate officer. For example, the president or chief executive officer of a corporation may also be a member of the board of directors.

In July of 2002, President Bush signed the Sarbanes-Oxley Act of 2002. This law applies generally to publicly traded companies and establishes new standards of accounting and financial reporting for those companies. A new Public Company Accounting Oversight Board has been charged with overseeing the auditing of public companies, as well as their auditors. The Act (often referred to as Sarbox or SOX) has dramatically changed the financial reporting requirements of public companies, including mandates that chief executive and chief financial officers must certify financial reports and that internal controls be in place to guard against improper methods of inflating company worth. It also has heightened the scrutiny of directors who are not independent of the corporation. All of this has impacted the D&O marketplace, which was in somewhat of a turmoil following the uncovering of major corporate scandals. The requirements of Sarbanes-Oxley has placed additional burdens on public companies and their management teams, and D&O underwriters now include review of Sarbanes-Oxley compliance when underwriting the coverage.

Directors who do not serve as corporate officers are not involved in the day-to-day operation and management of the entity. Rather, they are charged with overseeing long-range strategic matters. They do this through areas such as the appointment and removal of executive officers, the declaring of dividends, the monitoring of financial data, and the overseeing of merger and acquisition activity. There may be a conflict of interest – or at least the appearance of a conflict – when a director who also is a corporate officer must take action that affects his or her position with the company.

General Categories of Exposures

In general, shareholder suits are the most frequent and serious exposure for directors and officers of publicly traded companies. Shareholder suits usually are filed as *derivative suits*, which are brought by shareholders on behalf of the corporation. The shareholders normally must demand that the corporation file suit against the alleged wrongdoing of directors and officers, and the corporation usually must decline to do so, before a derivative suit is allowed. Such shareholder suits may be brought for various reasons, but they are frequently seen when the price of the corporation's stock drops and the shareholders allege that the actions of the directors and officers caused the loss in value.

Shareholder suits obviously are not a common problem for privately held and not-for-profit organizations because there are no outside shareholders in those types of business organizations. That may lead some directors and officers – especially those that serve privately held entities – to falsely believe that they are insulated from legal action. However, minority shareholder suits are always possible, even in family-owned businesses, and all types of organizations –

public, private, and not-for-profit – are exposed to claims from a variety of sources other than shareholders. These include claims filed by the corporation itself, or by its employees, customers, competitors, financial backers, or the government.

Varieties of Shareholder and Corporate Claims

Fiduciary Duty

Directors and officers of all three types of organizations have a *fiduciary duty* to the corporation and its shareholders; they must put the interests of the corporation above their own. Owing a fiduciary duty also means that the directors owe the organization – and its shareholders in a publicly traded organization – a high degree of good faith, candor, and loyalty. Directors may face personal liability if they are found to have breached this fiduciary duty in their dealings as board members.

For example, a group of directors may try to stop shareholder efforts to change the makeup of the board, executive management, or majority ownership. These directors may be sued for blocking such a change. In defending their attempts to impede the change, the directors may have to prove that they were acting in the best interest of the corporation – and not out of self-interest – in order to avoid a finding that they breached their fiduciary duty.

Negligence

In addition to having a fiduciary duty to the entity, directors and officers may be liable for losses that arise from negligence in their actions as board members. Many states have tempered this potential liability by adopting what is called the *business judgment rule*. The business judgment rule provides a shield against liability for those who act in good faith in making business decisions that subsequently prove faulty or detrimental to the organization. The business judgment rule, however, would not shield a director or officer who was grossly negligent or took action that was outside his duty as a director.

Bad Faith

The third general type of liability faced by directors is bad faith, sometimes called unauthorized conduct. Directors and officers are not shielded by the business judgment rule when they engage in bad faith actions or fraud, or when they operate outside the activities permitted by the company's articles of incorporation and bylaws. For example, a developer filed bankruptcy before completing a planned community that included a marina. The developer and the homeowners' association agreed on an allocation of expenses between the marina and the residential units that was voted on by board members who owned residential units. The marina club sued to invalidate the allocation, claiming that it was unreasonable. The bankruptcy court held that the business judgment rule did not protect the allocation, which was unreasonable, and substituted another allocation. On appeal, the court found that the board members' conflict of interest negated application of the business judgment rule because the board's action was unreasonable and in bad faith.[2]

Other Categories of Claims

Employee Claims

Employee claims of employment discrimination and/or wrongful discharge against directors and officers have skyrocketed in recent decades. Directors and officers frequently are targeted when such actions are filed with state or federal equal employment commissions or in the courts. The basis of many such claims is discrimination that arises from the employee's membership in a *protected group*. In general, state and federal employment laws prohibit employers from making employment decisions on the basis of an individual's

- race;

- gender;

- religion or creed;

- national origin;

- age; or

- disability.

These six categories often are referred to as *protected groups*. Employers that fall within the scope of such employment laws – which usually is determined by the number of employees – are precluded from discriminating against employees because of their membership in one of the groups. Individual states may add protected categories. For example, in Kentucky, employers are prohibited from discriminating against employees on the basis of tobacco usage.

In response to the escalating number and severity of such claims, a special type of insurance coverage – employment-related practices liability (ERPL) insur-

ance – was developed. Many D&O policies include coverage for ERPL claims against directors and officers within their forms. Others extend that coverage to managers who are not directors and officers and to claims against the organization (the entity) by attaching an ERPL endorsement. At times, a separate ERPL insurance policy may be more appropriate.

Employment-related claims are probably the greatest source of legal action against directors and officers, other than shareholder claims in publicly traded companies.

Claims from Those Outside the Organization

Customers, vendors, and competitors may allege that corporate officers or directors are personally liable for financial damages they incurred because the directors or officers were directly involved in an action. In other words, if a corporation decides to terminate a lease or draw up plans, an individual officer may be held personally liable if she was directly involved in the activity that led to the claimant's financial loss.

Competitors also may be the source of claims alleging personal liability. For example, corporate officers who control the day-to-day operations of an organization may be held personally liable for direct involvement in activities that involve unfair competition, stealing trade secrets, or patent infringement.

Various governmental agencies may be able to file actions against individual directors and officers for violation of certain laws if the individuals are directly involved in the alleged violations. Included among these would be violations of the Employee Retirement Income Security Act of 1974 (ERISA) and various federal environmental laws. For example, a corporate officer may be held liable for pollution violations if the officer was involved in the day-to-day operation of waste disposal that resulted in a violation.

Another situation in which directors and officers may be held personally liability, which has received increasing attention in recent years, is the theory of *deepening insolvency*. Deepening insolvency describes a process in which directors and officers may keep a business alive in the face of deepening financial problems, which leads to further extensions of credit. Instead of deciding to end the business, the executives are accused of failing to take reasonable action to cease operations. Keeping the business going and masking financial problems may lead creditors to become more deeply entrenched with the company. Directors and officers may face allegations of mismanagement and/or misrepresentation about the state of the business's finances.

BUSINESS USES

There are various methods that may help to pay for losses that involve a director's or officer's personal liability for their business decisions.

Corporate Indemnification

Corporate indemnification is one method of protecting directors and officers from their liability exposure from business management decisions. Most state legislatures have passed statutes that permit corporations to indemnify (secure against financial damage) directors and officers for their business decisions. The statutes are aimed at encouraging capable individuals to serve on corporate boards without fearing that their personal assets could be tapped to pay for liability arising from their good-faith business decisions.

There are two types of corporate indemnification:

- mandatory; and

- permissive.

Mandatory indemnification can be defined as an absolute statutory requirement that directors and officers be indemnified for their expenses to defend proceedings brought against them, as well as for settlements or judgments arising from such actions. *Permissive indemnification* involves situations in which a corporation is permitted, but not required, to indemnify directors and officers in situations where the individual is not entitled to mandatory indemnification. An example of permissive indemnification would be a proceeding in which a claim is settled before final judgment, with the claim being settled even though the executive acted in good faith. Since each state's laws vary as to mandatory and permissive indemnification, individual statutes should be reviewed for particular situations. In addition, corporate bylaws should be reviewed to determine whether they take full advantage of indemnification possibilities.

Corporate indemnification is important because it is the first line of protection available to directors and officers. It permits corporations to pay for the costs of defending suits against directors and officers for their good-faith actions, along with paying for judgments and settlements against them.

So Why Buy D&O Insurance?

If corporate indemnification is available to directors and officers, why should an organization spend the money to purchase a D&O liability policy?

In general, D&O policies fund the personal liability exposures of individuals serving as officers and directors, as well paying the corporation's expenses to indemnify those individuals. A D&O policy might not be necessary if corporate indemnification were assured. But, even in cases in which mandatory indemnification is required, the organization may not have sufficient funds to pay for the defense and settlement. And there are situations in which corporate indemnification is not required.

D&O insurance is necessary *in addition to* corporate indemnification provisions. It is just as valuable as the more common types of liability insurance – such as commercial general and auto liability policies – because it responds to claims for pure financial loss. In contract, general and auto liability policies only respond to damages that arise from bodily injury, property damage, or personal liability. In fact, most D&O policies exclude coverage for damages arising from bodily injury, property damage, or personal injury since these types of losses are more appropriately insured on the other types of liability insurance policies. Risk managers also should be aware that most personal umbrella policies will not respond to business claims against directors and officers who serve on for-profit boards of directors.

Terminology Refresher

Bodily injury means direct injury, sickness, disease, or death.

Financial loss means financial damages, settlements, judgment, and defense costs but does not usually include civil or criminal fines and taxes.

Property damage means physical injury to tangible property, along with loss of use of the property that is not physically injured.

And defending or settling a claim for financial loss may cost just as much – or even more – than defending a claim for bodily injury. Since the personal assets of directors and officers may be exposed by their service on an organization's board, most require that D&O insurance be provided before they will serve.

ADVANTAGES

1. D&O insurance may be required before individuals from outside of an organization will serve as directors. The insurance therefore facilitates the recruitment of outside directors.

2. D&O insurance may be the only protection that directors and officers have in the event of an organization's insolvency. If there are no funds available, there will be no corporate indemnification.

3. D&O insurance protects the assets of the corporation that otherwise would be needed to indemnify officers and directors for defense and settlement costs. Such lawsuits could unduly strain the organization financially.

4. Organizations that are organized as not-for-profit entities simply may not have enough funds available to defend a lawsuit against the board members and executives.

5. The cost of D&O insurance premiums could be miniscule when compared with the cost of defense and settlement of a serious claim.

6. Some D&O insurers may be able to offer or recommend resources – such as risk management consultants or legal firms that specialize in director and officer claims – of which an organization might not otherwise be aware.

7. Most D&O policies provide that the insured organization will control the defense of claims. This means that the organization must engage legal counsel and direct the defense of its directors and officers – with assistance from the D&O insurer. This is an advantage in that the personal reputations and assets of the directors and officers are on the line, and they probably will want to play a prominent role in their own defense.

8. The lengthy process of correctly completing a coverage application may lead to risk management initiatives that otherwise would be overlooked.

DISADVANTAGES

1. Although the premium for a D&O insurance policy may be very small when compared with the potential exposures, the coverage usually is called upon much less frequently than the more standard liability policies. Some may question the wisdom of investing in an insurance policy that is rarely used.

2. A great deal of time may be required to accurately complete a D&O insurance policy application, and those who sign the application must warrant that the information is correct. In signing the application

warranty, the officer pledges that the information supplied is true and complete.

3. There are no standard D&O policies. So risk managers must take time to review the coverage being provided on a specific form. Comparing various D&O insurance proposals may present an additional burden.

4. D&O insurance is a specialized practice area, and it is important to obtain information about the coverage from agents, brokers, and underwriters who are experienced in the area.

5. The cost of defense is included within the limit of liability on D&O policies. Other liability policies provide defense costs in addition to the limit of liability. Therefore, the D&O limit may have to be stretched to cover both defense and judgment or settlement costs.

6. D&O policies will not respond to all claims against directors and officers, and some may misunderstand the scope of what is covered.

7. Most D&O policies provide that the insured organization will control the defense of claims. This means that the organization must engage legal counsel and direct the defense of its directors and officers - with assistance from the D&O insurer. This is a disadvantage in that organizational resources will be tied up in the defense. In other words, the organization will not be able to just turn a claim over to the insurer and let it handle everything.

DESIGN FEATURES

There are three types of D&O policies that will be introduced in this chapter. They are those designed for private or closely held corporations, not-for-profit organizations, and publicly traded companies. We first discuss attributes that are common to all three types of policy, even though there would be variations in specific wording between different forms and insurance companies. We then discuss attributes that may apply to only one type of policy.

It is important to keep in mind that variations of these three types of policies are available. For example, schools and universities may purchase an educators legal liability (ELL) policy in lieu of a D&O policy. An ELL policy may provide additional coverage that is specifically designed for educational organizations.

It also is important to remember that D&O policies differ from insurer to insurer, and even within individual insurance companies. Therefore, the attributes discussed in this chapter apply in a general fashion to most forms. Individual coverage forms must be consulted, however, for specific details.

General Attributes of Most D&O Policies

Coverage Grants

Most policies provide at least two insuring agreements:

- *Coverage A (Side A Coverage)* – which provides coverage to directors and officers for losses that are not subject to corporate indemnification, and

- *Coverage B (Side B Coverage)* – which funds claims that are subject to corporate indemnification.

There usually is no *retention* or *deductible*, or a very small one, attached to Side A because that coverage applies to individual directors and officers for claims that do not qualify for corporate indemnification. A *retention* or *deductible* is the amount that the insured pays before the insurance policy begins to pay. The deductible for Side B may range from a thousand dollars upwards to tens or hundreds of thousands of dollars.

When a claim is received, the D&O insurer is put on notice. If the organization has amended its bylaws to maximize corporation indemnification and if the claim involves allegations that fall within the scope of that corporation indemnification, Side B will be triggered. However, if corporate indemnification is not permissible in the situation being claimed, Side A will be triggered. It should be noted, however, that most policies are written to state that Side B will be used for all claims that are *subject to the broadest application of the jurisdiction's corporate indemnification statutes, regardless of whether the corporation chooses to indemnify or not.* Therefore, Side B is the most common insuring agreement that comes into play.

Aggregate Limit of Liability

There is an aggregate limit of liability, which is the most that will be paid in any policy period – including defense costs – for all claims from both Side A and Side B. Defense costs are included within the limit of liability,

and risk managers should consider the possible cost of defense when choosing a coverage limit. In addition, claims arising from any extensions of coverage, such as endorsements that provide extended employment-related practices liability coverage, also will erode this aggregate limit. So determining the amount of coverage that should be purchased is a crucial exercise. Many organizations that need a high limit of liability will increase the retention or deductible in order to achieve a more reasonable premium. Individual insurers establish D&O coverage rates; there are no published class rates. Underwriter discretion is frequently permitted, and the interaction of limit and retention may be an important factor.

Once the aggregate limit is exhausted, a new policy must be purchased. Of course, if an aggregate limit is ever completely used up, underwriters will be more wary of the potential for claims and will correspondingly increase the premium or decrease the amount of coverage that is offered.

Claims–Made Coverage

D&O policies are almost universally written on a claims-made basis. This means that the policy applies to claims (to which coverage applies) that are made against an insured *and* reported to the insurer during the policy or discovery period. The *discovery period* is a period of time after the policy is canceled or nonrenewed (either because the company didn't renew it or the insurer refused to renew it) that the insured is given to discover claims that arise from wrongful acts (occurrences) that happened during the policy period. The insured is charged additional premium to purchase extended discovery periods.

Claims-made and reported coverage differs slightly. It specifies that the claim must be made against the insured and *must be reported to the insurance company* during the policy period.

Claims-made coverage may be contrasted to occurrence-based coverage, which is common in many other types of liability policies. With occurrence-based coverage, the policy that applied to the occurrence that caused the damage will respond regardless of when the claim is filed.

Claims–Made Versus Occurrence Comparison

The ABC Cosmetic Company is a publicly traded corporation with claims-made directors and officers liability insurance policies that run from January 1 through December 31 of each year. On December 1, 2003, the board of directors reviewed a proposal to sell one division, which produced organic hair-care products that had limited application. The board voted not to sell the division on December 15, 2003, but directed management to monitor the sales situation.

Within the next year, sales of the hair-care product fell drastically. The media publicized the company's problems, and, on December 12, 2004, ABC's stock price plummeted. Shareholders took legal action on February 20, 2005, against the corporation and its directors and officers, alleging that a sale of the division should have been executed when the opportunity arose and that the board's failure to act led to the plummeting stock price.

ABC received notice of the legal action on February 21, 2005, and notified its D&O carrier on February 23, 2005. If the D&O coverage was written on a claims-made basis, the policy that was in effect for the term of January 1-December 31, 2005, would apply to the claim because the *claim was received by the insured and reported to the insurance company* within that policy term. This is true even though the decision that is alleged to have caused the loss – the board decision not to sell the division – happened during the policy term of January 1-December 31, 2003.

Discovery Period Purchased

If ABC had nonrenewed its D&O policy on December 31, 2004 – or the insurer had refused to renew the policy – ABC may have purchased a one- or two-year *discovery period*. If the situation arose under this scenario and ABC had notified the insurer of problems with the stock on December 30, 2004, the claim would be received during the discovery period of the January 1-December 31, 2004, policy. The claim would be handled under that policy because it was received during that policy's discovery period.

No Discovery Period Purchased

If ABC had nonrenewed its D&O policy – or if the carrier nonrenewed it – and ABC did not purchase a replacement policy or a discovery period, what would the situation be? If the claim came in on February 21, 2005 (after the expiration of the last policy on December 31, 2004), there would be no coverage.

Occurrence-Based Option

If the coverage had been written on an occurrence basis, the policy that applied would be the one that was in effect when the occurrence that led to the claim happened. That would be the January 1-December 31, 2003, policy, which applied when the vote not to sell the division was taken.

Claim-Reporting Requirements

The policy's *Notice* or *Claim Reporting* provisions are an important part of the policy. In general, these clauses require that the insured organization or individual insured director or officer notify the insurer in writing of any claim within a certain timeframe from when the claim is received. Many policies specify that the claim must be reported "as soon as practicable." Others give a specific time period. Regardless of the amount of time given to report the claim, it must be reported before the end of the policy or discovery period (if a discovery period is applicable). A grace period of thirty or more days after policy expiration may be provided for claims that are received within the last few days of the policy period.

Example. XYZ Steel's current policy is due to expire on December 31, 2003. Its policy requires that claims be reported to the insurer as soon as practicable but no later than the policy expiration date (December 31, 2003). XYZ receives a D&O claim against two directors and the company president at 2 p.m. December 31, 2003. It would be impossible to file this claim *in writing* with the insurer before the policy expires. Because of such possible situations, many insurers have included a thirty-day grace period for claim reporting. These grace periods state that claims received within, say, the final thirty days of the policy period, must be reported in writing to the insurer within thirty days after the policy expires.

Again, individual policies should be reviewed for the time periods and reporting provision requirements.

Circumstances That May Result in a Claim

There also is a requirement that insureds notify the insurer when they become aware of any occurrence or circumstance that may reasonably be expected to result in a claim. The insured must notify the insurer in writing of the expectation, including the reasons for expecting it. Any claim that subsequently is received based on the reported circumstances will be considered to have been made when the notice of occurrence was given.

This type of requirement is common in claims-made policy forms. It is designed to make underwriters more aware of possible claim payments that will be needed so subsequent policies can be priced effectively. In addition, it serves to allocate claims to the most appropriate policy period. It must be noted, however, that insurers will not accept nonspecific information about circumstances that just might result in a claim. Most forms clearly state that insureds must provide specific information and details about the incident, along with why they believe that a claim may follow.

Definitions

The definitions section is very important, especially since forms differ so greatly from one to another. They play a critical role as coverage evolves and different insurers expand or contract policy provisions. It is impossible to discuss every conceivable definition in this chapter, but certain ones are introduced because they traditionally have a great impact on how coverage may apply. They are:

- claim;

- director or officer;

- insured;

- loss; and

- wrongful act.

Particular attention should be paid to these five definitions when reviewing a coverage form. However, risk managers should familiarize themselves with all the definitions on an organization's D&O policy in order to interpret the coverage correctly.

Claim

The definition of claim originally included written demands for monetary relief or nonmonetary relief and civil, criminal, or arbitration proceedings for monetary or nonmonetary relief. Current definitions, however, usually go much further and may add situations such as written demands for injunctive relief, regulatory proceedings, and civil, administrative, criminal, or regulatory investigations. Again, specific wording differs from form to form.

Director or Officer

The definition of director or officer may fall under terms such as insured persons, executive, individual insured, or similar wording. In essence, the individual directors and officers category usually include past, present, and future directors, officers, trustees, or governors of the organization, and past, present, and future members of management committees or management boards. With such general wording, individual directors and officers do not need to be named on the policy in order for coverage to apply.

Insured

The definition of insured may reference the individual directors and officers as explained previously. However, insured often is defined to include individual insureds and the organization—sometimes referred to as the entity.

Loss

The definition of loss varies among insurance companies. In general, however, loss includes damages, settlements, judgments, interest on judgments, and defense costs that arise from a situation to which the policy applies. Loss usually specifically excludes items such as fines and penalties, taxes, punitive damages (additional damages levied as a punishment), exemplary damages (additional damages levied to set an example), the multiplied portion of multiplied damages (awards that the court chooses to increase, or multiply, because the action was particularly onerous), amounts the insured is not financially liable for, and items that are considered uninsurable by law. Some forms exclude employment-related benefits and stock options from the definition of loss. As a general rule, items that the insured would have to pay regardless of the claim – such as wages or benefits – and items that are levied to punish the insured – such as punitive damages and fines – are excluded from the definition of loss.

This definition is important because it qualifies what types of costs and damages the policy will provide to covered insureds.

Wrongful Act

The definition of wrongful act is one of the most critical portions of the policy. Keep in mind that the policy responds to loss that arises from a claim against an insured for a wrongful act that the insured committed. Respective definitions of wrongful act can be quite lengthy. In essence, however, they include actions such as breach of duty, neglect, errors, mistakes, misstatements, misleading statements, and acts or omissions that insureds may commit in their capacities as directors, officers, or other insureds.

Exclusions

The exclusions sections of policies are always must-reads. The D&O policy is no exception. It is critical that all insureds – including the individual directors and officers –understand how the exclusion defines what is being covered.

In addition to reviewing the action section that is subtitled *Exclusions,* risk managers must keep in mind that exclusionary language may be included in other parts of the policy. For example, as noted previously, the definition of *loss* states what is *excluded* in addition to what is *included* in the meaning of loss.

Within the exclusions section of most policies are two basic types of exclusions: those that deal with corporate governance and those that are either uninsurable or better insured elsewhere. For example, good corporate governance standards would imply that those charged with governing an organization should not be entitled to gain profit or advantage from their positions if they are not legally entitled to it. Following this standard, there is an exclusion on nearly all D&O policies that voids coverage for claims arising from or attributable to the "gaining in fact of any profit or advantage to which the *Insured* was not legally entitled."[3]

Other common corporate governance exclusions include those that void coverage for payments to a director or officer without previous approval of the shareholders or members of the organization, deliberate criminal or fraudulent acts of an insured, profits to which the organization or an insured was not legally entitled, service as members of other boards unless specifically endorsed onto the policy, claims brought by one insured against the other(s), and the public offering of securities by privately held or not-for-profit organizations.

In regard to claims that are either uninsurable or better insured on other policies, most D&O forms include exclusions for bodily injury, property damage, and personal injury claims because they are better insured by other types of liability policies. There also frequently are exclusions for pollution liability, litigation or claims that were instigated before continuous D&O coverage was begun, and for violations of the Employment

Retirement Income Security Act of 1974 and similar laws. All of these are either not insurable or better insured elsewhere.

Limit of Liability

A noted previously, the coverage limit includes defense costs, which differs from many liability policies that offer defense costs in addition to the limit of liability. Most policies highlight this provision in the policy and, possibly, in the application form.

There also is an aggregate limit, which caps the amount that the insurer will pay for all claims – including defense costs – within the policy period.

Control of Defense

The insured, and not the insurance company, controls the defense of claims. The insurance company usually *has no duty to defend any insured* although it may end up paying for all or part of the defense. This means that insureds must defend themselves and contest claims that are made against them. However, the policy requires that insureds not admit or assume liability for any claims without approval from the insurer, and it also specifies that insureds must notify the insurance company of all claims and obtain written consent from the insurer before incurring defense costs. This is because, even though the insureds control and are responsible for their defense, the insurance company may ultimately pay these costs. Notifying the insurer of the claim and how the defense is being handled keeps the insurance company appraised of developments and aware of how serious the claim actually is. In addition, the D&O insurer will want to monitor the defense and may elect to participate in it and in settlement negotiations, especially if its money ultimately will be used.

Some policies include a provision stating that the insurance company will advance defense costs once the deductible or retention is satisfied.

Panel Counsel

Some D&O insurers require that defense attorneys for certain types of claims be chosen from preapproved lists, called *panel counsel* lists, which are attached to and form part of the policy. For example, an insurance company may have a panel counsel list of attorneys that are to be used in securities cases or in employment-related practices claims. If insureds choose attorneys that are not on the list, the insurer must preapprove them. These lists are made up of specialists in particular areas of law. In addition, their fee schedules have been negotiated in advance with the insurer. The use of panel counsel, according to some D&O underwriters, provides insureds with legal specialists at fee levels that are reasonable and set in advance.

Discovery Provisions

As noted in the section entitled "Claims-Made Coverage," D&O policies often have a built-in provision that allows the insured to extend the period for filing claims after policies have been nonrenewed by either the insured or the insurer. For example, the policy may provide that, for a preset percentage of the expiring premium, an insured may buy an extended discovery period of one or more years if the policy is not renewed. This is important because of the claims-made and reported aspect of the coverage, which means that the policy responds to claims that are made and reported to the insurer within the policy period. If a policy is not renewed, claims that are received after the policy expires as a result of actions taken by board members during the policy period would not be covered. There are two types of discovery clauses:

- unilateral discovery; and

- bilateral discovery.

When a unilateral discovery clause is provided in the policy, an extended discovery period is guaranteed to be available *only if* the policy is nonrenewed by the insurance company. Under a bilateral discovery clause, the extended discovery period is available if either the insured or the insurer nonrenew the policy. Most policies include the percentage of expiring premium that will be charged for various discovery period lengths.

Changing Carriers

The discovery clause may be important to insureds that, for one reason or another, decide to change D&O carriers. There are many reasons for such a change, including premium pricing considerations and the breadth or limit of coverage that is offered by a replacement insurer compared with that being offered by the expiring carrier.

If an insured decides to change insurers, the new carrier should be asked to provide *prior acts coverage*. Prior acts coverage means that the new policy will cover

claims that arise from wrongful acts that were committed before the new policy began. When prior acts coverage is provided on the new policy, the insured should not need to purchase an extended discovery period on the nonrenewed policy.

However, the replacement carrier may attach a *retroactive date*. When a retroactive date is attached to the replacement policy, the insuring agreements will respond to claims that are filed against the insured that arise from *wrongful acts that occurred between the retroactive date and the policy expiration date*. This means that there would be no coverage for a claim that is filed between the retroactive and policy expiration dates if the claim arose from board action that was taken prior to the retroactive date on the new policy. The insured would have to purchase the extended discovery period to cover such a possibility.

Changes in the Organization

In general, major changes in an organization – such as a merger or acquisition – should be reported to the D&O insurer as soon as possible. In the event of a merger or company sale, the policy may be invalidated upon completion of the deal, depending upon which party takes control of the newly formed organization. And most directors and officers want to be sure that claims received after the deal is completed – but based on their decision to merge – are covered by insurance. There often is automatic coverage for subsidiaries that are added to the organization, as long as the assets of the subsidiary are no more than 10-25% (as specified in the policy) of the total assets of the combined organization.

It always is a good risk management policy, however, to notify the D&O insurer when merger, consolidation, acquisition, or sale plans are gaining momentum.

Other Insuring Agreements

A somewhat recent development in the D&O insurance arena is that of offering coverage for the entity itself. One of the most common insuring agreements that may be offered in addition to Coverage A and B is

- *Coverage C (Side C)* – Organizational Entity Coverage

Not–for–Profit Entity Coverage

Entity coverage often is provided on insurance policies designed for not-for-profit entities. The theory behind this is that not-for-profit organizations may lack the financial assets to successfully defend a suit seeking financial damages that is filed against the organization. In addition to offering the coverage for the not-for-profit entity, these insuring agreements also may agree to advance defense costs for the organization.

Publicly Traded Entity Coverage

Side C entity coverage also may be included on policies designed for publicly traded companies. In this case, the coverage usually is restricted to entity coverage for *securities claims* only. A securities claim will be defined on the policy but generally would include claims alleging the violation of regulations or statutes regulating securities, including their purchase and sale. Securities claims often involve a drop in stock price or allegations of misleading information that encouraged the purchase or sale of that stock. Forms differ on how they handle administrative or regulatory proceedings involving securities. Some may provide coverage for such proceedings against the entity only if an insured director or officer also is named; others may exclude such regulatory proceedings entirely; and others may offer it regardless of whether an individual also is named in the suit. There also may be other significant limitations on the entity coverage for securities claims.

In the aftermath of corporate scandals at a number of publicly traded companies, the long-term viability of entity coverage came into question. Issues arose as to whether the D&O policy, which traditionally was dedicated to protecting the personal liabilities of individual directors and officers, possibly would revert to the bankruptcy estate in the event of the insured company becoming insolvent since the corporation had become a named insured on the policy. Issues such as this should be considered when selecting the type of coverages to include on a D&O policy.

The Allocation Issue

The presence or absence of entity coverage is important because of the allocation issue, which arises when part of a claim is covered and part is not. Defense and settlement costs must be allocated between the covered portion of the claim and the part that is not covered. In D&O insurance, there are two types of covered/uncovered situations:

- claims that involve covered and uncovered parties; and

- claims that involve covered and uncovered allegations.

The covered parties in D&O insurance usually are the directors and officers; the uncovered parties are the corporation or organization (the entity) and/or employees. This differs from other forms of liability insurance, in which the corporation is the named insured. In those policies, directors, officers, and employees also are insureds for coverage purposes. However, with D&O insurance, the directors and officers are the insureds, and there is no auxiliary coverage for the entity – unless it is specifically added to the policy, such as by adding a Coverage C, Entity, insuring agreement.

Therefore, when a claim is made against directors, officers, and the corporation for wrongful acts alleged against all of them, there has to be a decision as to how much coverage will be allocated to the individual insureds and how much will be allocated to the entity. There also has to be an allocation of defense costs.

Example. ABC Steel and its board take action that results in a shareholder claim. Assume that the claim is filed within the current policy period, and the allegations in the claim are essentially covered by the D&O policy. However, in addition to naming the seven directors and the executive officers, the claim also names the organization – ABC Steel Company. The relative fault of the covered parties (directors and officers) must be assessed against the relative fault of the uncovered party (ABC Steel). Some D&O policies may state that the insured and insurer agree to use their "best efforts" to arrive at a reasonable allocation of both defense and settlement costs. In some cases, a court may determine that the entire burden should be assigned to the directors and officers. ABC's policy would have to be reviewed to determine its stated position on the issue.

However, if ABC had purchased Coverage C, Entity Coverage, for securities claims, the allocation of costs and settlement may not be an issue.

It must be remembered, however, that entity coverage for publicly traded companies usually does not extend beyond securities claims. So other types of claims may trigger an allocation issue, even if Coverage C has been purchased.

Entity coverage also is often available for employment-related practices liability claims if a special ERPL endorsement is added to the policy. However, absent that endorsement, an allocation issue may arise if an ERPL claim is filed against both directors and the entity.

The same situation may result if a claim involves some allegations that are covered, and others that are not covered.

Coverage for Claims Arising from Initial Public Offerings (IPOs)

Private companies, as explained in the introductory section of this chapter, do not offer shares of their companies to the general public. However, a private company may decide to offer shares to the public in an effort to raise money or broaden its scope of operations. This first offering of stock is called an initial public offering. Companies that already have "gone public" may decide to offer additional shares of stock, which is called a secondary offering. Such stock offerings offer rich fodder for future claims, especially if the stock's value does not rise as much or as quickly as originally anticipated.

Private company D&O policies usually exclude coverage for IPOs. This is because the D&O underwriter wants to review and analyze the information that is developed to sell these initial shares. Most of the information about the IPO that the underwriter needs to review is contained in the prospectus, which is a document that describes the enterprise and is distributed to prospective investors. If the underwriter is not satisfied with how the offering is being made, he may decline to provide D&O coverage for it and the publicly traded operation. Some private company D&O policies may offer what is called securities coverage. In essence, this provides limited coverage for claims arising from certain types of securities. In addition, and perhaps most importantly, this policy provision states that the underwriter must offer a coverage proposal for the IPO as long as the private company notifies the underwriter of the IPO in advance, provides appropriate details, and pays the premium charged. The advance notice must be given to the underwriter at least thirty days (or some other preset number of days) before the IPO is scheduled. This is an important feature because it guarantees that coverage will be offered if the insured complies with the notification terms.

The Application

The application for coverage is an integral part of the D&O policy. It actually is attached to, and becomes a part of, the policy. Therefore, representations that are made in the application form the basis for coverage, and material misrepresentations may void coverage. Because of this, extreme care must be taken when completing the application.

A duly authorized officer of the organization must sign the application. In doing so, the officer warrants that the information is true and correct.

What happens if an officer warrants the application information and it later is determined that some material information was incorrect? If the officer knew of the information and falsely warranted the information, coverage probably will be voided for that individual. However, coverage for innocent insureds probably would not be voided. If the officer was not aware of the information – and had made reasonable efforts to fully complete the application – coverage probably would not be voided for him. However, the details of each situation would have to be reviewed to determine when coverage could be voided.

Some risk managers poll the board members, asking them to review the application to be sure material information is not omitted, in an effort to avoid a faulty application.

WHERE CAN I FIND OUT MORE ABOUT IT?

Corporate Governance in General

- Organization for Economic Cooperation and Development (OECD) and the OECD Principles of Corporate Governance, www.oecd.org.

Directors & Officers Liability Exposures and Insurance

- The Professional Liability Underwriting Society (PLUS), 4248 Park Glen Road, Minneapolis, MN 55416, Phone (952) 928-4644, http://plusweb.org/.

- Hagglund, Weimer, and Monteleone, *D&O: Guide to Risk Exposures & Coverage* (Cincinnati, OH: The National Underwriter Company, 1999).

- *D&O MAPS (Market Information, Analysis of Policies, and Policy Service)*, (Dallas, TX: International Risk Management Institute).

- *The D&O Book: A Comparison Guide to Directors & Officers Liability Insurance Policies* (Newport Beach, CA: Griffin Communications, Inc., 1993).

QUESTIONS AND ANSWERS

Question – What is the difference between the terms "claims-made" and "claims-made and reported" in regard to D&O policies?

Answer – A claims-made form will specify that it covers claims made against the insureds within the policy period or any applicable discovery period. A claims-made and reported form specifies that the claim must be made against the insured *and reported to the insurance company* during the policy period or any applicable discovery period.

Question – At one time, D&O policies included a *retroactive date*. There is little reference to retroactive dates now, but a new "date" has been introduced – a continuity date. Do they serve the same purpose?

Answer – Retroactive dates usually apply to all coverage grants on the policy. In order for coverage to apply, the wrongful act must occur between the retroactive and policy expiration dates, and the claim would have to be received during the policy period. In general, current D&O policies no longer have a retroactive date. Some have introduced *continuity dates*. Continuity dates usually apply to coverage agreements that have been added to the policy in more recent years and may not apply to all provisions of the policy. In some situations, litigation, proceedings, or investigations that an insured person knew about prior to the continuity date are excluded from coverage. In other situations, the continuity date acts like a retroactive date for a specific type of coverage and excludes claims that arise from wrong acts that an insured person knew about prior to the date.

For example, ABC Steel adds entity coverage for securities claims on January 1, 2003. At the time, the directors know about a securities claim. The insurer would affix a continuity date of January 1, 2003, to the entity coverage insuring agreement. This would exclude coverage for any possible costs or settlements arising from that particular securities claim.

Question – Is it always best to buy the broadest D&O coverage available and add provisions such as entity coverage, employment-related practices liability coverage, outside directorship, etc., to it?

Answer – Yes and no. Most risk managers and business owners are accustomed to looking for the broadest coverage at a certain premium level. However, it is important to keep in mind that D&O insurance is well named – it was designed primarily to protect the directors and officers. So every time coverage extensions are added, such as when entity or ERPL coverage is added, the amount of insurance available to the directors and officers is diluted. This is because the policies include an aggregate limit of liability and because defense costs are included within that aggregate. One way to get the best of both worlds might be to purchase a broad policy with many coverage extensions that would provide a certain limit of coverage – such as $10 million – and then add an additional tower of limits that is available for the individual directors and officers only.

CHAPTER ENDNOTES

1. See *Tools and Techniques of Charitable Planning* (Cincinnati, OH: The National Underwriter Company, 2001) for more information.

2. *Croton River Club, Inc., v. Half Moon Bay Homeowners Association, Inc.*, 52 F.3d 41(2d Cir. 1995).

3. American International Group, Executive and Organization Liability Insurance Policy exclusion 4. (a), Form 75879 (3/00).

END OF CHAPTER REVIEW

1. The allocation issue in directors and officers liability insurance involves a provision that states that the premium is to be paid by two separate entities.

    True   False

2. Most directors and officers liability insurance policies include Coverage A, which provides insurance for the individual directors and officers, and Coverage B, which funds claims that are filed against the corporation itself.

    True   False

3. Directors and officers liability insurance is not available for not-for-profit organizations.

    True   False

4. The Sarbanes-Oxley Act of 2002 establishes new standards of accounting and financial reporting for publicly traded companies.

    True   False

5. The aggregate limit of liability on a D&O policy is the most that will be paid in any policy period for all claims and defense costs.

    True   False

6. Coverage B is most frequently called upon in directors and officers liability claims because it provides coverage for claims that are subject to corporate indemnification of the directors and officers, and most states have adopted corporate indemnification.

    True   False

7. On a claims-made type of policy, the discovery period is the amount of time allotted to conduct discovery after a lawsuit is filed.

    True   False

8. D&O policies typically are written on an occurrence-based format.

    True   False

9. The application for coverage is attached to and made a part of a directors and officers liability policy.

    True   False

10. Private company D&O policies typically exclude coverage for initial public offerings.

    True   False

Chapter 14

PRODUCT/COMPLETED OPERATIONS LIABILITY INSURANCE

WHAT IS IT?

Products and completed operations liability insurance is but one element of the broader overall scope of general liability coverage that a business entity needs in its dealings with the public. A general liability policy does offer some coverage for products/completed operations exposures that a business entity faces, but often, those exposures are of such a nature that a separate and distinct coverage form is desirable.

As an example, a painting contractor who does not have an office or retail space that is frequented by customers could use a commercial general liability (CGL) coverage form, but the fact is that the true risk exposures facing the painter arise from his products and completed operations and not from his business premises.

Another example is a manufacturer that makes a certain product. No customers are on the manufacturing premises since sales are handled over the phone or through outside salesmen. The main connection with the public, and thus the greatest liability threat, arises from the product. The insured manufacturer (or the insurer) may wish to address the liability exposures through the use of a products/completed operations coverage form as opposed to simply a general liability form.

BASIS FOR PRODUCTS/COMPLETED OPERATIONS LIABILITY CLAIM

A person who is injured or whose property is damaged by a product or a completed operations may rest his claim against the responsible party on several bases; for example, negligence, breach of express or implied warranty, or strict liability.

Fundamentally, the same principles apply to a negligence claim involving products or completed operations as any other relationship. However, there is often a wide gap both in time and place between the two ultimate parties to such action – the manufacturer or producer of the product (or the one performing the operations) and the person who suffers harm from the product's use or mere existence of the completed operation. Hence, various legal doctrines have been published that, for the most part, make successful prosecution of such a claim more possible. As an example, it is now generally held that a manufacturer has a duty to exercise reasonable care in the manufacturing, designing, and packaging of its product; and, this duty is owed to anyone who may come in contact with the product, not merely the purchaser or consumer. Similarly, there is a duty on the part of a manufacturer to provide adequate warning of inherent dangers that are not obvious to the distributor or the consumer.

In the common type of products liability and completed operations liability claim based on alleged breach of warranty, the injured party counts on either an express or implied warranty. In an express warranty, for example, the manufacturer represents certain characteristics about its products to the customer. An implied warranty can be one of fitness or one of merchantability. A warranty of fitness is implied where the buyer makes known to the seller the purpose for which the use of the goods is intended, and indicates that the buyer is relying on the seller's skill or judgment to furnish appropriate goods; under such circumstances, there is an implied warranty that the goods are suitable for the purpose intended. An implied warranty of merchantability applies to any sale made by a merchant; in this instance, it is implied that the goods are of a quality comparable to that which is generally accepted in the merchant's line of trade. If any of these warranties are breached and bodily injury or property damage results, the resultant claim would be a products liability claim.

The doctrine of strict liability holds most sellers liable for injuries caused by defective and unreasonably dangerous products. The injured person is not required to prove negligence on the part of the seller or manufacturer, only that the product was defective when it left the control of the seller or manufacturer and that the defect was the ultimate cause of the injury or damage.

These same bases of negligence, breach of warranty, and strict liability can support a claim due to completed operations.

THE PRODUCTS/COMPLETED OPERATIONS COVERAGE FORM

If the business entity wants and can use a products/completed operations liability coverage form, there are two standard forms: CG 00 37 is the occurrence form and CG 00 38 is the claims-made type policy. An occurrence form simply means that for coverage to apply the injury or damage must occur during the policy period; a claim based on those injuries or damages can be made at any time during or after the policy period. A claims-made form also requires an occurrence to take place during the policy period, but in addition, the claim for damages has to be made during the policy period.

Both coverage forms offer to pay those sums that the insured becomes legally obligated to pay as damages because of bodily injury or property damage included within the products/completed operations hazard. "Products/completed operations hazard" is a defined term on both policies and means all bodily injury and property damage occurring away from the premises owned or rented by the named insured, and arising out of the product or work of the named insured. This definition makes the point that the products/completed operations coverage form is meant to apply to claims that occur off the insured's premises; it is not a premises or on-premises operations insurance coverage form.

The coverage forms have basically the same sections that a general liability (CGL) coverage form has: an insuring agreement, exclusions, supplementary payments, who is an insured, limits of insurance, conditions, and definitions. However, there are real differences between a general liability coverage form and a products/completed operations coverage form that should be noted.

The main difference in the insuring agreement section is stated above, namely, the products/completed operations form applies to products/completed operations hazards, not to all liability exposures that the insured faces. Also, when it comes to insuring agreements, CG 00 37 and CG 00 38 have one insuring agreement as opposed to the three found on the CGL form. They do not offer insurance coverage for personal and advertising injury liability or for medical payments.

In the exclusions section, the products/completed operations coverage form is notable for the absence of any references to "that particular part of real property on which you are performing operations," and "that particular part of any property that must be restored or replaced because your work was incorrectly performed on it." Both these items are found in the damage to property exclusion of the CGL form, but are not needed on the products/completed operations form since both items refer to ongoing operations. The products/completed operations form is for products and completed work, not ongoing operations.

Incidentally, note also that CG 00 37 and CG 00 38 do not have a pollution exclusion, an aircraft, auto, or watercraft exclusion, or a mobile equipment exclusion as does the CGL form. This is not surprising with reference to the pollution exclusion since an examination of the pollution exclusion on the CGL form shows that, under certain circumstances, the exclusion does not apply anyway to injury or damage arising out of the insured's products or completed operations. As for the auto and mobile equipment exclusions, if a loss involving an auto or aircraft or watercraft or mobile equipment can be shown to fit within the definition of "products/completed operations hazard", CG 00 37 and CG 00 38 will allow the coverage.

The products/completed operations coverage forms do have exclusions pertaining to damage to the named insured's products and work, and an exclusion preventing coverage for the expenses for a recall of the insured's products and work. Even though the products/completed operations coverage forms will apply to injury and damage caused by the insured's products and completed operations, damage to such products or work is something no insurance policy is meant to cover. These items are part of a business risk the insured is expected to handle itself.

The supplementary payments section simply lists the expense payments the insurer has agreed to pay in addition to the damages for which an insured may be found liable.

The "who is an insured" section describes who is applicable to seek coverage under the terms of the products/completed operations form.

The limits of insurance clauses serve as the guideposts on the amount that the insurer will pay under the products/completed operations form. The form has an aggregate limit and an each occurrence limit. The aggregate limit is the total amount the policy will pay because of bodily injury and property damage; that is, if the insured has chosen a $500,000 aggregate limit of insurance, that is the most that will be paid during the policy period regardless of the number of insureds on the policy or the number of claims made against the insured. The each occurrence limit is the most that the insurer will pay for damages arising out of one occurrence; that is, if there is a claim against the insured due to one product injuring one (or even several people), the most that will be paid will be the each occurrence limit. As long as the event can be shown to be just one occurrence, the each occurrence limit governs how much will be paid.

The conditions section of CG 00 37 and CG 00 38 contains the usual conditions that govern the contractual relationship between the insured and the insurer. One thing stands out though in the conditions of the products/completed operations form: the form is offered on a primary basis; there is no excess insurance clause as it exists on the CGL form.

The definitions section of the products/completed operations form is basically the same as the one on a standard CGL form, except the definition of products/completed operations hazard has to be emphasized and understood by the parties to the insurance contract. This is so because that phrase is a vital part of the insuring agreement. The products/completed operations coverage form applies to bodily injury and property damage included within the products/completed operations hazard; if the claim does not fit into the parameters of that defined term, the coverage form will not be useful to the insured. For example, if the insured's product harms someone after the person has purchased that product, the products/completed operations coverage form will respond to a claim. If a customer comes onto the insured's premises and injures himself in a slip and fall, the products/completed operations form will not respond to a claim. As another example, if the insured is a contractor and is building a wall at a customer's home and the wall falls after the insured has completed his work injuring a passerby, the products/completed operations form will apply. If that same wall were to fall while under construction, the products/completed operations form will not apply.

ADVANTAGES

1. Most of the risk exposures connected with making products and conducting operations have been transferred. The insured business does not have to worry about and plan for claims or lawsuits based on its products and completed operations, and so the time and money spent on responses to losses and claims can be spent on other items designed to aid the profitability and continuity of the business. Also, should a loss occur, or a lawsuit be filed against the insured, the company resources won't be spent paying for the loss or defense costs.

2. After a loss occurs or a lawsuit is filed, the insured can rely on the insurance company to handle almost if not all of the legal work and other paper work.

3. An insurance company could act as a loss control aid to the insured so that liability exposures can be discovered and analyzed, and preventive measures put into place so as to prevent losses.

DISADVANTAGES

1. Purchasing the products/completed operations coverage form does cost money, with the premium being more expensive as the risk exposure increases. For example, a manufacturer of off-road vehicles can expect to spend more premium dollars for products liability coverage than a manufacturer that makes coffee cups.

2. Through the language of the insurance contract, the insured has agreed to give up any control over the management and settlement of a claim or lawsuit made against it. It may be better for the insured from a profit standpoint or a public relations standpoint to settle a claim or a lawsuit as quickly as possible, but if the insurer does not choose to do so, the insured must live with the decision of the insurer. This may not fit in with the management style or future plans of the insured, but it is part of the insurance contract.

3. While it is true that products/completed operations liability insurance does provide financial protection for the insured business, that protection is limited by the policy's exclusions, definitions, and conditions. Not all of the insured's risk exposures will be covered by products/completed liability operations insurance, and those that are will be subject to the set policy limits of insurance.

QUESTIONS AND ANSWERS

Question – What are the bases on which a person who is injured or whose property is damaged by a product or completed operations may rest a claim?

Answer – Negligence, breach of express or implied warranty, or strict liability.

Question – What is an implied warranty of merchantability?

Answer – An implied promise by a merchant that his goods are of a quality comparable to that which is generally accepted in the merchant's line of trade.

Question – What is the definition of products/completed operations hazard?

Answer – All bodily injury and property damage occurring away from the premises owned or rented by the named insured, and arising out of the product or work of the named insured.

Question – What are the limits of insurance listed on the products/completed operations liability coverage form?

Answer – The form has an aggregate limit and an each occurrence limit of insurance.

Question – What coverages does the CGL form offer that the products/completed operations coverage form does not?

Answer – The products/completed operations liability coverage form does not offer personal and advertising injury liability or medical payments coverages.

END OF CHAPTER REVIEW

1. A person who is injured by a product can rest his claim against the responsible party only if that party was negligent.

    True   False

2. Under an express warranty, a manufacturer represents certain characteristics about its product to the customer.

    True   False

3. An implied warranty can be one of fitness or one of merchantability.

    True   False

4. Under the doctrine of strict liability, an injured person must prove negligence on the part of the seller or manufacturer of the product.

    True   False

5. Products/completed operation hazard is defined as bodily injury and property damage that occurs away from the premises owned by the named insured, and arising out of the product or work of the named insured.

    True   False

6. The products/completed operations liability coverage form applies to personal and advertising injury liability.

    True   False

7. The products/completed operations liability coverage form applies to damage to the insured's products and work.

    True   False

8. The aggregate limit of insurance is the most the insurance policy will pay during the policy period.

    True   False

Part 4:

HEALTH, DISABILITY, AND LTC INSURANCE

Chapter 15

OVERVIEW OF HEALTH–RELATED INSURANCE

WHAT IS IT?

An insurance contract is, simply put, a way to transfer some type of risk from one party to another. In the contract, one party, the insurance company, agrees to indemnify the other party, the insured, against certain types of losses.[1] With health insurance, disability income insurance, and long-term care insurance, the insurance company issuing the policies agrees to cover the insured person against the risk of financial loss due to illnesses, injury, or certain other conditions.

A complete financial plan is typically divided into three main areas: protection, liquidity, and investment.[2] The protection area is where health insurance, disability income insurance, and long-term care insurance fall. As mentioned above, all three of these coverages are designed to provide protection against financial loss. Health insurance protects the insured against potentially devastating medical and doctor's bills in the case of a serve injury or protracted illness while disability income insurance provides protection against the loss of income due to disability. Long-term care insurance protects against the high cost of daily care that can be needed for decades.

Other coverages that fall into the protection area of a financial plan include liability coverages, homeowners insurance, auto insurance, and life insurance.

WHEN IS THE USE OF THIS TOOL INDICATED?

In general terms, any risk can be handled in one of three ways: avoidance, retention, or insurance.[3] Simply avoiding a risk can be done if the risk is one that it is possible to avoid. For example, if a business is concerned about the potential liability of selling ladders to the public, this risk can be avoided by simply deciding not to sell ladders. However, it is generally not possible to avoid the risks of injury, illness, or disability covered by health insurance, disability income insurance, and long-term care insurance. While living a healthy lifestyle may help guard against the risk of illness, it cannot guarantee the insured will not encounter the need for some medical care. Also, the risks of disability and frailty cannot be easily avoided. These conditions may catch up to an individual despite his best efforts to remain healthy and avoid accidents. Thus, simply avoiding these risks is not a viable option.

The second method of handling risk is retention. Another term for this method is self-insuring. This method works well with a specific risk that has an ascertainable cost that is not too great. In our early example involving the sale of ladders, if the company could calculate the number of lawsuits that would likely be filed and the amount of damages awarded from these lawsuits, it would know the cost of selling ladders. The company could then retain this risk, setting aside a fund from which to pay the additional liability costs that would result from ladder sales. Of course, how workable a solution this might be would depend not only upon the accuracy of the calculation of the costs but also the relationship of the cost to the company's profits. If the cost to cover the additional liability claims exceeds the company's profits, retaining or self-insuring against the risk will not be a good choice. While it is theoretically possible to retain or self-insure against the risk of loss posed by illness or injury, from a practical viewpoint, most individuals do not have the financial means to set aside the hundreds of thousands of dollars that a serious illness or injury might require.

The third way to deal with the risk of illness, disability, and frailty is to purchase insurance. The purchase of a disability income policy, for example, transfers the economic risk of a disability from the individual to the insurance company. For the price of the policy's premium the individual has, in essence, transferred this risk to the insurance company. This method of dealing with risk works fairly well provided an insurance company will sell the coverage needed for a price that is not out of the individual's financial reach.

All three coverages – health insurance, disability income insurance, and long-term care insurance – are important to an individual's financial well-being. These coverages should be in place before an individual moves on to the liquidity and investment portions of his or her financial plan.

The first step in analyzing an individual's coverage needs is to determine what coverages are currently in place. For health insurance, disability income insurance, and long-term care insurance, this might involve checking to see if the individual has, or can obtain, these coverages through an employer or a spouse's employer. While this type of group coverage may not offer a high degree of choice of benefits and customization, it can often provide some coverage at an affordable rate. Also, for an individual in poor health, group coverage may be an option where individual coverage, with a greater degree of underwriting, may not be available. If group coverage through an employer is not currently in force, the next step is to look for existing individual policies.

After analyzing existing coverages, it is important to look at the cost of the coverage as well as whether the provisions of the insurance policy provide sufficient protection. This portion of the analysis will be different for each individual insured due to differing ages, family circumstances, employment considerations, and income levels. How the amount and type of health insurance, disability income coverage, and long-term care coverage should be arrived at is addressed in the following chapters.

BUSINESS USES

The primary use for these personal coverages in a business context is as employee benefits. Funded for the most part with group insurance contracts, health insurance and disability income coverage have become standard employee benefits, at least in larger corporations. With small businesses, these coverages are sometimes provided. Long-term care insurance can be provided as an employee benefit through the use of a group insurance contract. Since long-term care coverage is a newer coverage than health insurance and disability income insurance, it is offered by fewer employers.

ADVANTAGES

1. The policyholder can trade a known cost, the premium, for protection against the possibility of a potentially large loss. This quantifiable cost can be useful in personal financial planning as well as in planning for businesses.

2. The disability income insurance policy will provide a benefit payment equal to a certain percentage of the disabled individual's income for the duration of the disability or the length of the policy's benefit period, as explained below. This benefit payment will make it easier for the disabled individual to continue to support his family and meet basic living expenses.

3. The most immediately obvious advantage to having long-term care insurance in place when an individual finds the he or she needs care is that a greater amount of money will be available to pay for the care. This not only allows a spouse to continue to have the same level of income to meet living expenses, it may also provide the spouse who needs care with a greater number of options as to how and were the care will be provided. If the individual who needs care does not have a spouse, the existence of long-term care insurance coverage may result in the individual's (or the couple's) assets being passed down to children, grandchildren, or other heirs rather than used up to pay the cost of long-term care.

DISADVANTAGES

1. With personal insurance coverages, often the primary disadvantage is that the cost of the policy premiums can be significant. If an individual does not have the benefit of his employer paying the cost of health or disability income coverage, the cost or premium needed to buy the coverage could be substantial. This will typically be the case with self-employed persons. The premiums required to purchase long-term care insurance coverage can also be substantial, especially if the individual is older.

2. It may be that a particular individual will never use any of the benefits provided by a disability or long-term care insurance policy. It is less likely that the same would be said of the benefits provided by a health insurance policy.

3. The existence of the coverage may lead the policyholder to think that any loss or potential loss will be covered. Insurance policies often are written to exclude from coverage certain types of situations. A common example of this might be the definition of disability used in a disability income policy. If the insured person becomes disabled and cannot work in his own occupation but can work in another field, the policy may not pay full benefits, depending how the manner in which "disability" is defined in the policy.

TAX IMPLICATIONS

Health insurance, disability income insurance, and long-term care insurance all have potentially significant income tax advantages. These advantages generally reflect the belief that it is in the country's best interest to encourage these types of private insurance in order to decrease the demand on the government to pay for the care of the ill, the disabled, and the elderly. Specifically how these income tax advantages work is discussed in the next several chapters.

WHERE CAN I FIND OUT MORE ABOUT IT?

1. *The Health Insurance Primer* (Washington, D.C.: The Health Insurance Association of America, 2000).

2. *Social Security Manual* (Cincinnati, OH: The National Underwriter Company, published annually).

3. *All About Medicare* (Cincinnati, OH: The National Underwriter Company, published annually).

4. Jeff Sadler, *Disability Income: The Sale, The Product, The Market* (Cincinnati, OH: The National Underwriter Company, 1995).

5. Jeff Sadler, *How to Sell Long-Term Care Insurance: Your Guide to Becoming a Top Producer in an Untapped Market* (Cincinnati, OH: The National Underwriter Company, 2001).

6. United Seniors Health Council, *Planning for Long-Term Care* (New York, NY: McGraw-Hill, 2002).

7. Jeff Sadler, *The Long-Term Care Handbook*, 3rd ed. (Cincinnati, OH: The National Underwriter Company, 2003).

8. Jason G. Goetze, *Long-Term Care*, 3rd ed. (Chicago, IL: Dearborn Publishing, 1999).

9. LTC online, http://www.nationalunderwriter.com/LTC

10. *Tax Facts on Insurance & Employee Benefits* (Cincinnati, OH: The National Underwriter Company, published annually).

CHAPTER ENDNOTES

1. Leimberg, et al., *Tools & Techniques of Risk Management & Insurance* (Cincinnati, OH: The National Underwriter Company, 2002), p. 67.

2. Donald Ray Haas, *Financial Planning for the Baby Boomer Client* (Cincinnati, OH: The National Underwriter Company, 1998), p.57.

3. Leimberg, et al., *Tools & Techniques of Risk Management & Insurance* (Cincinnati, OH: The National Underwriter Company, 2002), p. 49. A fourth method, transfer of the risk by contract, does not apply to the coverages discussed in this chapter.

END OF CHAPTER REVIEW

1. An insurance contract is an agreement to share risk with another party.

   True   False

2. Protection is an important aspect of a complete financial plan.

   True   False

3. Avoidance is always available as a means of dealing with risk.

   True   False

4. Retention can be a viable option for dealing with reasonably ascertainable risks.

   True   False

5. An insurance contract involves accepting a known cost, the premium, to reduce the risk of incurring a large unknown cost.

   True   False

6. Insurance policies can eliminate the need to be concerned with risks.

   True   False

7. Health insurance, disability income insurance, and long-term care insurance all insure against risks of sickness, injury, and frailty.

   True   False

8. Group health and disability insurance have become standard employee benefits in many companies.

   True   False

Chapter 16

TYPES OF INDIVIDUAL HEALTH INSURANCE COVERAGE

WHAT IS IT?

Individual health insurance is a policy purchased by an individual that provides reimbursement for certain medical and hospital expenses in the event of the insured's illness or injury. It is generally issued by an insurance company. Many individuals obtain their health insurance through their employer. This type of coverage is usually provided using a group health insurance contract with the cost split between the employer and the employees.

There are two major types of health insurance plans: prepaid plans and postpaid plans. Prepaid plans pay the health care providers before the care is delivered. The most common type of prepaid plan is a health maintenance organization or HMO. Postpaid plans pay the health care providers or reimburse the insured individual after the care has been received. Traditional forms of health insurance coverage are postpaid plans.

Health insurance coverage was first offered in the 1920's. The first medical expense insurance policy was individual hospital expense insurance that covered only the cost of hospital expenses, not the cost of the doctor's services. This coverage was offered by the hospitals themselves and was the beginning of the Blue Cross plans.[1] The prevalence of employer-provided group health insurance increased significantly during the 1940's when employees were difficult to find but the employers were prohibited by the government from raising wages. Providing fringe benefits such as health insurance was not prohibited.[2] The first major medical coverage was introduced by the Liberty Mutual Insurance Company in 1949. This coverage was designed to supplement the basic medical expense plan coverage.[3]

WHEN IS THE USE OF THIS TOOL INDICATED?

Basic health insurance coverage is an essential part of any individual's financial security. The cost of a serious illness or injury can be, and often is, more than a single individual or family can afford.

In 2002, 52.2% of the United States population had health insurance through their employer, but 16.2% were uninsured.[4] In 1997, about 70% of the United States population had coverage provided by some form of private health insurance.[5] The rapidly-increasing cost of health care and health insurance has been a significant concern in the United States.

TAX IMPLICATIONS

Premiums paid for personally-owned health insurance are deductible as a medical expense to the extent that the premiums plus the taxpayer's other medical expenses exceed 7.5% of the taxpayer's adjusted gross income for the taxable year.[6] Benefits paid from a personally-owned health insurance policy are not taxable to the covered individual.[7] The taxation of health insurance is treated in greater detail in the following chapter.

DESIGN FEATURES

There are several different types of health insurance coverage. Although all are designed to provide reimbursement for expenses incurred as a result of sickness or injury, how the coverage and reimbursement is delivered differs. Following is a discussion of the major types of health insurance coverages including hospital-surgical coverage, major medical coverage, traditional indemnity coverage, preferred provider organizations (PPOs), health maintenance organizations (HMOs), and Medicare supplemental insurance.

Generally, medical expense coverage is designed to protect the insured person against financial losses by reimbursing the insured for the costs of surgery and hospitalization. The two major types of medical expense coverage are hospital-surgical insurance, also known as basic medical expense insurance, and major medical insurance. These two coverages are discussed below.

Hospital–Surgical Coverage

In conjunction with major medical coverage, hospital-surgical coverage provides coverage for hospitalization and surgery. As mentioned above, hospital-surgical coverage and major medical insurance together make up medical expense coverage which is sometimes referred to as basic medical expense insurance. This type of coverage can be offered on both an individual and a group basis.

With hospital-surgical coverage, certain expenses that are covered are defined in the policy. These expenses can differ from one policy to the next, but hospital-surgical coverage will usually cover hospital room and board charges; miscellaneous hospital charges including lab services, x-rays, and medicine; plus services of other hospital employees such as nurses, radiologists, and anesthetists. It also covers surgical charges, physicians' in-hospital charges, charges for outpatient services, and charges for maternity services.

What benefit does this type of coverage pay? Hospital-surgical coverage sets a limit, in one manner or another, on the amount it will pay for each benefit. The limit may be a certain dollar amount, such as $100 per day for hospital room and board charges, or the limit may be set at the usual and customary charge for a particular service. Also, some policies have a total limit on the amount of benefits that will be paid under the policy. For surgical charges this type of coverage sets a fee schedule that imposes an upper limit for various surgical procedures. This limit can be expressed as a cash amount or as portion of the policy's overall coverage amount. These types of policies also set a certain limit, usually a dollar limit, on what types of lab work the policy will reimburse.

Major Medical Coverage

As mentioned earlier, together with hospital-surgical coverage, major medical coverage makes up medical expense coverage. The two types of major medical coverage, which can be offered on both an individual basis and a group basis, are supplemental and comprehensive.

Supplemental major medical coverage is designed to supplement the basic hospital-surgical plan by covering expenses that the basic plan does not cover. In contrast, comprehensive major medical wraps up into a single plan all the coverages provided by the basic hospital surgical plan and a supplemental major medical plan. As you might expect, the comprehensive major medical plan is streamlined, easier to use, and does not have any overlapping of coverage from several different policies. For these reasons, the comprehensive major medical plan is more common than the other types of coverages.

Major medical policies cover specific services and supplies in much the same manner as the basic hospital-surgical policies. However, the major medical coverage tends to cover more services and to pay greater benefits. Similar to the basic hospital-surgical plan, the major medical coverage also has exclusions and limitation for various services.

With major medical coverage, there are two concepts that it is important to understand in relation to which and how much of certain services will be covered under the policy. These two concepts are the policy deductible and coinsurance.

A deductible is a certain amount of a covered expense that the policyholder must pay out of pocket. The deductible amount is not the same with each policy. One policy may have a deductible of $500 while another policy's deductible amount may be only $200. Sometimes, the policyholder can choose the deductible amount for the policy.

If a policyholder has major medical coverage with a deductible of $500 and he incurs a covered medical expense of $1,200, the policyholder must pay the first $500 dollars of the expense and the insurance policy will pay the remaining $700. Usually, deductible amounts are cumulative, so if the policyholder mentioned above incurs another covered expense of $400 later in the year, the policy will pay the entire $400 expense since the policyholder has already meet the $500 deductible for the year.

Coinsurance is a concept that typically applies to health insurance policies. It requires that both the policyholder and the insurance company pay a portion of each covered expense after the policy's deductible has been met. For example, if a covered expense is $2,000, after the policy deductible has been paid by the policyholder, the policyholder will pay a portion of the $2,000 out of pocket and the insurance company will cover the remainder. Often, coinsurance is a 20/80 split, with the policyholder paying 20% of the covered amount ($400 in the example) and the insurance company paying 80% ($1,600 in the example). Usually, there is an overall coinsurance maximum for the policyholder for the year. After the policyholder has paid this maximum amount, such as $1,000, in coinsurance for the year, the insurance company will pay 100% of subsequent covered expenses.

Finally, most major medical expense policies set a maximum limit on the amount that the policy will pay out in benefits during the insured person's lifetime.

This limit is generally quite high, perhaps as much as $5,000,000.

Traditional Indemnity

This type of coverage, known as traditional or hospital indemnity insurance, pays a specified dollar amount for each day the insured is in the hospital. With some policies, the applicable time period may be a week or a month rather than per day. The benefits paid by hospital indemnity coverage are not based upon the insured person's actual medical expenses. They are paid in addition to other types of insurance payments. These payments are intended to provide the hospitalized person with funds to pay expenses not covered by other types of insurance as well as other incidental expenses, childcare costs, housekeeping services, etc. A typical benefit amount under this type of coverage ranges from $100 to $400 per day.[8]

Health Maintenance Organization (HMO)

An HMO is a type of managed care organization. It is an organization of physicians and other health care providers that provide health care on a prepaid basis. It is generally considered to be an alternative to traditional health insurance coverage.

One advantage of the HMO is that it often covers more types of health care services than the traditional policy and often has lower copayments and deductibles. On the other hand, HMOs impose limits as to which doctors and which hospitals an insured individual may use. Some HMOs emphasize preventative care to a greater extent than does traditional health insurance coverage.

Preferred Provider Organization (PPO)

Like an HMO, a preferred provider organization or PPO is a type of managed care organization. A PPO contracts between the sponsor and health care providers to treat plan members. A PPO can also be a group of health care providers who contract with an insurer to treat policyholders according to a set fee schedule. A PPO might consist of a single hospital and its practicing physicians that contract with a large employer while another PPO might consist of a national network of physicians, hospitals, and labs that contract with insurers or employer groups. A PPO often provides discounts from standard fees and incentives for plan enrollees to use the contracting providers.

Medicare Supplemental Insurance

This type of supplemental coverage pays for expenses not covered by Medicare. Other names for this type of coverage are MedSupp policies and Medigap polices. Medicare is a program of the federal government that pays for health care for individuals age 65 and older. Medicare has two primary parts: Part A and Part B.

Part A of Medicare pays benefits for hospitalization, skilled nursing facilities, home health services, and hospice care. It is provided, without cost, to everyone age 65 and older who is eligible for Social Security benefits. If an individual with Medicare Part A coverage is hospitalized, the individual must pay the deductible and all of the charges for the first 60 days. For days 61 through 90, the individual must pay a copayment for each day in the hospital. After the 90th day, the individual is again responsible for the hospital expenses. In addition, each person has a lifetime reserve benefit available of up to 60 additional days of hospitalization coverage where the individual pays only a copayment.

Medicare Part A also pays benefits for skilled nursing care for the first 100 days if the individual spent at least three days in the hospital prior to the skilled care. The costs of the first 20 days are paid in full while the costs of the next 80 days require the individual to make a copayment. Home health services and hospice care are also covered by Medicare Part A.

In contrast to Part A of Medicare, Part B is a voluntary program that requires participants to pay a premium. It provides coverage for doctor's bills, surgical procedures, hospital outpatient services, and medical supplies. The amount of payment for the various expenses paid by Medicare Part B is determined based on what is considered reasonable for the area in which the services are provided.

In 1990, the federal government required that all Medicare supplement policies, which provide coverage for certain expenses not covered by Medicare, must be standardized. There are ten standard types of policies that may be sold. These ten polices are designated with the letters A through J. Plan A offers the least amount of benefits and is generally referred to as the "core" plan. Plans B through J provide a mix of additional benefit options. Plan J provides the most coverage available for this type of policy.[9]

The "core" plan must contain these benefits[10]:

- Hospital Insurance (Part A) coinsurance for the 61st day through the 90th day of hospitalization;

- Hospital Insurance coinsurance for the 91st day through the 150th day of hospitalization;

- Hospital Insurance expenses for an extra 365 days in the hospital;

- Hospital Insurance (Part A) and Medical Insurance (Part B) deductible for the cost of the first three pints of blood; and

- Medical Insurance (Part B) coinsurance (20% of allowable charges).

An individual has six months after turning age 65 to open-enroll in a Medigap policy. During this time period, the insurance company cannot deny Medigap coverage to an individual or charge a greater premium if the individual has had health problems. Further, Medigap policies are guaranteed renewable which means that the insurance company must continue the policy provided the premiums are paid in a timely manner. This is true even if the insured individual is in poor health.[11]

ALTERNATIVES

1. One alternative to the purchase of health insurance is self-funding. In other words, an individual saves sufficient funds to pay any medical expenses out of pocket and completely forgoes the purchase of any commercial health insurance policy. This is typically difficult for the average person to do since a major illness or accident can happen at any time and conceivably result in medical and doctors' bills that run into the hundreds of thousands of dollars. Most individuals cannot realistically save this amount and set it aside for possible medical bills.

2. A second alternative to individually-purchased health insurance is group health insurance coverage. A common type of coverage, this is usually provided by an employer or perhaps through an association. Typically, there is an open-enrollment period where all eligible employees can accept coverage without showing evidence of insurability. The cost of the insurance is usually paid for by both the employer and the individual employee.

WHERE CAN I FIND OUT MORE ABOUT IT?

1. *The Health Insurance Primer* (Washington, D.C.: The Health Insurance Association of America, 2000).

2. *Social Security Manual* (Cincinnati, OH: The National Underwriter Company, published annually).

3. *All About Medicare* (Cincinnati, OH: The National Underwriter Company, published annually).

QUESTIONS AND ANSWERS

Question – What are the various types of deductibles used with major medical health insurance policies?

Answer – Generally, there are two basic types of deductibles used with major medical coverage: the all cause deductible and the per cause deductible. With an all cause deductible, all expenses incurred for all illnesses or accidents apply to a single deductible amount. Once this deductible amount has been met for the year, all covered expenses will be paid by the insurance company.

With the per cause deductible, the policyholder must meet the deductible amount for each illness or accident. Any expenses attributable to an illnesses or accident will be paid in full after the deductible is met, typically, for a two-year period. Because of its simplicity, the all cause deductible is more commonly used than the per cause deductible.

Question – What is the difference between a corridor deductible and an integrated deductible?

Answer – Both of these deductible types are used to coordinate medical benefits paid by a major medical plan with benefits paid by the basic hospital-surgical plan that the major plan supplements. When the medical expenses incurred by the policyholder are greater than the benefits that will be paid by the basic plan, a corridor deductible must be met before the supplemental major medical plan will pay any benefits. For example, if the total medical expense incurred is $3,000 and the basic plan will pay only $1,500, the corridor deductible must be met by the policyholder before the supplement plan will pay any benefits. If the corridor deductible is equal to $500, the first $1,500 of the expenses is paid by the basic plan, the next $500 is paid by the policyholder as a deductible, and the remaining $1,000 is paid by the supplement plan.

In contrast, the integrated deductible is easier to understand. This type of deductible can be met by either payments made by the policyholder or by benefit payments made by the basic coverage policy.

Question – What is critical illness insurance?

Answer – Critical illness insurance pays a lump sum to the insured person if he suffers one of the serious illnesses or injuries set forth in the policy. Typical conditions covered by critical illness insurance are heart attack, heart bypass, major organ transplant, stroke, kidney failure, paralysis, cancer, Alzheimer's disease, multiple sclerosis and the loss of sight, hearing, or speech.[12]

Critical illness policies pay the lump sum benefit without regard to the insured person's actual medical expenses or any other medical insurance benefits he may be entitled to. The lump sum may be different for different illnesses or injuries within one policy.

Question – What are the additional benefits that can be offered by Medigap policies above the "core" plan?

Answer – Beyond the "core" benefits offered in the Plan A Medigap policy, the following additional benefits can be offered in the other plans[13]:

- the entire hospital insurance deductible;

- the per day coinsurance for days 21 through 100 of skilled nursing home care under hospital insurance;

- the medical insurance deductible;

- 80% of the "balance billing" paid by Medical Insurance beneficiaries whose doctors do not accept assignments;

- 100% of the lawful balance billing;

- 50% of outpatient prescription drug costs;

- 80% of the Medicare-eligible costs of medically necessary emergency care when the insured is traveling outside the United States;

- up to $120 per year for certain screening and preventative measures; and

- some short-term at-home assistance benefits.

CHAPTER ENDNOTES

1. *The Health Insurance Primer* (Washington, D.C.: The Health Insurance Association of America, 2000), p. 163.
2. Ibid, p. 164.
3. Ibid, p. 165.
4. Ibid, p. 170.
5. Ibid, p. 9.
6. IRC Sec. 213(a).
7. IRC Sec. 104(a)(3).
8. *The Health Insurance Primer* (Washington, D.C.: The Health Insurance Association of America, 2000), p.34.
9. Ibid, p. 40.
10. *2004 All About Medicare* (Cincinnati, OH: The National Underwriter Company, 2004), p. 99.
11. Ibid, pp. 97-98.
12. *The Health Insurance Primer* (Washington, D.C.: The Health Insurance Association of America, 2000), p. 35.
13. *All About Medicare* (Cincinnati, OH: The National Underwriter Company, 2004), p. 97.

END OF CHAPTER REVIEW

1. Many individuals obtain their health insurance through an employer-sponsored group health plan.

   True   False

2. Individuals may not purchase individual health insurance policies that reimburse for medical and hospital expenses.

   True   False

3. The first health insurance offered was individual hospital expense insurance that covered the cost of hospital expenses, but not the cost of the doctor's services.

   True   False

4. Premiums paid for personally-owned health insurance are never deductible as a medical expense.

    True   False

5. Major medical coverage tends to cover more services and to pay greater benefits than hospital-surgical insurance.

    True   False

6. A policy deductible is the amount of a covered expense that the policyholder must pay out of pocket.

    True   False

7. Coinsurance never applies once a policy deductible is met.

    True   False

8. HMOs and PPOs are types of managed care organizations.

    True   False

9. Medicare Part A provides coverage for doctor's bills, surgical procedures, outpatient services, and medical supplies.

    True   False

10. Medigap policies vary widely from state to state.

    True   False

Chapter 17

TAXATION OF INDIVIDUAL HEALTH INSURANCE COVERAGE

WHAT IS IT?

Individual health insurance is a policy purchased by an individual that provides reimbursement for certain medical and hospital expenses in the event of the insured's illness or injury. It is generally issued by an insurance company. Many individuals obtain their health insurance through their employer. This type of coverage is usually provided using a group health insurance contract with the cost split between the employer and the employees.

There are two major types of health insurance plans: prepaid plans and postpaid plans. Prepaid plans pay the health care providers before the care is delivered. The most common type of prepaid plan is a health maintenance organization or HMO. Postpaid plans pay the health care providers or reimburse the insured individual after the care has been received. Traditional forms of health insurance coverage are postpaid plans.

BUSINESS USES

Health insurance has been used in a business setting for quite a few years. Typically, an employer purchases health insurance coverage for employees through a group health insurance policy. In some instances, individual health insurance policies are purchased by employers to provide coverage for employees.

The first group health insurance policy was purchased by Montgomery Ward and Company in 1910. The policy provided weekly benefits for employees who were unable to work due to illness or injury.[1] The prevalence of employer-provided group health insurance increased significantly during the 1940's when employees were difficult to find but the employers were prohibited by the government from raising wages. Providing fringe benefits such as health insurance was not prohibited.[2]

The first major medical coverage was introduced by the Liberty Mutual Insurance Company in 1949. This coverage was designed to supplement the basic medical expense plan coverage.[3] At first, the cost of group health insurance coverage was little enough that employers typically paid the full premium for all employees and, sometimes, even retirees.

In the last several decades health care and health insurance costs have increased significantly. Today, most employers ask employees to contribute toward the cost of group health insurance coverage.

TAX IMPLICATIONS

Taxation of Individual Health Insurance Premiums

An individual who itemizes deductions on his income tax return may deduct the net unreimbursed expenses he has paid during the taxable year for medical care of himself, his spouse, and his dependents to the extent that these expenses exceed 7.5 percent of his adjusted gross income.[4] Generally, this includes premiums paid for medical expense insurance (hospital, surgical, and medical expense reimbursement coverage). In other words, the individual must subtract 7.5 percent of his adjusted gross income from the total of unreimbursed medical expenses he has paid during the taxable year and only the balance, if any, is deductible.

"Medical care" is defined generally as the amounts paid "for the diagnosis, cure, mitigation, treatment or prevention of disease or for the purpose of affecting any structure or function of the body." The cost of transportation required primarily for this medical care is also included.[5] However, cosmetic surgery is not included unless it is necessary to correct an injury resulting from an accident or a disfiguring disease.[6]

While premiums for medical expense insurance (hospital, surgical, and medical expense reimbursement coverage) qualify as deductible expenses for medical care, premiums for nonmedical benefits (disability income, accidental death, and dismemberment) are not deductible.[7]

Since the deduction is available only for expenses paid for medical care for the individual, his spouse, and his dependents, if the insurance premiums provide for medical expenses of other individuals as well (as in the case of automobile insurance), no deduction is allowed where the portion of the premium applicable to the medical care of the taxpayer, his spouse, and his dependents is not separately stated.[8]

Taxation of Individual Health Insurance Benefits

Generally, benefits paid from personal health insurance are exempt from income tax. This includes dismemberment and sight loss benefits and hospital, surgical, and other medical expense reimbursement. There is no limit on the amount of benefits that can be received tax-free under personally-owned health insurance.[9] Note, however, that health insurance benefits are tax-exempt not only if received by the insured, but also if received by a person having an insurable interest in the insured.[10]

Medical expense reimbursement benefits must be taken into account in calculating an individual's medical expense deduction. Since only unreimbursed expenses are deductible, the total amount of medical expenses paid during the taxable year must be reduced by the total amount of reimbursements received in the taxable year.[11]

Taxation of Group Health Insurance – Employees

Generally, the value of health insurance coverage provided under an employer-sponsored health plan, including premiums paid by an employer on health insurance for an employee, is excludable from the employee's income.[12] Under this general rule, the coverage or premiums on medical expense insurance and dismemberment and sight loss coverage for the employee, his spouse and dependents are tax-exempt to the employee.[13] There is no specific limit on the value of health insurance coverage that may be excluded from the employee's gross income.

Retired employees, also, can exclude employer-paid health insurance premiums from income.[14] Medicare premiums paid by an employer for 65-year-old employees are also excludable from the employees' income.[15]

If an employer reimburses employees for premiums that the employees pay on personally-owned medical expense insurance, the reimbursements are excludable from the employees' gross income.[16] However, where

the employer simply pays the employee a sum which may be used to pay the premium but is not required to be so used, the sum is taxable to the employee.[17]

This exclusion from income for employer-paid health insurance premiums is available only to active employees and not to self-employed individuals. By special statutory provision, however, full-time life insurance salespersons are treated as employees for this purpose if they qualify as employees under the social security law.[18] However, if an employer purchases health insurance for independent contractors, the independent contractors must report the premium payments as taxable.[19]

If an employee has the option to take compensation in cash or have it applied as premiums for health insurance, the amount is included in gross income because constructively received and the premiums are deductible as if personally paid.[20] A properly-structured cafeteria plan, discussed below, can avoid this result.

Taxation of Group Health Insurance – Employer

Generally, an employer can deduct as a business expense all premiums paid for individual health insurance for one or more employees. This includes premiums for medical expense insurance for the employee as well as for the employee's spouse and dependents. An employer can also deduct, as a business expense, premiums paid for group health insurance covering employees, their spouses, and their dependents.

The premiums are deductible by the employer only if the benefits are payable to the employees or their beneficiaries; the deduction is not allowable if the benefits are payable to the employer.[21] But, where the spouse of the employer is a bona fide employee and the employer is covered as a family member, the premium is deductible.[22]

A sole proprietor or partnership can deduct premium payments for group health insurance for employees. The deduction is for the entire amount of the premiums and extends to health insurance for the employees, their spouses, and their dependents. However, a sole proprietor or partner cannot take this deduction for his own health insurance coverage if he is eligible for health insurance coverage through a plan that is offered by an employer of himself or his spouse.[23]

Amounts paid by employers to active and retired employees for reimbursement of Medicare premiums are also deductible.[24]

To be deductible to the employer, the health insurance premium plus all other compensation received by the employee must be considered as reasonable compensation for the employee's services. The question of reasonable compensation is most commonly raised in relation to stockholder-employees of close corporations. It appears that where health insurance is provided for only the stockholder-employees of a corporation, the IRS may consider the premium payments to be nondeductible dividends.

ALTERNATIVES

1. One alternative to the purchase of health insurance is self-funding. In other words, an individual saves sufficient funds to pay any medical expenses out of pocket and completely forgoes the purchase of any commercial health insurance policy. This is typically difficult for the average person to do since a major illness or accident can happen at any time and conceivably result in medical and doctors' bill that run into the hundreds of thousands of dollars. Most individuals cannot realistically save this amount and set it aside for possible medical bills.

2. A second alternative to individually-purchased health insurance is group health insurance coverage. A common type of coverage, this is usually provided by an employer or perhaps through an association. Typically, there is an open-enrollment period where all eligible employees can accept coverage without showing evidence of insurability. The cost of the insurance is usually paid for by both the employer and the individual employee.

3. Cafeteria plans offer another method of providing employees with health insurance coverage. Generally, participants in a cafeteria plan may choose among two or more benefits consisting of cash and qualified benefits. If the plan meets all the applicable requirements, the participants are not taxed on the value of the plan's benefits. One of the benefits which may be offered on the cafeteria plan "menu" is health insurance.[25]

WHERE CAN I FIND OUT MORE ABOUT IT?

1. *The Health Insurance Primer*, published by The Health Insurance Association of America, Washington, D.C., 2000.

2. *Tax Facts on Insurance & Employee Benefits*, The National Underwriter Company, Cincinnati, Ohio, 2004.

QUESTIONS AND ANSWERS

Question – How are health insurance benefit payments made to Health Maintenance Organizations (HMOs) taxed?

Answer – Health insurance benefit payments paid directly to HMOs are taxed in the same manner as traditional health insurance benefits. That is, generally, the benefit payments are not taxable to the policyholder.

Question – When must health insurance coverage continue to be offered to an employee?

Answer – Since 1986, the Consolidated Omnibus Budget Reconciliation Act (COBRA) has required that any group health plan maintained by an employer provide for continuation of coverage to certain employees and certain family members who would otherwise lose coverage under certain circumstances. These requirements are generally referred to as the COBRA requirements.

The COBRA requirements mandate that each "qualified beneficiary" who would lose coverage under a plan subject to the requirements as a result of a "qualifying event" must be permitted to elect, within the "election period," "continuation coverage" under the plan.[26] The Code sets forth several time periods applicable to COBRA coverage. Generally, coverage must be extended for 18, 29, or 36 months, depending upon the triggering event.[27]

The group health plan may require payment of a premium by the qualified beneficiary for continuation coverage. However, the premium charged cannot be more than 102% of the cost of the plan.[28]

If an employer fails to make continuation coverage available the penalty is an excise tax of $100 per day for the noncompliance period with respect to each qualified beneficiary.[29]

CHAPTER ENDNOTES

1. *The Health Insurance Primer*, published by The Health Insurance Association of America, Washington, D.C., 2000, p. 161.
2. *The Health Insurance Primer*, published by The Health Insurance Association of America, Washington, D.C., 2000, p. 164.
3. *The Health Insurance Primer*, published by The Health Insurance Association of America, Washington, D.C., 2000, p. 165.
4. IRC Sec. 213(a).
5. IRC Sec. 213(d)(1).

6. IRC Sec. 213(d)(9).

7. IRC Sec. 213(d)(1)(C).

8. Rev. Rul. 73-483, 1973-2 CB 75.

9. IRC Sec. 104(a)(3).

10. *Castner Garage, Ltd.,* 43 BTA 1 (1940), Acq.

11. Rev. Rul. 56-18, 1956-1 CB 135.

12. IRC Sec. 106.

13. Treas. Reg. §1.106-1; Treas. Reg. §1.79-3(f)(3).

14. Rev. Rul. 62-199, 1962-2 CB 38.

15. Rev. Rul. 67-360, 1967-2 CB 71.

16. IRC Sec. 106.

17. Rev. Rul. 75-241, 1975-1 CB 316.

18. IRC Sec. 7701(a)(20).

19. Rev. Rul. 56-400, 1956-2 CB 116; see also IRC Sec. 3508.

20. Rev. Rul. 75-539, 1975-2 CB 45.

21. Treas. Reg. §1.162-10(a).

22. Rev. Rul. 71-588, 1971-2 CB 91; TAM 9409006.

23. IRC Sec. 162(l); Treas. Reg. §1.162-10(a).

24. Rev. Rul. 67-315, 1967-2 CB 85.

25. IRC Sec. 125(d)(1).

26. IRC Sec. 4980B(f)(1); Treas. Reg. §54.4980B-1, A-1.

27. IRC Sec. 4980B(f).

28. IRC Sec. 4980B(f)(2)(C).

29. IRC Sec. 4980B(b).

END OF CHAPTER REVIEW

1. Employer-provided group health insurance increased significantly during the 1940's, when many employers were prohibited by the federal government from raising wages.

    True   False

2. An individual who itemizes deductions may deduct his net unreimbursed medical expenses for the year to the extent the expenses exceed 7.5% of his adjusted gross income.

    True   False

3. Cosmetic surgery is never deductible as a medical expense.

    True   False

4. Benefits paid from personal health insurance are generally taxable to the extent they exceed medical expenses.

    True   False

5. The value of employer-paid health insurance is usually includable in an employee's income.

    True   False

6. Independent contractors must report in income health insurance premium payments paid by an employer.

    True   False

7. An employer can deduct as a business expense premiums paid for group health insurance covering employees, their spouses, and their dependents.

    True   False

8. A sole proprietor or partner cannot deduct his own health insurance premiums if he is eligible for health insurance coverage through a plan that is offered by an employer of himself or his spouse.

    True   False

9. Cafeteria plans often allow participants to choose between receiving cash and contributions toward health insurance premiums.

    True   False

10. Many group health plan maintained by employers must offer continuation coverage to certain employees and family members who would otherwise lose coverage.

    True   False

Chapter 18

STANDARD PROVISIONS OF INDIVIDUAL DISABILITY INCOME INSURANCE

WHAT IS IT?

A disability income insurance policy is purchased so that if the insured individual becomes disabled, he or she will receive benefit payments. Disability may result from either an injury or an illness. The benefit is intended to replace the individual's salary during the period of disability.

A disability income benefit may be provided through a group insurance plan obtained through the individual's employer or it may be purchased as an individual policy by the insured individual. Although there are similarities between various disability income policies, there are also differences from one policy to the next. It is important to remember that a disability income policy is a contract and that, as with any contract, the provisions may vary. Before purchasing a disability income policy, the potential policyholder should carefully review and understand the policy's provisions.

WHEN IS THE USE OF THIS TOOL INDICATED?

Generally, disability income coverage is an important component of an individual's protection coverage. If an individual is an employee, such coverage may be provided by the employer. Other individuals may provide their own coverage.

Especially for the self-employed individual, individual disability income coverage is a vital benefit. In the event of a disability, unless disability income coverage is in place, the self-employed individual will probably not receive any income with which to meet living expenses.

Despite the importance of this coverage, many working individuals do not have disability income coverage. According to one source, only 27% of American income earners have disability income insurance.[1] Another source concludes that about 82% of American workers either have no long-term disability income insurance or believe that the coverage they do have is not sufficient.[2] This low level of coverage may be partially attributable to the fact that many life insurance companies have stopped selling disability income coverage in recent years. In 2003, only 26 companies offered disability income insurance compared to 350 companies in 1990.[3]

ADVANTAGES

The most obvious advantage of disability income insurance is that the policy will provide a benefit payment equal to a certain percentage of the disabled individual's income for the duration of the disability or the length of the policy's benefit period, as explained below. This benefit payment will make it easier for the disabled individual to continue to support his family and meet basic living expenses.

DISADVANTAGES

If an individual does not have the benefit of his employer paying the cost of disability income coverage, the cost or premium needed to buy the coverage could be substantial. This will typically be the case with self-employed persons.

TAX IMPLICATIONS

Disability income policies offer some income tax advantages. While premiums paid by an individual for an individually owned disability income policy are generally not deductible from income for income tax purposes,[4] disability income benefit payments received from personally purchased policies are exempt from income tax.[5] The taxation of disability income policies is addressed in greater detail in the following chapter.

DESIGN FEATURES – STANDARD PROVISIONS

Occupational Definitions and Applications

How the policy defines "disability" is a critical element of the coverage. Whether an individual policyholder will receive benefit payments is closely linked to this definition. Generally, there are three ways that disability income policies define "disability": total disability, partial disability, and residual disability.

Total disability – The broadest definition of total disability is centered around the concept of "own occupation." This is the best definition of disability from the policyholder's point of view. Here the insured policyholder must be unable to perform the major functions of his own regular occupation.[6] In other words, if a surgeon in unable to perform surgery, he is considered disabled for purposes of this type of definition. As mentioned earlier in this chapter, this inability to perform the duties of his occupation may be the result of either an injury or an illness.

Technically, an insured individual with this definition of disability could become disabled and unable to work in his own occupation, begin collecting disability benefits, return to work in another field, and still continue to collect disability benefits. In response to this possibility, some policies use a "modified" own occupation definition of disability. This modified definition generally provides that an insured who becomes disabled and cannot work in his own occupation will receive benefits unless that individual decides (and is able) to return to employment in another occupation. Still other policies use a definition of total disability that provides that the insured is considered disabled and will receive benefits if, for the first few policy years, he cannot work in his own occupation and then after this short time period, the insured must be unable to work in any occupation for which he is suited by education and training to continue to be considered disabled and receive benefit payments. Thus, if the surgeon mentioned above, could work in a research setting or a teaching setting, he might not qualify to continue receiving disability income benefits.

Partial disability – A partial disability is one in which the insured individual cannot perform some of the duties of his own occupation, but can perform other duties of his own occupation. After a period of total disability, when the insured can return to work and perform some of his duties, the policy will pay a partial disability income benefit such as 50% of the total disability benefit payment.

Residual disability – Some disability income policies will pay a benefit for a residual disability. These policies provide benefits based on how much income an individual has lost. Some policies simply require a loss of earnings as the result of a disability caused either by an accident or an illness. Others may require a prior period of total disability.[7]

The second type of residual disability provision comes into play in a situation where an individual is first totally disabled and then recovers to the point where he can resume work but not at the same income level as before the disability. The residual disability benefit will pay the difference between the insured's pre-disability income and the amount he is able to earn after the disability. This type of benefit is probably most easily understood with an example.

Example. Assume that Mr. Jones earns $8,000 per month before he becomes disabled. After six months, he is able to return to work but earns only $5,000. The residual disability benefit would pay Mr. Jones $3,000 per month, the difference between the $8,000 pre-disability amount and the current monthly income of $5,000.

A policy may pay residual disability benefits on a pro rata basis according to the percentage of pre-disability earnings lost, or may pay benefits on a sliding scale based on earnings lost. For example, with a pro rata policy, an individual with a $3,000 monthly disability benefit who loses 60% of his pre-disability earnings would receive an $1,800 monthly benefit (60% of $3,000). With a sliding scale policy, an individual with a loss of earnings between 20% and 50% might receive a 50% benefit. With a loss of earnings between 50% and 80%, he might receive a pro rata benefit amount. With lost earnings of greater than 80%, he might receive 100% of the full disability benefit.

Recurrent disability – This definition of disability addresses when a period of disability is deemed to have ended. Generally, if the insured policyholder has been found to be totally disabled and then his condition improves to the point where he is no longer disabled, this provision says that if a new period of disability begins within six months of the end of the prior period, the two periods are deemed to be one continuous period of disability. If this is the case, then the insured policyholder does not have to satisfy the elimination period again.

Benefit Period

The benefit period for a disability income policy, as with long-term care insurance, is the period of time for which benefit payments will be made. The disability income payments will be paid for the length of the benefit period that is selected when the policy is purchased, assuming the disability continues for this entire time. Generally, the shorter the benefit period selected, the lower the premium for the disability income coverage.

Typically benefit periods for disability income coverage are offered for a certain length of time, such as one year or five years or until a certain age such as 65 or 70. After this age, the disabled individual will likely be receiving retirement benefits from retirement plans and government programs such as Social Security. At one time it was possible to select a lifetime benefit period under a disability income policy, but this is not widely available today. Of course, it is best to purchase the longest benefit period that the individual can reasonably afford.

Elimination Period

The elimination period is the period of time after disability begins until the disability income policy begins paying disability benefits. An individual disability income policy will typically offer the purchaser a choice of several elimination periods at the time the policy is purchased. And, as might be expected, the longer the elimination period that is selected, the lower the premium for the coverage.

While the effect of the policy premium is one item to consider in selecting an elimination period, the amount of assets the individual has that can be used to meet living expenses during a period of disability must also be taken into account. If assets are sufficient to pay living expenses for 60 days but not necessarily 90 days, then 60 days may be the best elimination period to select. While companies may offer elimination periods from 30 days up to as long as 2 years, the most commonly selected period is 90 days.[8]

Benefit Amount

The benefit amount of a disability income policy is, just as it sounds, the amount of the benefit that the insured individual receives each month in the event he becomes disabled. In arriving at the needed benefit amount, it is important to consider other sources of income that a disabled individual may having during the disability, as well as the living and health care expenses that must be met. Some sources that may provide income during disability include Social Security disability payments, group disability income provided by an employer, workers' compensation, and income earned by a spouse.

Renewability

The renewability feature of a disability income policy dictates whether and at what premium rate the policy may be renewed. This feature is an important one to understand. There are several types of renewability provisions: noncancelable; guaranteed renewable; and conditionally renewable.

Noncancelable – One type of renewability provision is the noncancelable type. Here the policy owner has the right to renew coverage at the same rate, unusually until age 65. In other words, the policy owner will not see an increase in his policy premiums regardless of whether there have been any claims under the policy or not. In effect, a noncancelable policy offers premiums that are guaranteed, at least to age 65. As one might expect, with a noncancelable policy the premium may be higher than it would if the policy were not noncancelable. Generally, a disability income policy that is noncancelable and guaranteed renewable is considered the best type of policy to purchase.[9]

Guaranteed renewable – This type of renewability provision is similar to the noncancelable feature except that with the guaranteed renewable provision the insurance company can increase the premium that the insured must pay for the policy. However, an increase in premium cannot be made on individual policies. Rather, the insurance company must increase the premium on all policies that fall within a particular category. A disability income policy with the guaranteed renewable provision may prove to be more affordable to purchase since the insurance company may feel that it can charge a lower premium initially than it could on a disability income policy with a noncancelable renewability provision.

Conditionally renewable – Under this type of renewability provision, the insurance company imposes certain conditions that the policyholder must meet in order to be able to renew the policy. One fairly common requirement is that the policyholder must be employed full-time in order to renew coverage. Also, the insurance company may raise rates under this type of plan.

Riders

As with life insurance policies, disability income policies may offer additional and optional benefits that can be added to the base policy by purchasing a rider.

Waiver of premium – The waiver of premium provision or rider allows a policyholder to stop paying premiums once he begins receiving disability income benefits. Thus, the policy will continue in force during a period of disability.

Automatic benefit increases – This provision is similar to the inflation protection provision in a long-term care insurance policy. Basically, this provision automatically increases the benefit payable under the policy by a certain percentage each year. The percentage is usually based on the Consumer Price Index (CPI).

ALTERNATIVES

Alternatives to disability income coverage include self-insuring against the possibility of a disability, purchasing a life insurance policy with a waiver of premium benefit or rider, purchasing critical illness insurance, and being able to qualify to receive Social Security disability income payments.

WHERE CAN I FIND OUT MORE ABOUT IT?

1. *Tax Facts on Insurance & Employee Benefits* (Cincinnati, OH: The National Underwriter Company, published annually).

2. Jeff Sadler, *Disability Income: The Sale, The Product, The Market*, 2nd ed. (Cincinnati, OH: The National Underwriter Company, 1995).

3. *Social Security Manual* (Cincinnati, OH: The National Underwriter Company, published annually).

QUESTIONS AND ANSWERS

Question – What definition of disability must be satisfied to qualify for Social Security disability benefits?

Answer – Disability for Social Security purposes is defined as the inability to engage in any substantial gainful activity by reason of any medically deter-

minable physical or mental impairment that can be expected to result in death or can be expected to last for a period of not less than 12 months. This is a fairly difficult definition to meet since it requires that the disabled individual not only be unable to work at his previous occupation but be unable to engage in any kind of gainful employment.

Question – What is the "regular care and attendance of a physician" requirement?

Answer – Generally, an element of meeting the definition of "disability" under a disability income policy is that the insured person must be under the care of a qualified physician in order to continue to receive disability income benefit payments.

CHAPTER ENDNOTES

1. Department of Labor statistics referred to in "The Once-Huge Throng of DI Providers has Evaporated," by W. Harold Petersen, *The National Underwriter*, Life and Financial Services ed., March 1, 2004, p. 14.

2. Survey completed by the Consumer Federation of America and the American Council of Life Insurance, cited in "Consumer, Insurer Groups Work to Inform Americans About Disability Income Insurance," *The National Underwriter*, NU Online News Service, April 23, 2001.

3. W. Harold Petersen, "The Once-Huge Throng of DI Providers has Evaporated," *The National Underwriter*, Life and Financial Services edition, March 1, 2004, p. 14.

4. IRC Sec. 213(d)(1).

5. IRC Sec. 104(a)(3).

6. Jeff Sadler, *Disability Income: The Sale, The Product, The Market*, 2nd ed. (Cincinnati, OH: The National Underwriter Company, 1995), p. 105.

7. Jeff Sadler, *Disability Income: The Sale, The Product, The Market*, 2nd ed. (Cincinnati, OH: The National Underwriter Company, 1995), p. 106.

8. Jeff Sadler, *Disability Income: The Sale, The Product, The Market*, 2nd ed. (Cincinnati, OH: The National Underwriter Company, 1995), p. 30.

9. Marcia Little, "Replacing Existing DI: What You Should Know," The National Underwriter, Life and Financial Services ed., March 1, 2004, p. 19.

END OF CHAPTER REVIEW

1. Disability income insurance is intended to replace an individual's salary during a period of disability.

   True   False

2. Most Americans have sufficient disability income insurance coverage.

   True   False

3. All disability income policies define "total disability" using standard language.

    True   False

4. Some disability income policies provide partial disability benefits for individuals who can perform some, but not all, the duties of their own occupation.

    True   False

5. If Mr. Jones returns to work from a period of total disability, but is able to earn less than before, he might benefit from a policy with a "residual disability" benefit.

    True   False

6. Disability income policies typically pay benefits for life.

    True   False

7. Shorter elimination periods typically result in lower policy premiums for disability income policies.

    True   False

8. With a "guaranteed renewable" policy, the insurance company cannot increase the premiums on individual policies.

    True   False

9. Disability income policies may offer automatic benefit increases to protect against inflation.

    True   False

10. The definition of disability for Social Security requires the inability to perform any substantial gainful activity for a period of not less than 12 months.

    True   False

Chapter 19

TAXATION OF INDIVIDUAL DISABILITY INCOME INSURANCE

WHAT IS IT?

Disability income insurance provides a benefit payment when the insured individual is unable to work due to a disability. The benefit is intended to replace the individual's salary during the period of disability. However, the benefit payment is not typically equal to 100% of the individual's salary. Most policies replace about 60 to 65% of income. A disability income benefit may be provided through a group insurance plan obtained through the individual's employer or it may be purchased as an individual policy by the insured individual.

WHEN IS THE USE OF THIS TOOL INDICATED?

If an individual's family depends on his or her income to meet their living expenses, disability income insurance should be considered as part of a sound financial plan. Often, if an individual is an employee, such coverage is provided by the employer. A self-employed individual must often provide his or her own coverage.

Especially for the self-employed individual, individual disability income coverage is a vital benefit. In the event of a disability, medical insurance will likely cover the cost of medical care but, unless disability income coverage is in place, the self-employed individual will not receive any income with which to meet his and his family's living expenses.

The risk of disability, particularly at younger ages when an individual may have young children, is greater than one might think. For example, at age 30 a male is 4 times more likely to become permanently disabled than he is to die. At age 40 this figure is 2.9 times more likely and at age 50, a man is 2.3 times more likely to encounter a disability than he is to die.[1] Plus, while many disabled individuals do recover from their disability, the length of time that recovery can take can be substantial. For example, nearly 70% of individuals who become disabled at age 35 remain disabled after two years and 90 days.[2]

BUSINESS USES

Group disability income insurance coverage is a fairly typical benefit provided to employees by large and medium size employers as part of the benefits package. It is probably accurate to say that this is a benefit that employees expect from employers, with the possible exception of smaller businesses.

Another type of disability insurance is used in conjunction with buy-sell agreements. If a shareholder/employee becomes disabled and, after a certain period of time, it appears that the disability will continue, this insurance coverage provides a sum with which the disabled shareholder's interest in the business is bought out. This allows the shareholder/employee to recover the value of his interest in the business and allows the business to hire a replacement for the disabled person and move forward with its business activities.

ADVANTAGES

The most obvious advantage of disability income insurance is that the policy will provide a benefit payment equal to a certain percentage of the disabled individual's income for the duration of the disability. This benefit payment will make it easier for the disabled individual to continue to support his or her family and meet basic living expenses.

DISADVANTAGES

If an individual does not have the benefit of his or her employer paying the cost of disability income coverage, the cost or premium needed to buy the coverage could be substantial. This will typically be the case with self-employed persons.

TAX IMPLICATIONS

Disability Income Premium Payments

Generally, premiums paid by an individual for an individually owned disability income policy are not considered premiums paid for medical care and, thus, are not deductible from income for income tax purposes.[3]

Premiums paid by an employer for disability income policies provided to employees are deductible to the employer in the year paid.[4] This deduction is available for both individual disability income policies and group disability income policies.

Disability Income Benefit Payments

Generally, disability income benefits from personally purchased policies are exempt from income tax. Further, there is no limit on the amount of disability income benefits that can be received tax-free under personally owned disability income policies.[5]

On the other hand, disability income payments received from a disability income policy paid for by an employer are fully includable in gross income and taxable to the employee.[6] If benefits are received under a plan under which an employee has contributed to the cost, the portion of the disability income attributable to the employee's contributions will be received income-tax free.[7] However, if an employee chooses in advance to reimburse his employer for premiums paid on a disability income policy, any benefit payments that he receives while disabled are entitled to be excluded from income.[8]

If the disability income insurance is financed partly by the employer and partly by the employee, only that portion of the disability income benefits attributable to the employer's premium payments is includable in the employee's income.

Example. Suppose the employee pays one-third of the premium and his employer pays the remaining two-thirds of the premiums. If the employee becomes disabled, one-third of the benefits received from the policy will be tax-exempt and two-thirds of the disability income benefit will be taxable.[9]

If the premiums are paid by the employer but are not excludable from the employee's gross income in the year they are paid, any disability income benefits received will be tax-exempt.[10]

Where benefit amounts are determined by other methods, the income taxation of benefit payments may differ. For example, benefits from a plan for injured football players where the benefit amount was determined by the number of seasons played rather than the type and severity of the injury as required were not

excludable from income.[11] Further, benefits determined as a percentage of a disabled employee's salary rather than the nature of his injury are not typically excludable from income.[12]

Tax Credit for the Elderly and the Permanently and Totally Disabled

Section 22 of the Internal Revenue Code offers an income tax credit to "qualified individuals" who were totally disabled when they retired. The amount of the credit is 15% of the taxpayer's IRC Section 22 amount.[13] "Disability income" is defined as the taxable amount an individual receives under an employer plan as wages or payments in place of wages for the period he is absent from work due to disability.[14]

Qualified individuals are those who are age 65 or older or who are under age 65, retired on disability, and considered permanently and totally disabled.[15] "Permanent and total disability" is the inability "to engage in any substantial gainful activity by reason of any medically determinable physical or mental impairment which can be expected to result in death or which has lasted or can be expected to last for a continuous period of not less than 12 months."[16]

To determine the amount of the credit, the individual must determine his "Section 22" amount for the taxable year. The credit equals 15% of that amount; however, since it is a nonrefundable credit, it may not exceed the taxpayer's income tax liability for the taxable year.[17]

The base "Section 22" amount is $5,000 for a single taxpayer or married taxpayers filing jointly if only one spouse qualifies for the credit; $7,500 for married taxpayers filing jointly if both qualify; and $3,750 for married taxpayers filing separately.[18] The base figure (or the amount of disability income in the case of individuals under age 65 if that is less) is reduced dollar-for-dollar by one-half of adjusted gross income in excess of $7,500 (single taxpayer); $10,000 (joint return); or $5,000 (married filing separately).[19]

Gift, Estate, and Generation–Skipping Transfer Taxation

Basically, there is no effect on disability income premiums or benefit payments from the gift tax, the estate tax, and the generation-skipping transfer tax. An individual can make a gift of any amount of cash that the recipient will use to pay disability income premiums.

Such a gift would be considered a present interest gift and, as such, would qualify for the gift tax annual exclusion of $11,000 (in 2004, as indexed). Since disability income benefits are paid only during the policyholder's life, after his or her death, nothing remains to be transferred to an heir or beneficiary.

ALTERNATIVES

The only real alternative to disability income coverage is to self-insure against the possibility that an individual will become disabled and unable to work. Any funding vehicle that allows funds to be withdrawn as needed and without significant tax penalties or surrender charges is an appropriate place to put the funds that will be used to provide an income in the event of a disability.

Another alternative that may provide some assistance during a period of disability is a life insurance policy with a waiver of premium benefit or rider. In the event of a permanent disability, this benefit will pay the premiums due on the life insurance policy. Not only is this a financial benefit in that the disabled policyholder does not have to pay the premiums, it is also a benefit in that it keeps the policy in force. A disabled policyholder may find that he or she is unable to purchase additional life insurance after becoming disabled.

Another possible alternative to disability income insurance is critical illness insurance. This type of insurance pays a lump sum benefit to the insured individual upon the diagnosis of a covered critical illness. Most policies of this type cover a number of different critical illnesses including strokes, heart attacks, certain cancers, kidney failure, and Alzheimer's disease.

Finally, a disabled individual may qualify to receive disability payments from Social Security. It is important to note that the definition of "disability" used by the government is a fairly conservative one that can be difficult to meet. Generally, for purposes of receiving social security disability income benefits, the individual must be unable to engage in any substantial gainful activity by reason of a mental or physical disability. The disability must be expected to end in death or to last for a period of at least 12 months. In other words, to receive disability income benefits from Social Security, an individual must be disabled to the point where he or she cannot work at any job, not just unable to work at his or her previous job or profession.[20]

WHERE CAN I FIND OUT MORE ABOUT IT?

1. *Tax Facts on Insurance & Employee Benefits* (Cincinnati, OH: The National Underwriter Company, published annually).

2. Jeff Sadler, *Disability Income: The Sale, The Product, The Market*, 2nd ed. (Cincinnati, OH: The National Underwriter Company, 1995).

QUESTIONS AND ANSWERS

Question – Are disability income benefit payments subject to FICA and FUTA tax?

Answer – Payments made to a disabled employee by either an employer or an insurance company are subject to social security tax (FICA) and federal unemployment tax (FUTA) for the first six months after the last month in which the employee worked for the employer. After six months, such payments are exempt from social security and federal unemployment tax.[21] However, if the benefit payments are made from a plan to which the employee contributed, the portion of such payments attributable to the employee's contributions is not subject to social security tax.[22]

Question – Are disability income benefit payments subject to income tax withholding?

Answer – While an employer is generally required to withhold income tax from disability income benefit payments, withholding is not required on benefit payment amounts that can be excluded from the employee's income. Further, if the disability benefit payments are made by an insurance company or other entity under an accident or health plan, no withholding of income tax is required.[23]

Question – How is a disability income benefit received under a life insurance policy treated for income tax purposes?

Answer – When disability income benefits are received under a disability rider attached to a life insurance policy, the amount is treated as a separate accident or health benefit, and not as proceeds from the life insurance policy. Thus, such benefit payments are excludable from income as "amounts received through accident or health insurance... for personal injury or sickness."[24]

Question – What is disability buy-out insurance?

Answer – Another type of disability income insurance is generally referred to as disability buy-out insurance. This type of coverage provides funds, upon the total and permanent disability of a shareholder or partner, to be used to buy out the disabled individual's interest in the business.

There may be certain requirements that must be met before a business can purchase this type of coverage. For example, a business might be required to have been in business for a certain amount of time before disability buy-out insurance will be issued.

CHAPTER ENDNOTES

1. Donald F. Cady, *2004 Field Guide to Estate Planning, Business Planning, & Employee Benefits* (Cincinnati, OH: The National Underwriter Company, 2004), p. 251.
2. Donald F. Cady, *2004 Field Guide to Estate Planning, Business Planning, & Employee Benefits* (Cincinnati, OH: The National Underwriter Company, 2004), p. 330.
3. IRC Sec. 213(d)(1).
4. Treas. Reg. §1.162-10(a).
5. IRC Sec. 104(a)(3).
6. *Cash v. Comm.*, TC Memo 1994-166. See also *Crandall v. Comm.*, TC Memo 1996-463.
7. Treas. Reg. §1.105-1(c).
8. See IRC Sec. 104(a)(3); *Bouquett v. Comm.*, TC Memo 1994-212.
9. IRC Sec. 104(a)(3).
10. IRC Sec. 104(a)(3).
11. See IRC Sec. 105(c)(2); *Beisler v. Comm.*, 814 F.2d 1304 (9th Cir. 1987).
12. *Colton v. Comm.*, TC Memo 1995-275; *Charles Webster v. Comm.*, 94-2 USTC ¶50,586 (M.D. Tenn. 1994).
13. IRC Sec. 22(b).
14. IRC Sec. 22(c)(2)(B)(iii).
15. IRC Sec. 22(b).
16. IRC Sec. 22(e).
17. IRC Sec. 22(a).
18. IRC Sec. 22(c)(2)(A), 22(e)(1).
19. IRC Sec. 22(d).
20. *2004 Social Security Manual* (Cincinnati, OH: The National Underwriter Company, Cincinnati, Ohio, 2004), p. 76.
21. IRC Secs. 3121(a)(4), 3306(b)(4).
22. See IRC Sec. 6051(f)(2)(B); Treas. Reg. §31.6051-3(b)(4).
23. Treas. Reg. §31.3401(a)-1(b)(8); Rev. Rul. 77-89, 1977-1 CB 300.
24. IRC Sec. 104(a)(3).

END OF CHAPTER REVIEW

1. Premiums paid by an individual for an individual disability income policy are generally tax deductible.

   True   False

2. Premiums paid by an employer for disability income policies provided to employees are generally deductible to the employer in the year paid.

   True   False

3. Benefits received from employer-provided disability income policies are fully includable in gross income and taxable to the employee.

   True   False

4. Benefits received from personally purchased disability income policies are fully includable in gross income and taxable to the individual.

   True   False

5. Benefits received from disability income policies for which the employer and the employee shared the cost are includable in gross income on a pro rata basis.

   True   False

6. Disability income benefits that are includable in an employee's gross income are subject to FICA and FUTA taxes for the first six months after the last month worked.

    True   False

7. Individuals who are age 65 or older or who are retired on total disability may qualify for a tax credit for a portion of disability income benefits received.

    True   False

8. Disability income benefits on personally purchased disability income policies are subject to FICA and FUTA taxes for the first six months of benefit payments.

    True   False

9. Insurance companies paying disability income benefits are not required to withhold income tax from payments.

    True   False

10. Disability buy-out insurance can be used to provide funds to "buy out" a disabled partner or shareholder.

    True   False

Chapter 20

LONG–TERM CARE POLICY COVERAGE AND SELECTION

■

WHAT IS IT?

Long-term care insurance is coverage that is available on either an individual or a group basis that pays for personal care needs and other services for individuals who are limited in their abilities to perform the activities of daily living for themselves. The policy typically pays for care that is provided in the individual's home, in an assisted living facility, or in a nursing home.

In other words, long-term care is, generally, care provided for individuals who can no longer perform certain activities for themselves. These activities are referred to as "activities of daily living" or ADLs and include eating, bathing, toileting, dressing, moving between a chair and the bed, and remaining continent.

ADVANTAGES

1. The most immediately obvious advantage to having long-term care insurance in place when an individual finds that he or she needs care is that a greater amount of money will be available to pay for the care. This not only allows a spouse to continue to have the same level of income to meet living expenses, it may also provide the spouse who needs care with a greater number of options as to how and where the care will be provided

2. If the individual who needs care does not have a spouse, the existence of long-term care insurance coverage may result in the individual's assets being passed down to children, grandchildren, or other heirs rather than used up to pay the cost of long-term care.

DISADVANTAGES

1. Probably the greatest perceived disadvantage to purchasing a long-term care insurance policy is the cost. The premiums required to purchase coverage can be substantial, especially if the individual is older.

2. Also, another disadvantage is that, even though most individuals need some type of long-term care

during their lifetime, it may be that a particular individual will never use any of the benefits provided by a long-term care insurance policy.

TAX IMPLICATIONS

The tax implications of purchasing a long-term care policy and receiving benefit payments from such a policy are covered in detail in a later chapter. For now, it is sufficient to note that how a policy is taxed depends upon whether it is a qualified long-term care policy or a nonqualified long-term care policy.

If the policy is a qualified policy, generally, premiums paid to purchase the policy are eligible for income tax deduction[1] to the extent that the premiums, when added to the other amounts the taxpayer has paid for the medical care of the taxpayer, his spouse or dependents, exceed 7.5% of adjusted gross income.[2] However, the deduction for long-term care insurance and services is subject to an additional dollar amount limitation that increases with the age of the insured individual. In 2004, for persons age 40 or less the limitation amount is $260. For ages 41 through 50, the limitation amount is $490; for ages 51 through 60, the limitation amount is $980; for ages 61 through 70, the limitation amount is $2,600 and for those over 70, the limitation amount is $3,250.[3]

Benefit payment amounts received from a qualified long-term care insurance contract are generally not includable in income.[4] However, there is a limit on the amount of qualified long-term care benefits that may be excluded from income. Generally, if the total periodic long-term care payments received from all policies and any periodic payments received that are treated as paid by reason of the death of the insured exceed a per diem limitation, the excess must be included in income.[5] This per diem limitation is equal to the greater of the dollar amount limitation or the otherwise-unreimbursed costs incurred for qualified long-term care services provided for the insured. For 2004, the dollar amount limitation is $230 per day.[6]

As far as the nonqualified long-term care insurance policy, the taxation of premiums paid for and benefits received from such a contract is uncertain. However, generally, it is believed that tax benefits applicable to the qualified contracts are not applicable to nonqualified long-term care insurance contracts.

WHEN IS THE USE OF THIS TOOL INDICATED?

In determining whether long-term care insurance is appropriate for an individual client, several items should be taken into account. First, when asked about how they would pay for long-term care should it be needed, many individuals are surprised to learn that these costs are not necessarily going to be covered by Medicare or some other government program. Neither are most long-term care costs covered by private health insurance or by Medicare supplement policies. Medicare will pay care for skilled care for a limited number of days but if long-term care is needed beyond this period, the individual must bear the cost himself. In other words, the individual must use all his personal assets, with some limited exceptions if there is a spouse, to pay for long-term care. After the individual's assets and/or income have been used up or "spent down," the individual may qualify for Medicaid to begin paying the long-term care costs.

Generally, some type of long-term care insurance should be considered if the individual has sufficient assets that it would be some time before the individual had spent down his assets and could qualify for Medicaid. In other words, individuals with few assets may not need this type of coverage. On the other end of the continuum, individuals with a great deal of wealth may prefer simply to pay for their care, if long-term care is needed, rather than purchase long-term care insurance coverage. It is the individuals with an amount of assets that fall between these two points – with some assets that they wish to preserve for spouses and children but not sufficient assets that paying for care is of no concern – that will want to carefully consider the purchase of some type of long-term care insurance coverage.

HOW DO I SELECT THE BEST OF ITS TYPE?

Appropriateness of Coverage

Whether to purchase long-term care insurance is a personal decision and, much like the decision to purchase life insurance, depends upon an individual's concern for the financial situation of his spouse and family after death. Generally, the risk that long-term care insurance protects against is the risk of a long nursing home stay. Such a stay could use up most or even all of an individual's assets, leaving little or nothing for surviving family members. While not all of us will enter a nursing home, one study predicts that men have a 33% chance of entering a nursing home sometime during their lives while women have a 52% chance. However, the same study found that men have only a 4% chance of staying in a nursing home more than five years while women have only a 13% chance of staying more than five years.[7] Another estimate is that 40% of individuals will not need long-term care insurance.[8]

As with many purchases, the cost of long-term care insurance coverage is a primary item to consider. An individual with few assets may decide that the cost of purchasing the coverage is too great in view of his present income and assets. One recommendation as to when the purchase of long-term care insurance coverage should be considered states that household income should be at least $35,000 with assets of at least $75,000 before a purchase of long-term care insurance coverage should be considered.[9]

Yet another item to consider when looking at whether long-term care insurance coverage is appropriate for a particular client is when, under a given policy, benefits will be paid out. In general terms, qualified long-term care insurance policies can only have certain "benefit triggers" upon the occurrence of which benefit payments begin.

With a qualified contract, one benefit trigger is generally referred to as the ADL (activities of daily living) benefit trigger. This benefit trigger is activated when a person becomes classified as chronically ill, which means the individual has been certified as being unable to perform, without substantial assistance, at least two activities of daily living (ADLs) for at least 90 days or when a person has a similar level of disability.

In addition, there is a second benefit trigger that a qualified long-term care policy may have. Under this benefit trigger, called the cognitive impairment trigger, benefits may be paid if the individual requires substantial supervision to protect himself from threats to his health and safety due to severe cognitive impairment. The existence of this condition must have been certified by a health care practitioner within the previous 12 months.

In contrast to the qualified long-term care insurance policy, a common benefit trigger used in nonqualified long-term care contracts is the "medical necessity" benefit trigger. Under this provision, benefit payments can begin if the insured person's physician certifies that it is medically necessary for the individual to begin receiving long-term care.

Comparing and Selecting Policies

Long-term care insurance policies typically cover the cost of skilled, intermediate, and custodial care in nursing homes. In addition, long-term care insurance often covers home care services, assisted living, and adult daycare. The costs of hospice care, counseling, and other community-type services may be covered as well. However, it is important to remember that a long-term care insurance policy is a contract and that, as with any contract, the provisions may vary. Before purchasing a long-term care insurance policy, the potential purchaser should carefully review and understand what services are covered by the policy.

The cost of long-term care can be significant and, for some, a coverage that is not justified in view of the relationship between the cost of coverage and the individual's assets and income level. In addition, the various elements that make up a typical long-term care policy can be adjusted in many ways. This not only allows for some variance in premium amounts but also a range in terms of the benefit amounts that will be paid, the length of time benefits will continue, and the length of time before benefits will begin once long-term care has become necessary.

When comparing different long-term care policies, there are four basic elements of the policy that any comparison should begin with: (1) the daily benefit amount; (2) the benefit period; (3) the elimination or waiting period; and (4) the policy's provisions to protect against inflation. Also a consideration is whether the policyholder should purchase a qualified long-term care policy or a nonqualified policy. Each of these policy provisions is discussed in greater detail in a subsequent chapter. Here, following a brief summary, we will discuss how to compare policies by looking at these provisions.

The daily benefit amount is, basically, the specific daily amount that the individual purchases the policy for. For example, a particular long-term care insurance policy may pay a benefit amount of $120 per day or $200 per day. Some policies will provide a different daily dollar amount for different types of long-term care. Whether an individual desires coverage that will pay the daily benefit regardless of what the actual long-term care expenses are or whether he would rather have

coverage that pays only the daily benefit amount up to the actual cost of the care is a first consideration. The first type of coverage is generally referred to as an indemnity type of plan while the second type of coverage is a reimbursement type of coverage. The primary advantage of electing a reimbursement type of coverage is that it is typically less expensive. The main advantage of the indemnity type of coverage is that it may cover items that are considered "extra" or "add-on" coverages in addition to the basic cost of care.

The benefit period is the period of time over which a long-term care policy will pay a benefit. It can be a set number of years, such as three years or five years, or it can be for lifetime. Which benefit period is selected by an individual policyholder is often a function of affordability. Of course, the lifetime benefit period is always preferable since this benefit period would insure that a person who needs skilled care for quite a long time would not use up the full amount of the policy's benefits. However, often this length of coverage is significantly more expensive than a shorter benefit period such as three or five years. Statistics show that the average stay in a nursing home lasts about 2.5 years.[10] If a policyholder is admitted to a nursing home and stays the average amount of time, a five-year benefit period would result in the cost of the stay being covered. How long of a benefit period a particular policyholder will elect is dependent on price. Other factors to consider are the current age of the individual and his or her family history. A younger purchaser of long-term care insurance, perhaps in his or her 50's may have a greater interest in a longer benefit period than an older purchaser. Along the same lines, an individual who has a family history of an illness that results in a need for nursing home care, such as Alzheimers, may be more interested in a longer benefit period than someone without such a family history.

The elimination period is the number of days that the individual must wait after long-term care begins before the policy will start to pay benefits. Generally, the shorter the elimination period, the higher the premium, but it is a good idea to actually check the difference in premium amounts between the various choices of elimination periods. In effect, unless a policyholder elects a zero-day elimination period and, thus, will receive "first day" coverage, the policyholder is choosing how long a period of time he will self insure. Assuming the daily benefit amount is $200 per day and the policyholder chooses a 30-day elimination period, he has elected to self insure for $6,000 (30 days x $200 per day). If he elects a longer elimination period of 90 days, the self insured amount is $18,000 (90 days x $200 per day).

The inflation protection provision in a long-term care policy typically provides that the amount paid in benefits will increase by a fixed percentage each year. There are several different ways that the amount by which the benefits will increase can be calculated. The younger the policyholder is at the time the long-term care insurance coverage is purchased, the greater the possible effect of inflation. A purchaser in his or her 50's may hold a policy for 20 years before any benefits are paid out. A daily benefit amount that seems more than adequate at the time of purchase may be woefully inadequate two decades down the road. One study predicts that by 2030, the cost of one year in a nursing home will be about $190,000 per year and the adult day care will cost $220 per day. A policy purchased today with a $150 per day benefit would pay only about $54,750 of the cost of such a nursing home stay.[11]

Purchasing inflation protection that uses the simple inflation method to calculate the benefit amount increase is probably the most affordable of the inflation protection alternatives. Under this method, the benefit amount is increased each year by a certain percentage, often 5%, of the original benefit amount. Most purchasers of long-term care policies should at least consider including this benefit as part of their policy. Another type of inflation protection, called compound inflation, increases the benefit amount each year by a percentage, such as 5%, of the previous year's benefit amount. This method typically results in a greater benefit payable after the policy has been in force at least a few years but typically the cost for the compound inflation protection is greater than the cost for simple inflation protection.

Also a consideration is whether the policyholder should purchase a qualified long-term care policy or a nonqualified policy. Two of the main differences between these two types of policies are the income taxation of the premium and the benefits and the benefit triggers, as discussed earlier in the chapter. Generally, if a policy is a qualified policy, premiums paid to purchase the policy are eligible for income tax deduction[12] to the extent that the premiums when added to the other amounts the taxpayer has paid for the medical care of the taxpayer, his spouse or dependents exceed 7.5% of adjusted gross income.[13] However, the deduction for long-term care insurance and services is subject to an additional dollar amount limitation that increases with the age of the insured individual.[14]

Benefit payment amounts received from a qualified long-term care insurance contract are generally not includable in income.[15] However, there is a limit on the amount of qualified long-term care benefits that may be excluded from income.[16]

As far as the nonqualified long-term care insurance policy, the taxation of premiums paid for and benefits received from such a contract is uncertain. However, generally, it is believed that tax benefits applicable to the qualified contracts are not applicable to nonqualified long-term care insurance contracts.

ALTERNATIVES

1. One alternative to the purchase of a long-term care insurance policy is the accelerated death benefits that may be available from a life insurance policy. Typically, a life insurance policy may provide that it will pay a certain portion of the policy's death benefit prior to the insured individual's death if the insured is terminally ill. The funds can be used for any purpose including medical care and living expenses. One drawback of relying solely upon this feature is that the individual's heirs will not receive the full death benefit of the policy and the amount they do receive may not be sufficient to cover the needs that the policy was originally sold to address.

2. A second alternative to a stand-alone long-term care insurance policy is the purchase of a combination policy. This is a life insurance policy and a long-term care insurance policy rolled into a single product and offering the potential of multiple benefits.

3. Of course, an individual may decide not to purchase long-term care insurance and instead plan to rely on the government benefits through the Medicare and Medicaid programs. One drawback to this plan is that the insured may not have a great deal of choice about where he or she receives care. Another drawback is that much of the insured's assets will have to be spent to pay for care before he or she can qualify to receive Medicaid benefits. (There are exemptions available for certain assets.)

4. Another alternative to the purchase of long-term are insurance is to rely on the individual's spouse and other family members to provide needed care.

5. Finally, an individual may simply plan to pay for any long-term care services that are needed by using existing assets to pay these costs.

WHERE CAN I FIND OUT MORE ABOUT IT?

1. Jeff Sadler, *How to Sell Long-Term Care Insurance: Your Guide to Becoming a Top Producer in an Untapped*

Market (Cincinnati, OH: The National Underwriter Company, 2001).

2. United Seniors Health Council, *Planning for Long-Term Care*, (McGraw-Hill, 2002).

3. Jeff Sadler, *The Long-Term Care Handbook* (Cincinnati, OH: The National Underwriter Company, 2004).

4. LTC Online, http://www.nationalunderwriter.com/LTC/

5. Jason G. Goetze *Long-Term Care*, 3rd ed. (Chicago, IL: Dearborn Publishing, 2001).

QUESTIONS AND ANSWERS

Question – What are the activities of daily living?

Answer – The most common activities of daily living are: (1) eating; (2) toileting; (3) transferring; (4) bathing; (5) dressing; and (6) continence. To be considered a qualified long-term care insurance contract, a policy must take into account at least five of these ADLs in determining whether a person is a chronically ill individual under the ADL benefit trigger as defined above.[17]

Question – What are the most frequently-asked questions about the purchase of long-term care insurance?

Answer – According to the LTC Learning Institute,[18] the top five questions asked by participants in long-term care seminars are:

1. What is the best age to buy LTC insurance?

2. Is this insurance portable to another state?

3. How much would LTC insurance cost me?

4. What happens to all the money I paid if I never need LTC?

5. What if the company I'm insured with goes out of business?

Question – What are the disclosure requirements applicable to the sale of long-term care insurance policies?

Answer – A long-term care insurance policy must meet certain requirements of the National Association of Insurance Commissioners (NAIC) long-term care insurance model regulations pertaining to application forms and replacement coverage, reporting requirements, marketing filing requirements, marketing standards, the appropriateness of the recommended purchase, and the standard format outline of coverage.[19] Further, a policy must meet certain requirements of the NAIC long-term care insurance model act relating to requirements for certificates under group plans, policy summary, monthly reports on accelerated death benefits, and the incontestability period.[20]

In addition, a long-term care insurance policy that is approved must be delivered to the policyholder within 30 days of the approval date. Further, if a claim under a long-term care insurance policy is denied, the issuer must provide a written explanation of the reasons for the denial and make available all information relating to the denial within 60 days of a written request from the policyholder.[21]

The penalty for not meeting these requirements is a tax equal to $100 per insured for each day that these requirements are not met for each qualified long-term care insurance contract.[22]

Question – What types of care does "home health care" provide?

Answer – Home health care, a service that is covered under most long-term care policies, generally encompasses several types of care including adult day care, respite care, caregiver training benefits, care coordinator, and equipment advice and home modification. Adult day care is paid for by the policy if one of the benefit triggers is activated and a dependent adult is taken to a center that typically provides intermediate or custodial type care. Respite care is basically a relief for the primary caregiver of a dependent adult. Generally, this type of care takes place in the individual's home. Caregiver training is a benefit provided to train a family member to provide the care needed, typically in the individual's home. This allows the care to be provided by a family member or friend. The care coordinator benefit provides payment for the assistance of a coordinator to help the individual needing care and his or her family find out about and take advantage of community and locally-provided long-term care services. Finally, some policies will provide payment to make certain modifications to an individual's home, such as putting in a wheel chair ramp or grab bars in the bathtub. The company is willing to put such provisions in the policy on the theory that it is less expensive to pay for these modifications and let the individual remain at home than it would be to pay for care in some type of facility.

CHAPTER ENDNOTES

1. IRC Sec. 213(d)(1).

2. IRC Sec. 213(a).

3. The age is the individual's attained age before the close of the taxable year. IRC Sec. 213(d)(10)(A); Rev. Proc. 2003-85, 2003-49 IRB 1184.

4. See IRC Sec. 104(a)(3); IRC Sec. 105(b).

5. IRC Sec. 7702B(d).

6. Rev. Proc. 2003-85, 2003-49 IRB 1184.

7. *Planning for Long-Term Care*, United Seniors Health Council, McGraw Hill, 2002, p. 83, citing "Medical Care, 1997."

8. Benjamin Lipson, "Ways to Help Consumers Evaluate LTC Insurance," *National Underwriter*, Life & Financial Services Edition, August 19, 2002.

9. *Planning for Long-Term Care*, United Seniors Health Council, McGraw Hill, 2002.

10. *How to Sell Long-Term Care Insurance*, by Jeff Sadler, The National Underwriter Company, 2001.

11. "Study Finds Rising Long-Term Care Costs, Demographics Will Make 'Aging in Place' Harder than Boomers Think," PR Newswire, April 26, 2000 cited in *How to Sell Long-Term Care Insurance*, by Jeff Sadler, The National Underwriter Company, 2001, p. 62.

12. IRC Sec. 213(d)(1).

13. IRC Sec. 213(a).

14. The age is the individual's attained age before the close of the taxable year. IRC Sec. 213(d)(10)(A); Rev. Proc. 2003-85, 2002-49 IRB 1.

15. See IRC Sec. 104(a)(3); IRC Sec. 105(b).

16. Rev. Proc. 2003-85, 2003 49 IRB 1.

17. IRC Sec. 7702B(c)(2)(B).

18. LTC Learning Institute referred to in How to Sell Long-Term Care Insurance, by Jeff Sadler, The National Underwriter Company, 2001, p. 79.

19. IRC Sec. 4980C(c)(1)(a).

20. IRC Sec. 4980C(c)(1)(b).

21. IRC Sec. 4980C(c).

22. IRC Sec. 4980C(b)(1).

END OF CHAPTER REVIEW

1. Long-term care insurance pays for personal care services for individuals who are limited in performing certain "activities of daily living."

   True   False

2. Long-term care policies may only pay for care provided in an assisted living facility or a nursing home.

   True   False

3. Long-term care insurance may help prevent a spouse from being impoverished by long-term care expenses.

   True   False

4. Long-term care premiums are much more expensive for older individuals.

   True   False

5. Medicare will pay for a limited amount of skilled long-term care following a hospital stay.

   True   False

6. Medicaid requires an individual to "spend down" most of his personal assets to pay for long-term care.

   True   False

7. Accelerated death benefits from a life insurance policy may be an alternative to a long-term care policy.

   True   False

8. Some insurance companies offer policies that combine life insurance and long-term care benefits.

    True   False

9. The NAIC does not set any disclosure or marketing standards for long-term care insurance policies.

    True   False

10. Most long-term care policies provide benefits for home health care services.

    True   False

Chapter 21

STANDARD PROVISIONS OF LONG–TERM CARE INSURANCE

WHAT IS IT?

Long-term care insurance is coverage that is available on either an individual or a group basis that pays for personal care needs and other services for individuals who are limited in their abilities to perform the activities of daily living for themselves. A policy typically pays for care that is provided in the individual's home, in an assisted living facility, or in a nursing home.

In other words, long-term care is, generally, care provided for individuals who can no longer perform certain activities for themselves. These activities are referred to as "activities of daily living" or ADLs and include eating, bathing, toileting, dressing, moving between a chair and the bed, and remaining continent.

Long-term care insurance policies typically cover the cost of skilled, intermediate, and custodial care in nursing homes. In addition, long-term care insurance often covers home care services, assisted living, and adult daycare. The costs of hospice care, counseling, and other community-type services may be covered as well. However, it is important to remember that a long-term care insurance policy is a contract and that, as with any contract, the provisions may vary. Before purchasing a long-term care insurance policy, a potential purchaser should carefully review and understand what services are covered by the policy.

WHEN IS THE USE OF
THIS TOOL INDICATED?

Approximately 44% of Americans age 65 or older will be confined to a nursing home at some time. Further, more than 50% of these individuals will remain in a nursing home for at least one year.[1] Since the average cost of staying in a nursing home was $56,000 in 2001, even a stay of a single year can result in significant costs.[2] Health care delivered in the insured's home can also be costly. On average a year of home care cost between $12,000 and $16,000 in 2001. This type of care includes an aid coming to the individual's home three days a week for two or three hours per day. Home health care services provided by more skilled caregivers, such as physical therapists, cost even more.[3]

Generally, individuals in nursing home and their families pay for about 33% of nursing home costs out of their own funds.[4] One study concluded that only 27% of older Americans were found to have sufficient assets to be able to pay the cost of a three-year nursing home stay (which was estimated to be about $150,000).[5] While long-term care insurance benefits may seem to be paid only to the elderly, in fact, 40% of the benefits paid from such policies are paid for care provided to adults between the ages of 18 and 64.[6]

Further, studies show that if a woman reaches age 65, she has a better than 50% chance of needing extended care before her death. Plus, it is interesting to note that 75% of nursing home residents are women.[7]

ADVANTAGES

1. If one spouse requires long-term care, the other spouse will be in a better position to pay for the care than if the policy had not been purchased. Thus, this provides some peace of mind and perhaps some options to the spouse who continues to live independently.

2. The fact that the policy can provide benefits to pay for long-term care may result in the individual's (or couple's) assets being passed down to children, grandchildren, or other heirs rather than used up to pay the cost of long-term care. For some, the ability to leave an inheritance to the next generation is an important consideration.

3. The availability of long-term care insurance benefits may offer an individual who needs care a greater number of options regarding how and where to obtain the care needed. For some, this can also provide some peace of mind. If a long-term care policy is available to pay for care, this may reduce the need for individuals to rely on family members to provide the care. Caring for an older relative can place a significant burden on children who may be working and raising their own children at this same time.

4. The purchase of a qualified long-term care policy can offer some potential income tax advantages, as discussed in a later chapter.

DISADVANTAGES

1. Probably the greatest perceived disadvantage to purchasing a long-term care insurance policy is the cost. The premiums required to purchase coverage can be substantial, especially if the individual is older.

2. Even though most individuals need some type of long-term care during their lifetime, it may be that a particular individual will never use any of the benefits provided by a long-term care insurance policy.

DESIGN FEATURES – STANDARD PROVISIONS

With long-term care insurance, it is vital that the person selling the product understands the structure of the particular long-term care policy being sold. While long-term care policies from different companies do have certain similarities, they are not all exactly the same. Many policies pay a fixed dollar amount for each day that the covered individual is in a nursing home or receiving other types of care. Also, many policies have a "pooled dollar" amount that pays for a combination of benefits among various care facilities. Most long-term care policies do not pay for the cost of drugs and medical care, although these costs may be covered by the individual's private health insurance policy or, if the individual is eligible, by Medicare.

There are other aspects of a long-term care policy that are important to understand, as well. Generally, gaining an understanding of the policy structure involves becoming familiar with the choice of maximum daily benefit, the benefit length, the type of inflation benefit, as well as the elimination period.[8] These elements and others are discussed below.

Eligibility

Most companies will issue a policy between the ages of 18 and 84, if the individual applying for the policy meets certain underwriting requirements. Certain pre-existing conditions (a health condition the insured person already had when the policy was applied for) may cause an individual to be rejected for coverage. Alternatively, the company may issue the policy but impose a time limit before any benefits will be paid that relate to the pre-existing condition. It is important to remember that clients will tend to think of insurability in terms of mortality but not morbidity. Long-term care insurance underwriting looks at medical conditions that may not be fatal but could result in a need for long-term care. This outlook may be different than the one a client has about his or her current health status.[9]

Benefit Amount

This is basically the specific daily amount for which the individual purchases the policy. A policy may provide for any benefit amount. It could be $100 per day or $200 per day. Some policies will provide a different daily dollar amount for different types of long-term care. For example, a policy may pay a benefit of $120 per day for nursing home costs but only pay a benefit of $75 per day for home health care. The person purchasing the policy typically has several possible benefits to choose from. Many considerations should come into making this decision, including what level of coverage the purchaser can afford.

Another factor that impacts the selection of the benefit amount is where in the country the individual lives (or, perhaps, plans to retire or relocate to). For example, average daily nursing home rates in 2000 ran as high as $295 per day in New York City to as little as $90 per day in a small town in Minnesota.[10]

With a reimbursement type policy, the insurance company will pay the cost of the long-term care up to the maximum daily benefit amount while an indemnity policy will pay the daily benefit amount without regard to the actual cost of the care.[11]

Benefit Period

This is the period of time over which the long-term care policy will pay a benefit. It can be a set number of years, such as three years or five years, or it can be for lifetime. This second type of benefit period is often referred to as a "lifetime benefit." As one might guess, electing benefits to be paid for life results in a higher premium than a policy that limits benefit payments to a certain number of years. Thus, which type of benefit period to elect must be based on the affordability of the policy as well as the preference of the potential purchaser.

Typically, current policies offer a "pot of money" approach to a benefit period. Here, the pot of money available is calculated by multiplying the number of years the policy will pay benefits by the maximum daily benefit amount. The resulting number is then multiplied by 365. This result is the amount of benefits the insurance company will pay over the life of the policy. For example, a policy with a benefit length of five years and a maximum daily benefit of $120 will result in a benefit limit of $219,000 (5 x 120 x 365 = $219,000.)

Elimination Period

Also called a waiting period, the elimination period is the number of days that the individual must wait after long-term care begins before the policy will start to pay benefits. Almost all policies offer a choice of at least two elimination period lengths. Many policies offer more choices such as, for example, elimination periods of 20 days, 50 days, or 100 days. Often it is possible to have no elimination period or a 0-day period. This results in "first day" coverage.

Typically, the shorter the waiting period, the higher the premium will be for the policy. The elimination days may be consecutive calendar days beginning with the first day the individual receives care. Some policies have a once-in-a-lifetime waiting period while other policies require that a new waiting period begins each time a new period of care begins.

Inflation Period

Generally, if a long-term care insurance policy has some type of inflation protection coverage, the amount paid in benefits increases by a fixed percentage each year. Several types of inflation coverage are available. Included here are compound inflation coverage and simple inflation coverage plus the policyholder typically has the option of not having any inflation protection coverage. Younger buyers generally will want to at least consider the purchase of compound inflation coverage while older buyers may be sufficiently protected against increases in the cost of long-term care by purchasing the simple inflation coverage.

Compound inflation protection coverage increases the daily maximum benefit by a certain percentage, often 5%, of the proceeding year's amount. A simple inflation protection rider increases the maximum daily benefit by 5% of the original daily maximum benefit amount. Thus, over time, a policy providing compound inflation protection will be providing a greater maximum daily benefit amount than the same policy that provides inflation protection using the simple inflation coverage method.

Example. If two policies begin with a $100 maximum daily benefit and 5% inflation protection, after twenty years, the simple inflation protection policy would be paying a maximum daily benefit amount of $200 while the compound inflation protection policy's maximum daily benefit would have reached $265.[12]

Yet another way to protect against inflation is the use a cost-of-living inflation rider, sometimes referred to as a COLI rider. With this type of approach, the maximum daily benefit amount is increased based on the increases in some type of cost of living index such as the Consumer Price Index or CPI. Usually, when an increase is offered, the policyholder has the option to either accept it or decline it. With some riders, no futher increases are offered once one is declined. With other riders, increases are offered for a certain number of years or until the insured person reaches a certain age. Generally, the premium for the policy increases whenever a cost-of-living rider increase is accepted by the policyholder.

It is important to at least consider adding some type of inflation protection to a long-term care insurance policy since some costs, particularly those related to health care, have been increasing faster than inflation. Further, depending upon the age of the insured individual at the time of purchase, the benefits of a long-term care policy may not be paid out for several decades. Over this amount of time, inflation can have a significant impact on the cost of care.

Benefit Triggers

"Benefit trigger" is a shorthand term for the set of circumstances that must occur before a long-term care policy will begin to pay benefits. If a long-term care insurance policy is a "qualified" policy, the benefit triggers are dictated in the Internal Revenue Code.[13] (The differences between a qualified long-term care contract and a nonqualified long-term care contract are covered in a subsequent chapter.)

With a qualified contract, one benefit trigger is generally referred to as the ADL (activities of daily living) benefit trigger. This benefit trigger is activated when a person becomes classified as chronically ill, which means the individual has been certified as being unable to perform, without substantial assistance, at least two activities of daily living (ADLs) for at least 90 days or when a person has a similar level of disability.

In addition, there is a second benefit trigger that a qualified long-term care policy may have. Under this benefit trigger, called the cognitive impairment trigger, benefits may be paid if the individual requires substantial supervision to protect himself from threats to his health and safety due to severe cognitive impairment. Further, the existence of this condition must have been certified by a health care practitioner within the previous 12 months.

A common benefit trigger used in nonqualified long-term care contracts is the "medical necessity" benefit trigger. Under this provision, benefit payments can begin if the insured person's physician certifies that it is medically necessary for the individual to begin receiving long-term care. Thus, many nonqualified products offer what is sometimes referred to as the "triple trigger" of benefits. In other words, the insured individual can begin receiving benefits if any one of three tests is met:

1. the insured individual is not able to perform two of five activities of daily living (ADLs);

2. the insured suffers a medically diagnosed cognitive impairment; or

3. a physician certifies the need for long-term care services. (This is the medical necessity benefit trigger.)

While the nonqualified policies typically offer more ways to begin receiving benefits, the qualified type of long-term care insurance policy offers potential income tax advantages. Most policies being sold today are of the qualified variety.[14]

Other Benefit Provisions

Accelerated payment plans – These types of plans permit the holder of a long-term care policy to pay the policy premiums in a shorter time frame than over his or her lifetime. The total policy premium might be paid in a single premium or over a period of years continuing until the policyholder reaches age 65. Not all policies offer this premium payment method.

Waiver of premium – The waiver of premium provision allows a policyholder to stop paying premiums once he or she begins receiving benefits, although with some policies not all benefits will relieve the policyholder of the duty to pay premiums. For example, receiving home health care may not trigger relief from continuing to pay premiums but receiving skilled care

in a facility might mean that no more premiums will be due under the policy.

Restoration of benefits – This provision is often offered in the form of an optional rider to a long-term care policy. It provides that the policy will be "restored" to the original policy maximum benefit after benefits are received for some period of time less than the maximum benefit length period. Usually, for the restoration of benefits to occur, the insured must not have been receiving benefits for a certain length of time because he or she has recovered from the condition that made the long-term care benefits necessary.

Nonforfeiture benefits – Some policies offer this benefit, which is designed to allow a policyholder to stop paying premiums into the policy without losing all benefits and coming away from the situation having paid premiums but having no current coverage. Much like the nonforfeiture provisions in a life insurance policy, the nonforfeiture provision in a long-term care policy allows the policyholder to stop paying premiums and receive a lesser amount of coverage under the policy. Often, the same daily benefit amount will be paid but it will be paid for a shorter time period. This benefit is usually an optional benefit with an additional cost.

Survivorship benefit – This benefit is available only to married couples and provides, generally, that at the death of one spouse, the surviving spouse will receive a paid-up long-term care policy. This benefit, which may be offered either as part of the base policy or as a rider, may state that the survivorship benefit will be provided only if, upon the spouse's death, no prior benefits have been paid out of the policy. Another requirement that may be imposed is that the policy has been in force for a certain number of years before the survivorship benefit will take effect.

Premium refund at death – Some policies will provide that a refund of premium will be made upon the policyholder's death. Often, the amount returned is equal to the amount of premiums paid for the policy less the total of any claims paid under the policy. This is typically an optional benefit.

ALTERNATIVES

1. One alternative to the purchase of a long-term care insurance policy is the accelerated death benefits that may be available from a life insurance policy. Typically, a life insurance policy may provide that it will pay a certain portion of the policy's death

benefit prior to the insured individual's death if the insured is terminally ill. The funds can be used for any purpose including medical care and living expenses. One drawback of relying solely upon this feature is that the individual's heirs will not receive the full death benefit of the policy and the amount they do receive may not be sufficient to cover the needs that the policy was originally sold to address.

2. A second alternative to a stand-alone long-term care insurance policy is the purchase of a combination policy. This is a life insurance policy and a long-term care insurance policy rolled into a single product and offering the potential of multiple benefits.

3. Of course, an individual may decide not to purchase long-term care insurance and instead plan to rely on the government benefits through the Medicare and Medicaid programs. One drawback to this plan is that the insured may not have a great deal of choice about where he or she receives care. Another drawback is that much of the insured's assets will have to be spent to pay for care before he or she can qualify to receive Medicaid benefits. (There are exemptions available for certain assets.)

4. Another alternative to the purchase of long-term are insurance is to rely on the individual's spouse and other family members to provide needed care.

5. Finally, an individual may simply plan to pay for any long-term care services that are needed by using existing assets to pay these costs.

WHERE CAN I FIND OUT MORE ABOUT IT?

1. Jeff Sadler, *How to Sell Long-Term Care Insurance: Your Guide to Becoming a Top Producer in an Untapped Market*, (Cincinnati, OH: The National Underwriter Company, 2001).

2. United Seniors Health Council, *Planning for Long-Term Care* (New York, NY: McGraw-Hill, 2002).

3. Jeff Sadler, *The Long-Term Care Handbook*, 3rd ed. (Cincinnati, OH: The National Underwriter Company, 2003).

4. LTC Online, http://www.nationalunderwriter.com/LTC/

5. Goetze, Jason G., *Long-Term Care,* (Dearborn Publishing, 3rd edition, 2001).

QUESTIONS AND ANSWERS

Question – Why should an individual buy a long-term care insurance policy since Medicare will pay the cost of this type of care?

Answer – Contrary to the belief of many individuals, Medicare does not cover the cost of long-term care. It will pay for certain types of care for a limited number of days, but if long-term care is needed beyond this period, the individual must bear the cost himself. In other words, the individual must use all his personal assets, with some limited exceptions if there is a spouse, to pay for long-term care. After these assets and/or income have been used up or "spent down," the individual may qualify for Medicaid to begin paying the long-term care costs.

Question – Will a long-term care insurance policy cover all the costs associated with providing long-term care?

Answer – Generally, no. Most long-term care policies do not pay for the cost of drugs and medical care, although these costs pay be covered by the individual's private health insurance policy or, if the individual is eligible, by Medicare.

Question – At what age should an individual consider the purchase of a long-term care insurance policy?

Answer – Typically, the average age that individuals begin thinking about the purchase of long-term care insurance is in the mid-60s. It may make sense, however, to at least consider the purchase at an earlier age since premiums are typically lower at younger ages and it may be easier for an individual to meet the company's underwriting standards at a younger age.

Question – What if I want to return or cancel a long-term care insurance policy after I have purchased it?

Answer – Typically, after an individual receives a policy, he or she has 30 days in which to return the policy to the insurance company for a full refund of premium.

Question – What are accelerated death benefits and how can they be used as an alternative to long-term care insurance?

Answer – An accelerated death benefit is a provision found in many permanent life insurance policies. Basically, this provision allows a portion of the policy death benefit to be paid to the insured individual before his death if he is terminally ill. If the policy provision meets certain requirements, the distribution can be received free of income tax.[15]

Generally, any amount received under a life insurance contract on the life of a terminally ill insured or a chronically ill insured is received free of income tax. It is treated as an amount paid by reason of the death of the insured, which is not includable in gross income. Thus, an accelerated death benefit meeting certain requirements will generally be received free of income tax. However, amounts paid to a chronically ill individual are subject to the same limitations that apply to long-term care benefits. Generally, this is a limitation of $230 (as indexed for 2004) per day in benefits.[16] Accelerated death benefits paid to terminally ill individuals are not subject to this limit.

For purposes of accelerated death benefits, a terminally-ill individual is a person who has been certified by a physician as having an illness or physical condition that can reasonably be expected to result in death within 24 months following the certification.[17] Further, a chronically ill individual is a person who is not terminally ill and who has been certified as being unable to perform, without substantial assistance, at least two activities of daily living (ADLs) for at least 90 days or a person with a similar level of disability.[18]

There is one exception to this general rule of non-includability for accelerated death benefits. The rules outlined above do not apply to any amount paid to any taxpayer other than the insured if the taxpayer has an insurable interest in the life of the insured because the insured is a director, officer, or employee of the taxpayer or if the insured is financially interested in any trade or business of the taxpayer.[19]

Question – Can the holder of a long-term care insurance policy increase or decrease the policy benefits after the policy has been issued?

Answer – It is generally possible to decrease the benefits payable under a long-term care policy after the policy has been issued. However, most companies will not as readily agree to increase the benefits

payable under the policy. Generally, an increase in benefits will only be made after the policyholder has submitted a new application and provided proof of insurability.

CHAPTER ENDNOTES

1. The National Association of Insurance Commissioners as referred to in *A Consumer Guide to Long-Term Care Insurance*, published by The Insurance Marketplace Standards Association.

2. The U.S. Department of Labor as referred to in *A Consumer Guide to Long-Term Care Insurance*, published by The Insurance Marketplace Standards Association.

3. The National Association of Insurance Commissioners as referred to in *A Consumer Guide to Long-Term Care Insurance*, published by The Insurance Marketplace Standards Association.

4. *A Consumer Guide to Long-Term Care Insurance*, published by The Insurance Marketplace Standards Association.

5. 2000 study by James R. Knickman and Emily Snell of the Robert Wood Johnson Foundation as referred to in *A Consumer Guide to Long-Term Care Insurance*, published by The Insurance Marketplace Standards Association.

6. The General Accounting Office as referred to in *A Consumer Guide to Long-Term Care Insurance*, published by The Insurance Marketplace Standards Association.

7. According to LIMRA International as referred to in *A Consumer Guide to Long-Term Care Insurance*, published by The Insurance Marketplace Standards Association.

8. Nancy P. North, "The Importance of Proper Structure in Long-Term Care Insurance," *Journal of Financial Service Professionals* (May, 2001).

9. Nancy P. North, "The Importance of Proper Structure in Long-Term Care Insurance," *Journal of Financial Service Professionals* (May, 2001).

10. Jeff Sadler, *How to Sell Long-Term Care Insurance* (Cincinnati, OH: The National Underwriter Company, 2001), p. 62.

11. Nancy P. North, "The Importance of Proper Structure in Long-Term Care Insurance," *Journal of Financial Service Professionals* (May, 2001).

12. The policy used in this example had a six year benefit period. Nancy P. North, "The Importance of Proper Structure in Long-Term Care Insurance," *Journal of Financial Service Professionals* (May, 2001).

13. IRC Sec. 7702B.

14. Jeff Sadler, *How to Sell Long-Term Care Insurance* (Cincinnati, OH: The National Underwriter Company, 2001), p. 173.

15. IRC Sec. 101(g).

16. IRC Secs. 101(g)(3)(D), 7702B(d).

17. IRC Sec. 101(g)(4)(A).

18. IRC Secs. 101(g)(4)(B), 7702B(c)(2)(A).

19. IRC Sec. 0101(g)(5).

END OF CHAPTER REVIEW

1. Most insurance companies will issue long-term care policies on any healthy individual regardless of age.

   True   False

2. Underwriting for long-term care insurance may consider different risk factors than underwriting for life insurance.

   True   False

3. Long-term care policies are typically purchased for a specific daily benefit amount.

   True   False

4. Long-term care policies always pay a daily benefit amount without regard to the cost of care.

   True   False

5. Long-term care policies generally limit the length of time for which benefits will be paid.

   True   False

6. Long-term care policies typically limit total benefit payments to an amount equal to the daily benefit amount times the policy benefit period in days.

   True   False

7. Longer elimination periods generally result in higher premiums on long-term care insurance policies.

   True   False

8. Long-term care insurance policies generally offer a rider that increases policy benefits by a fixed percentage each year.

   True   False

9. Qualified long-term care insurance contracts pay benefits when an individual is either chronically ill or suffers from severe cognitive impairment.

   True   False

10. Non-qualified long-term care insurance contracts may additionally provide benefits when a physician certifies the need for long-term care services.

    True   False

Chapter 22

TAXATION OF LONG–TERM CARE INSURANCE

In previous chapters, long-term care and long-term care insurance have been defined and placed within the framework of a thorough financial plan. Also, the standard provisions of a long-term care policy have been summarized and reviewed. As may have become apparent, the provisions of a long-term care policy are determined, in large extent, by the income tax requirements that must be satisfied for a policy to be considered a "qualified long-term care policy." If this definition is not met, the policy does not receive income tax benefits relating to premiums and benefits, as discussed in greater detail below.

WHAT IS IT?

First, let's consider the question, "What is a qualified long-term care insurance policy?"

The definition is found in Section 7702B of the Internal Revenue Code. This section was added to the Code by the Health Insurance Portability and Accountability Act of 1996.[1] In addition to setting forth the definition of a qualified contract, this legislation addressed the income taxation of long-term care premiums and benefits. Most of the long-term care provisions discussed in this section are effective for taxable years beginning after December 31, 1996.

Before August of 1996, the taxation of long-term care insurance was uncertain. While the 1996 legislation clarified taxation of long-term care insurance contracts that are considered to be qualified, it did not address the income taxation of contracts that do not meet the definition and are, generally, referred to as "nonqualified" long-term care insurance policies.

The Definition of "Qualified" Long–Term Care Insurance Contract

As one might expect, since it is found in the Internal Revenue Code, the definition of a "qualified long-term care insurance contract" is complex. It is also one of the most important elements to consider in looking at long-term care insurance since the income taxation of a qualified contract can be significantly more beneficial than the income taxation of a nonqualified contract.

Generally, a long-term care insurance contract meets the definition of a "qualified" contract if:[2]

1. the only insurance protection provided under the contract is coverage of qualified long-term care services;

2. the contract does not pay or reimburse expenses incurred for services that are reimbursable under Title XVIII of the Social Security Act (or would be reimbursable but for the application of a deductible or coinsurance amount);

3. the contract is guaranteed renewable;

4. the contract does not provide for a cash surrender value or other money that can be paid, assigned or pledged as collateral for a loan or borrowed;

5. all premium refunds and dividends under the contract are to be applied as a reduction in future premiums or to increase future benefits; and

6. the contract satisfies certain consumer protection provisions concerning model regulation and model act provisions, disclosure, and nonforfeitability.

In addition to these six general requirements, a long-term care policy must meet certain additional requirements to be considered a "qualified" contract.[3] These include certain provisions of the National Association of Insurance Commissioners (NAIC) long-term care insurance model regulation dealing with such issues as guaranteed renewal or noncancellability, prohibitions on limitations and exclusions, extension of benefits, continuation or conversion of coverage, replacement of policies, unintentional lapse, disclosure, post-claims underwriting, minimum standards, the requirement to offer inflation protection, and the prohibition against preexisting conditions and probationary periods in replacement policies. In addition, a long-term care contract must meet certain provisions of the NAIC long-term care insurance model act relating to preexisting conditions and prior hospitalization as well as certain nonforfeiture provisions.

Disclosure Requirements for a Qualified Long–Term Care Insurance Contract

Additionally, a long-term care insurance contract must comply with certain disclosure requirements.[4] Generally, for a level premium policy the contract must offer the policyholder a nonforfeiture provision that:

1. is properly captioned;

2. provides for a benefit available in the event of a default in the payment of premiums and the amount of the benefit may be adjusted only as necessary to reflect changes in claims, persistency and interest as reflected in changes in rates for premium paying contracts approved for the same contract form; and

3. provides for at least one of the following options: (a) reduced paid-up insurance; (b) extended term insurance; (c) shortened benefit period; or (d) other similar approved offerings.[5]

In addition, a long-term care insurance policy that is approved must be delivered to the policyholder within 30 days of the approval date.[6] Further, if a claim under a long-term care insurance policy is denied, the issuer must provide a written explanation of the reasons for the denial and make available all information relating to the denial within 60 days of a written request from the policyholder.[7] A policy will be considered to meet the disclosure requirements, if the policy states that it is intended to be a qualified long-term care insurance contract under IRC Section 7702B(b).[8] The penalty for not meeting these requirements is a tax of $100 per insured for each day that these requirements are not met for each qualified long-term care insurance contract.[9] If a failure is due to reasonable cause and not willful neglect, the penalty tax may be waived.[10]

Definition of "Qualified Long–Term Care Services"

As mentioned above, under the definition of a qualified long-term care insurance contract, one of the requirements to be qualified is that under the contract the only insurance protection provided is coverage of qualified long-term care services. Generally, "qualified long-

term care services" are defined as "… necessary diagnostic, preventive, therapeutic, curing, treating, mitigating, and rehabilitative services and maintenance or personal care services which…" are required by a chronically ill individual and are provided under a plan of care set forth by a licensed health care practitioner.[11] Thus, a long-term care insurance contract cannot be a qualified contract unless it covers only qualified long-term care services for a chronically ill individual.

Definition of "Chronically Ill Individual"

There is a specific definition of a "chronically ill individual." This is a person who has been certified as being unable to perform, without substantial assistance, at least two activities of daily living (ADLs) for at least 90 days or a person with a similar level of disability. This is often referred to as the ADL benefit trigger. The activities of daily living are eating, toileting, transferring, bathing, dressing, and continence. To be considered a qualified long-term care insurance contract, a policy must take into account at least five of these ADLs in determining whether a person is a chronically ill individual under the ADL benefit trigger.[12]

In addition, a person may be considered chronically ill if he requires substantial supervision to protect himself from threats to his health and safety due to severe cognitive impairment and this condition has been certified by a health care practitioner within the previous 12 months. This is called the cognitive impairment trigger.[13]

BUSINESS USES

Group long-term care plans are offered by a few employers to employees and even to parents of employees but not on a wide-spread basis. Generally, where an employer makes this type of plan available, participating employees pay the full cost to obtain long-term care coverage themselves.

TAX IMPLICATIONS

Qualified vs. Nonqualified Long–Term Care Contracts

The discussion below of the tax consequences associated with long-term care insurance contracts is applicable to qualified contracts. The taxation of premiums paid for and benefits received from nonqualified long-term care insurance contracts is uncertain. However, most authorities believe that tax benefits applicable to the qualified contracts are not applicable to nonqualified long-term care insurance contracts.

Long-Term Care Insurance Premiums

Generally, premiums paid to purchase a qualified long-term care insurance contract are eligible for income tax deduction.[14] This is so because the Internal Revenue Code[15] states that amounts paid for qualified long-term care services or any qualified long-term care insurance contract are considered to be "medical care." Amounts paid for the medical care of a taxpayer, his spouse or dependents are deductible subject to the 7.5% adjusted gross income floor.[16]

However, the deduction for long-term care insurance and services is subject to an additional dollar amount limitation that increases with the age of the insured individual. In 2004, for persons age 40 or less, the limitation amount is $260. For ages 41 through 50, the limitation amount is $490; for ages 51 through 60, the limitation amount is $980; for ages 61 through 70, the limitation amount is $2,600 and for those over 70, the limitation amount is $3,250.[17] These limitation amounts are indexed annually.[18]

Long-Term Care Insurance Benefits

A "qualified long-term care insurance contract" issued after December 31, 1996, is treated as an accident and health insurance contract.[19] Thus, amounts (other than dividends or premium refunds) received under a qualified long-term care insurance contract are treated as amounts received for personal injuries and sickness and are treated as reimbursement for expenses actually incurred for medical care.[20] Amounts received for personal injuries and sickness are generally not includable in income.[21]

However, as with the deductibility of long-term care premiums, there is a limit on the amount of qualified long-term care benefits that may be excluded from income. Generally, if the total periodic long-term care payments received from all policies and any periodic payments received that are treated as paid by reason of the death of the insured exceed a per diem limitation, the excess must be included in income.[22] This per diem limitation is equal to the excess of the greater of the dollar amount limitation or the costs incurred for qualified long-term care services provided for the insured

over the total payments received as reimbursement for qualified long-term care services for the insured. For 2004, the dollar amount limitation is $230 per day.[23] It is adjusted for inflation annually.[24]

Long-Term Care Insurance Owned by Self-Employed Individuals

Because premiums paid for qualified long-term care insurance contracts come within the definition of medical care, long-term care insurance premiums are eligible for deduction from income by self-employed persons.[25] The amount of long-term care insurance premiums that may be deducted is subject to the dollar amount limitations discussed above.

In addition, there is a further limitation. The deduction for long-term care insurance premiums is not available to a self-employed individual for any calendar month in which he is eligible to participate in any subsidized health plan maintained by any employer of the self-employed individual or his spouse, if the employer plan provides coverage for qualified long-term care services.[26]

Generally, sole proprietors, partners and S corporation shareholders owning more than 2% of the S corporation's shares may take advantage of this deduction.

Gift Tax Consequences of Long-Term Care Insurance

Neither the purchase of a long-term care policy nor the receipt of benefits from such a policy will trigger federal gift tax consequences. It is possible to incur gift tax liability if the funds to purchase a long-term care policy are given by one individual to another. In this instance, any gift amount over the annual gift tax exclusion ($11,000 per donee in 2004) may result in a gift tax liability on the part of the person making the gift.[27]

Estate Tax Consequences of Long-Term Care Insurance

Generally, the purchase of a long-term care insurance policy will not have any significant estate tax implications. One indirect effect on the estate plan of the policy purchaser is that since the policy may pay for long-term care needs in the future, other property and funds that the policy purchaser owns may not have to be used to pay for care and, thus, will remain in the policy purchaser's estate. If the estate is of sufficient value upon the death of the policy owner, it may be subject to federal estate tax. However, this depends upon the action or lack of action that Congress may take regarding the repeal of the federal estate tax. Currently, the estate tax is scheduled to be repealed beginning in 2010. If no action is taken to extend or make permanent this repeal, in 2011 the estate tax will be reinstated.[28]

Generation Skipping Transfer Tax Consequences of Long–Term Care Insurance

As with the estate tax discussion above, the purchase of a long-term care insurance policy will not have any significant generation skipping transfer tax consequences.

DESIGN FEATURES

As it relates to the income taxation of a long-term care insurance contract, an important design feature to consider is whether the policy is a "qualified" long-term insurance contract. A policy that is not "qualified" is generally referred to as "nonqualified." In addition to the different income tax treatment for these two types of long-term care contracts, as discussed earlier in this chapter, another significant difference between the qualified and the nonqualified contracts is the "benefit triggers." A benefit trigger is the name for the events and/or circumstances that must occur before the policy will begin to pay long-term care benefits.

For qualified contracts, the benefit triggers are specified in the governing section of the Internal Revenue Code.[29]

One benefit trigger for a qualified contract is the ADL (activities of daily living) benefit trigger. This benefit trigger is activated when a person becomes classified as chronically ill, which means the individual has been certified as being unable to perform, without substantial assistance, at least two activities of daily living (ADLs) for at least 90 days or a person with a similar level of disability.

In addition, a person may be considered chronically ill if he requires substantial supervision to protect himself from threats to his health and safety due to severe cognitive impairment and this condition has been certified by a health care practitioner within the previous 12 months. This is called the cognitive impairment trigger.[30]

For purposes of the ADL benefit trigger, taxpayers may rely upon certain safe-harbor definitions. First, the term "substantial assistance" is defined to mean "hands-on assistance" and "standby assistance." Further, "hands-on assistance" is the physical assistance of another person without which an individual would not be able to complete an ADL. "Standby assistance" is defined to mean the presence of another individual that is needed to prevent an individual from injury while performing an ADL.[31]

For purposes of the cognitive impairment benefit trigger, there are several safe-harbor definitions that may be relied upon. A "severe cognitive impairment" is defined as a loss or deterioration in intellectual capacity that is similar to Alzheimer's disease and like forms of irreversible dementia and is measured by clinical evidence and standardized tests that reliably measure impairment in short-term or long-term memory, orientation to people, places or time and deductive or abstract reasoning. Further, "substantial supervision" is defined as continual supervision by another person that is needed to protect the severely cognitively impaired person from threats to his health or safety.[32]

QUESTIONS AND ANSWERS

Question – How is "medical care" defined for purposes of deducting premiums paid to purchase a long-term care policy?

Answer – Internal Revenue Code section 213(d) states that "'medical care' means amounts paid...for qualified long-term care services...or for any qualified long-term care insurance contract..." Thus, as mentioned above, amounts paid for long-term care services may be deducted from income, provided that the 7.5% of adjusted gross income floor is met.

However, it is important to note that an amount paid for qualified long-term care services will not be treated as paid for medical care if the service is provided by the individual's spouse or a relative. A "relative" is generally any individual who can be considered a dependent for tax purposes. Also, the service may not be provided by a corporation or partnership that is related to the individual.[33]

Question – Are there income tax reporting requirements applicable to long-term insurance contracts?

Answer – Yes. Any person paying long-term care benefits must file a return that sets forth:

1. the aggregate amount of long-term care benefits paid by the person to any individual during any calendar year;

2. whether or not such benefits are paid, either fully or partially, on a per diem or other periodic basis without regard to the expenses incurred during the period;

3. the name, address, and taxpayer identification number (TIN) of such individual; and

4. the name, address, and TIN of the chronically ill or terminally ill individual for whom the benefits are paid.[34] Additionally, any person paying long-term care benefits must provide a written statement to each individual whose name is reported under the above requirement. The statement must show the name, address, and phone number of the information contact of the person making the payments and the aggregate amount of long-term care benefits paid to the individual that is required to be shown on the above-mentioned return. This written statement must reach the individual on or before January 31 of the year following the calendar year for which the return was required.[35] Although, the code section which contains these reporting requirements does not specify, presumably the term "person" is used to encompass not only individuals but also companies paying long-term care benefits.[36]

For purposes of these reporting requirements "long-term care benefits" are any payment under a product that is advertised, marketed or offered as long-term care insurance and any payment that is excludable from gross income under IRC Section 101(g).[37]

Question – Can long-term care insurance be offered in a cafeteria or IRC Section 125 plan?

Answer – Generally, no. Any product that is advertised, marketed or offered as long-term care insurance is not a qualified benefit under a cafeteria plan.[38]

Question – Can long-term care insurance be offered through a flexible spending arrangement (FSA)?

Answer – After 1996, employer-provided coverage for long-term care services provided through a flexible spending arrangement (FSA) is included in the employee's gross income.[39]

Question – Do the COBRA continuation coverage requirements that apply to group health insurance plans also apply to employer-provided long-term care plans?

Answer – No, the COBRA continuation coverage requirements do not apply to plans under which substantially all of the coverage is for long-term care services.[40]

CHAPTER ENDNOTES

1. P.L. 104-491.
2. IRC Sec. 7702B(b).
3. IRC Sec. 7702B(g).
4. IRC Sec. 4980C(d).
5. IRC Sec. 7702B(g)(4).
6. IRC Sec. 4980C(c)(2).
7. IRC Sec. 4980C(c)(3).
8. IRC Sec. 4080C(d).
9. IRC Sec. 4980C(b)(1).
10. IRC Sec. 4980C(b)(2).
11. IRC Sec. 7702B(c)(1).
12. IRC Sec. 7702B(c)(2)(B).
13. IRC Sec. 7702B(c)(2)(A).
14. IRC Sec. 213(d)(1).
15. IRC Sec. 213(d).
16. IRC Sec. 213(a).
17. The age is the individual's attained age before the close of the taxable year. IRC Sec. 213(d)(10)(A); Rev. Proc. 2003-85, 2002-49 IRB 1.
18. IRC Sec. 213(d)(10)(B).
19. IRC Sec. 7702B(a)(1).
20. IRC Sec. 7702B(a)(2).
21. See IRC Sec. 104(a)(3); IRC Sec. 105(b).
22. IRC Sec. 7702B(d).
23. Rev. Proc. 2003-85, 2003 49 IRB 1.
24. IRC Sec. 7702B(d)(5).
25. IRC Secs. 162(l), 213(d).
26. IRC Sec. 162(l).
27. IRC Sec. 2503(b).
28. IRC Sec. 2010; EGTRAA 2001, Sec. 901.
29. IRC Sec. 7702B.
30. IRC Sec. 7702B(c)(2)(A).
31. Notice 97-31, 1997-1 CB 417.
32. Notice 97-31, 1997-1 CB 417.
33. Within the meaning of IRC Sections 267(b) or 707(b). IRC Sec. 213(d)(11).
34. IRC Sec. 6050Q(a).
35. IRC Sec. 6050Q(b).
36. IRC Sec. 6050Q.
37. IRC Sec. 6050Q(c).
38. IRC Sec. 125(f).
39. IRC Sec. 106(c)(1).
40. IRC Sec. 4980B(g)(2).

END OF CHAPTER REVIEW

1. Qualified long-term care insurance contracts must provide coverage only for qualified long-term care services.

    True   False

2. Qualified long-term care insurance contracts must be guaranteed renewable.

    True   False

3. Qualified long-term care insurance contracts may accumulate a cash surrender value.

    True   False

4. Premiums for qualified long-term care insurance contracts are fully deductible as medical expenses, to the extent medical expenses exceed 7.5% of adjusted gross income.

    True   False

5. A chronically ill individual is one who is unable to perform, without substantial assistance, at least two "activities of daily living," for at least 90 days.

    True   False

6. Subject to certain limits, benefits payment amounts received from a qualified long-term care insurance policy are generally not includable in income.

    True   False

7. Benefits from qualified long-term care insurance contracts are includable in income to the extent they exceed the greater of the annual indexed amount and the otherwise-unreimbursed costs incurred for qualified long-term care services.

    True   False

8. The taxation of benefits paid by nonqualified long-term care insurance contracts is uncertain.

    True   False

9. Long-term care insurance may be offered as a benefit under a cafeteria plan.

    True   False

10. COBRA continuation coverage requirements do not apply to plans under which substantially all of the coverage is for long-term care services.

    True   False

APPENDICES

Appendix A

EXPLANATION OF INSURANCE COMPANY RATINGS

DEMOTECH FINANCIAL STABILITY RATINGS

Financial Stability Ratings®
http://www.demotech.com/

A" Regardless of the severity of a general economic downturn or a deterioration in the insurance cycle, insurers earning a Financial Stability Rating® of "A double prime" possess <u>Unsurpassed</u> financial stability related to withstanding a general economic downturn or deterioration of an underwriting cycle. **The distinction between A double prime and A prime may be related to the magnitude of policyholders' surplus, market share or national presence.**

A' Regardless of the severity of a general economic downturn or a deterioration in the insurance cycle, insurers earning a Financial Stability Rating® of "A prime" possess <u>Unsurpassed</u> financial stability related to withstanding a general economic downturn or deterioration of an underwriting cycle.

A Regardless of the severity of a general economic downturn or a deterioration in the insurance cycle, insurers earning a Financial Stability Rating® of "A" possess <u>Exceptional</u> financial stability related to withstanding a general economic downturn or deterioration of an underwriting cycle.

S Regardless of the severity of a general economic downturn or a deterioration in the insurance cycle, insurers earning a Financial Stability Rating® of "S" possess <u>Substantial</u> financial stability related to withstanding a general economic downturn or deterioration of an underwriting cycle.

M Regardless of the severity of a general economic downturn or a deterioration in the insurance cycle, insurers earning a Financial Stability Rating® of "M" possess <u>Moderate</u> financial stability related to withstanding a general economic downturn or deterioration of an underwriting cycle.

L Insurers earning a Financial Stability Rating® of "L" are <u>Licensed</u> by state regulatory authorities.

However, in our opinion, the ability of these title insurers to withstand a deterioration in general economic conditions is below average.

FITCH RATINGS
(formerly Duff and Phelps)

Fitch Insurer Financial Strength Rating
http://www.fitchratings.com/

AAA Insurers assigned this highest rating are viewed as possessing EXCEPTIONALLY STRONG capacity to meet policyholder and contract obligations. For such companies, risk factors are minimal and the impact of any adverse business and economic factors is expected to be extremely small.

AA Insurers are viewed as possessing VERY STRONG capacity to meet policyholder and contract obligations. Risk factors are modest, and the impact of any adverse business and economic factors is expected to be very small.

A Insurers are viewed as possessing STRONG capacity to meet policyholder and contract obligations. Risk factors are moderate, and the impact of any adverse business and economic factors is expected to be small.

BBB Insurers are viewed as possessing GOOD capacity to meet policyholder and contract obligations. Risk factors are somewhat high, and the impact of any adverse business and economic factors is expected to be material, yet manageable.

BB Insurers are viewed as MODERATELY WEAK with an uncertain capacity to meet policyholder and contract obligations. Though positive factors are present, overall risk factors are high, and the impact of any adverse business and economic factors is expected to be significant

B Insurers are viewed as MODERATELY WEAK with an uncertain capacity to meet policyholder and contract obligations. Though positive factors are present, overall risk factors are high, and the impact of any adverse business and economic factors is expected to be very significant.

CCC, CC, C Insurers rated in any of these three categories are viewed as VERY WEAK with a very poor capacity to meet policyholder and contract obligations. Risk factors are extremely high, and the impact of any adverse business and economic factors is expected to be insurmountable. A 'CC' rating indicates that some form of insolvency or liquidity impairment appears probable. A 'C' rating signals that insolvency or a liquidity impairment appears imminent.

DDD, DD, D These ratings are assigned to insurers that have either failed to make payments on their obligations in a timely manner, are deemed to be insolvent or have been subjected to some form of regulatory intervention. Within the DDD-D range, those companies rated 'DDD' have the highest prospects for resumption of business operations or, if liquidated or wound down, of having a vast majority of their obligations to policyholders and contractholders ultimately paid off, though on a delayed basis (with recoveries expected in the range of 90-100%). Those rated 'DD' show a much lower likelihood of ultimately paying off material amounts of their obligations in a liquidation or wind down scenario (in a range of 50-90%). Those rated 'D' are ultimately expected to have very limited liquid assets available to fund obligations, and therefore any ultimate payoffs would be quite modest (at under 50%).

MOODY'S INSURANCE FINANCIAL STRENGTH RATINGS

Insurance Financial Strength Ratings Definitions
http://www.moodys.com/cust/default.asp

Aaa Insurance companies rated "Aaa" offer exceptional financial security. While the financial strength of these companies is likely to change, such changes as can be visualized are most unlikely to impair their fundamentally strong position.

Aa Insurance companies rated "Aa" offer excellent financial security. Together with the "Aaa" group they constitute what are generally known as high grade companies. They are rated lower than "Aaa" companies because long-term risks appear somewhat larger.

A Insurance companies rated "A" offer good financial security. However, elements may be present which suggest a susceptibility to impairment sometime in the future.

Baa Insurance companies rated "Baa" offer adequate financial security. However, certain protective elements may be lacking or may be characteristically unreliable over any great length of time.

Ba Insurance companies rated "Ba" offer questionable financial security. Often the ability of these companies to meet policyholder obligations may be very moderate and thereby not well safeguarded in the future.

B Insurance companies rated "B" offer poor financial security. Assurance of punctual payment of policyholder obligations over any long period of time is small.

Caa Insurance companies rated "Caa" offer very poor financial security. They may be in default on their policyholder obligations or there may be present elements of danger with respect to punctual payment of policyholder obligations and claims.

Ca Insurance companies rated "Ca" offer extremely poor financial security. Such companies are often in default on their policyholder obligations or have other marked shortcomings.

C Insurance companies rated "C" are the lowest rated class of insurance company and can be regarded as having extremely poor prospects of ever offering financial security.

Note: Moody's applies numerical modifiers 1, 2, and 3 in each rating classification: the modifier 1 indicates that the security ranks in the higher end of its generic rating category; the modifier 2 indicates a mid-range ranking and the modifier 3 indicates that the issue ranks in the lower end of its generic rating category.

STANDARD & POOR'S INSURANCE RATINGS

Insurer Financial Strength Rating Definitions
http://www2.standardandpoors.com/
Secure Rating Range: AAA to BBB

Note: An insurer rated "BBB" or higher is regarded as having financial security characteristics that outweigh any vulnerabilities, and is highly likely to have the ability to meet financial commitments.

Insurer Financial Strength Rating Definitions

An insurer rated 'BBB' or higher is regarded as having financial security characteristics that outweigh any vulnerabilities, and is highly likely to have the ability to meet financial commitments.

AAA An insurer rated 'AAA' has EXTREMELY STRONG financial security characteristics. 'AAA' is the highest Insurer Financial Strength Rating assigned by Standard & Poor's.

AA An insurer rated 'AA' has VERY STRONG financial security characteristics, differing only slightly from those rated higher.

A An insurer rated 'A' has STRONG financial security characteristics, but is somewhat more likely to be affected by adverse business conditions than are insurers with higher ratings.

BBB An insurer rated 'BBB' has GOOD financial security characteristics, but is more likely to be affected by adverse business conditions than are higher rated insurers.

BB An insurer rated 'BB' or lower is regarded as having vulnerable characteristics that may outweigh its strengths. 'BB' indicates the least degree of vulnerability within the range; 'CC' the highest. An insurer rated 'BB' has MARGINAL financial security characteristics. Positive attributes exist, but adverse business conditions could lead to insufficient ability to meet financial commitments

B An insurer rated 'B' has WEAK financial security characteristics. Adverse business conditions will likely impair its ability to meet financial commitments.

CCC An insurer rated 'CCC' has VERY WEAK financial security characteristics, and is dependent on favorable business conditions to meet financial commitments.

CC An insurer rated 'CC' has EXTREMELY WEAK financial security characteristics and is likely not to meet some of its financial commitments.

R An insurer rated 'R' is under regulatory supervision owing to its financial condition. During the pendency of the regulatory supervision, the regulators may have the power to favor one class of obligations over others or pay some obligations and not others.

NR An insurer designated 'NR' is NOT RATED.

Plus (+) or minus (-) signs following ratings from 'AA' to 'CCC' show relative standing within the major rating categories.

WEISS SAFETY RATINGS

Insurer and HMO Safety Ratings
http://www.weissratings.com/

A **Excellent.** The company offers excellent financial security. It has maintained a conservative stance in its investment strategies, business operations and underwriting commitments. While the financial position of any company is subject to change, we believe that this company has the resources necessary to deal with severe economic conditions.

B **Good.** The company offers good financial security and has the resources to deal with a variety of adverse economic conditions. It comfortably exceeds the minimum levels for all of our rating criteria, and is likely to remain healthy for the near future. However, in the event of a severe recession or major financial crisis, we feel that this assessment should be reviewed to make sure that the firm is still maintaining adequate financial strength.

C **Fair.** The company offers fair financial security and is currently stable. But during an economic downturn or other financial pressures, we feel it may encounter difficulties in maintaining its financial stability.

D **Weak.** The company currently demonstrates what we consider to be significant weaknesses which could negatively impact policyholders. In an unfavorable economic environment, these weaknesses could be magnified.

E **Very Weak.** The company currently demonstrates what we consider to be significant weaknesses and has also failed some of the basic tests that we use to identify fiscal stability. Therefore, even in a favorable economic environment, it is our opinion that policyholders could incur significant risks.

F   **Failed.** The company has failed and is either 1) under supervision of state insurance commissioners; 2) is in the process of liquidation; or 3) has voluntarily dissolved after disciplinary or other regulatory action by state insurance commissioners.

+   **The plus sign** is an indication that the company is at the upper end of the letter grade rating.

-   **The minus sign** is an indication that the company is at the lower end of the letter grade rating.

U   **Unrated Companies.** The company is unrated for one or more of the following reasons: (1) total assets are less than $1 million; (2) premium income for the current year was less than $100,000; or (3) the company functions almost exclusively as a holding company rather than as an underwriter; or (4) we do not have enough information to reliably issue a rating.

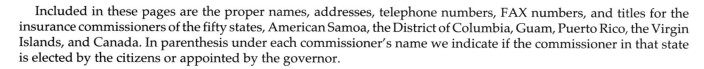

Appendix B

INSURANCE DIRECTORIES

Included in these pages are the proper names, addresses, telephone numbers, FAX numbers, and titles for the insurance commissioners of the fifty states, American Samoa, the District of Columbia, Guam, Puerto Rico, the Virgin Islands, and Canada. In parenthesis under each commissioner's name we indicate if the commissioner in that state is elected by the citizens or appointed by the governor.

In some cases two addresses are shown. If one of them is a post office box, mail will usually arrive the quickest by using it. If an overnight express service is being used, use of the street address is often required. Note that there may be different zip codes for the two addresses.

We also provide email and/or Web site addresses where available. If no separate email address is shown, keep in mind that email can be sent through and/or messages can be posted on most Web sites.

NATIONAL ASSOCIATION OF INSURANCE COMMISSIONERS (NAIC)

Executive Headquarters

2301 McGee St., #800
Kansas City MO 64108
(816) 842-3600
FAX: (816) 783-8175
http://www.naic.org

NAIC

Federal & International Relations Office

444 N. Capitol Street, Suite 701
Washington DC 20001
(202) 624-7790
FAX: (202) 624-8579

NAIC

Securities Valuation Office (SVO)

1411 Broadway, 9th Floor
New York, NY 10018
(212) 398-9000
FAX: (212) 382-4207

ALABAMA

Walter A. Bell
Insurance Commissioner
(Appointed)
201 Monroe St., Ste. 1700
Montgomery AL 36104
Commissioner: (334) 269-3550
FAX: (334) 241-4192
Licensing: (334) 241-4126
Licensing FAX: (334) 240-3282
Consumer Hot Line: (334) 241-4141
http://www.aldoi.gov

ALASKA

Linda S. Hall
Director of Insurance
(Appointed)
Alaska Division of Insurance
550 W. 7th St., #1560
Anchorage AK 99501
Director: (907) 269-7900
FAX: (907) 269-7910
Licensing: (907) 465-2515
Licensing FAX: (907) 465-2816
http://www.dced.state.ak.us/insurance
9th Floor State Office Bldg.
333 Willoughby Avenue
P.O. Box 110805
Juneau AK 99811
(907) 465-2515
FAX: (907) 465-3422

AMERICAN SAMOA

Elisara T. Togiai
Insurance Commissioner
(Appointed)
Office of the Governor
Pago Pago AS 96799
Commissioner: 011 (684) 633-4116
FAX: 011 (684) 633-2269
http://www.samoanet.com/asg/

ARIZONA

Christina Urias
Director of Insurance
(Appointed)
2910 N. 44th St., Ste. 210
Phoenix AZ 85018
Director: (602) 912-8400
FAX: (602) 912-8452
Licensing: (602) 912-8470
Licensing FAX: (602) 912-8473
Consumer Hot Line: (602) 912-8444
http://www.state.az.us/id
400 W. Congress, #152
Tuscon AZ 85701

ARKANSAS

Mike Pickens
Insurance Commissioner
(Appointed)
1200 W. Third St.
Little Rock AR 72201
Commissioner: (501) 371-2600
WATS: (800) 282-9134
FAX: (501) 371-2618
Licensing: (501) 371-2750
http://www.state.ar.us/insurance

CALIFORNIA

John Garamendi
Commissioner of Insurance
(Elected)
300 Capitol Mall, Ste. 1500
Sacramento CA 95814
Commissioner: (916) 492-3500
FAX: (916) 445-5280
Consumer Hot Line: (800) 927-4357
http://www.insurance.ca.gov
Licensing
320 Capitol Mall
Sacramento CA 95814
Licensing: (415) 904-6072 and (916) 322-3555

COLORADO

Doug Dean
Commissioner of Insurance
(Appointed)
1560 Broadway, Ste. 850
Denver CO 80202
Commissioner: (303) 894-7499
WATS: (800) 930-3745
FAX: (303) 894-7455
Licensing: (800) 275-8247
Licensing FAX: (303) 894-7455
http://www.dora.state.co.us/insurance

CONNECTICUT

Susan Cogswell
Insurance Commissioner
(Appointed)
P.O. Box 816
Hartford CT 06142
153 Market St., 7th Fl.
Hartford CT 06103
Commissioner: (860) 297-3800
FAX: (860) 566-7410
Licensing: (860) 297-3845
Licensing FAX: (860) 297-3978
Consumer Hot Line: (800) 203-3447
http://www.state.ct.us/cid

DELAWARE

Donna Lee H. Williams
Insurance Commissioner
(Elected)
841 Silver Lake Blvd.
Dover DE 19904
Commissioner: (302) 739-4251
FAX: (302) 739-6278
Licensing: (302) 739-4254
Licensing FAX: (302) 739-5280
Consumer Hot Line: (800) 282-8611
http://www.state.de.us/inscom

DISTRICT OF COLUMBIA

Larry Mirel
Superintendent of Insurance
(Appointed)
810 First St., N.E., #701
Washington DC 20002
Superintendent: (202) 727-8000
FAX: (202) 535-1196
Licensing: (202) 727-8000
Licensing FAX: (202) 727-8055
http://disr.washingtondc.gov/main.shtm

FLORIDA

Tom Gallagher
Chief Financial Officer
Kevin M. McCarty, Director
Office of Ins. Regulation
(Elected/Appointed)
200 E. Gaines St.
Tallahassee FL 32399
Commissioner: (850) 413-3100
FAX: (850) 413-4993
Licensing: (850) 413-3135
Consumer Hot Line: (800)342-2762
http://www.fldfs.com

GEORGIA

John W. Oxendine
Insurance Commissioner
(Elected)
2 Martin Luther King, Jr. Dr.
West Tower, Ste. 704
Atlanta GA 30334
Commissioner: (404) 656-2070
FAX: (404) 657-8542
Licensing: (404) 656-2101
Licensing FAX: (404) 656-0874
http://www.gainsurance.org/
HERE HERE HERE

GUAM

Artemio B. Ilagan, Director
Dept. of Revenue and Taxation
Government of Guam
Building 13-1 Mariner Ave.
Tiyan Barrigada GU 96913
Commissioner: (671) 475-5000
FAX: (671) 472-2643
Note: the International Code of "011" is no longer
required to call Guam.
http://www.gov.gu

HAWAII

J.P. Schmidt
Insurance Commissioner
(Appointed)
Dept. of Commerce & Consumer Affairs
P.O. Box 3614
Honolulu HI 96811
Commissioner: (808) 586-2790
Licensing: (808) 586-2788
FAX: (808) 586-2806
http://www.state.hi.us/dcca/ins

IDAHO

Mary L. Hartung
Director of Insurance
(Appointed)
700 W. State St., 3rd Fl.
Boise ID 83720
Director: (208) 334-4250
FAX: (208) 334-4398
Licensing: (208) 334-4341
http://www.doi.state.id.us

ILLINOIS

J. Anthony Clark
Director of Insurance
(Appointed)
320 W. Washington St., 4th Fl.
Springfield IL 62767
Director: (217) 782-4515
TDD: (217) 524-4872
FAX: (217) 782-5020
http://www.ins.state.il.us

INDIANA

Sally McCarty
Commissioner of Insurance
(Appointed)
311 W. Washington St., Ste. 300
Indianapolis IN 46204
Commissioner: (317) 232-2385
FAX: (317) 232-5251
Licensing: (317) 234-1138
Licensing FAX: (317) 232-5251
http://www.in.gov/idoi/

IOWA

Therese Vaughan
Insurance Commissioner
(Appointed)
330 E. Maple St.
Des Moines IA 50319
Commissioner: (515) 281-5705
FAX: (515) 281-3059
WATS: (877) 955-1212
Licensing: (515) 281-7757
http://www.iid.state.ia.us

KANSAS

Sandy Praeger
Commissioner of Insurance
(Elected)
420 S.W. Ninth St.
Topeka KS 66612
Commissioner: (785) 296-3071
Consumer Hot line: (800) 432-2484
FAX: (785) 296-2283
http://www.ksinsurance.org

KENTUCKY

Janie A. Miller
Insurance Commissioner
(Appointed)
P.O. Box 517
Frankfort KY 40602
215 W. Main St.
Frankfort KY 40601
Commissioner: (502) 564-3630
FAX: (502) 564-1453
Licensing: (502) 564-6004
Licensing FAX: (502) 564-6030
Consumer Hot Line: (800) 595-6053
http://doi.ppr.ky.gov/kentucky/

LOUISIANA

J. Robert Wooley
(Elected)
P.O. Box 94214
Baton Rouge LA 70804-9214
1702 N. 3rd. St.
Baton Rouge LA 70802
Commissioner (225) 342-5900
FAX: (225) 342-3078
Licensing: (225) 342-0860
Consumer Hot Line: (800) 259-5300 or
(800) 259-5301 (in state)
http://www.ldi.state.la.us

MAINE

Alessandro A. Iuppa
Superintendent of Insurance
(Appointed)
34 State House Station
Augusta ME 04333
Superintendent: (207) 624-8475
WATS: (800) 300-5000
FAX: (207) 624-8599
http://www.state.me.us/pfr/ins/ins_index.htm

MARYLAND

Alfred W. Redmer, Jr.
Insurance Commissioner
(Appointed)
525 St. Paul Pl., 2nd Fl.
Baltimore MD 21202
Commissioner: (410) 468-2000
Outside Baltimore Metro Area: (800) 492-6116
FAX: (410) 468-2020
Licensing: (410) 468-2006
Licensing: (800) 492-6116
Licensing FAX: (410) 468-2399
Consumer Hot Line: (800) 492-6116
http://www.mdinsurance.state.md.us

MASSACHUSETTS

Julianne Bowler
Commissioner of Insurance
(Appointed)
One South Station, 5th Fl.
Boston MA 02210
Commissioner: (617) 521-7794
TDD: (617) 521-7490
FAX: (617) 521-7575
Consumer Help Line: (617) 521-7777
Licensing: (617) 521-7794
Licensing fax: (617) 521-7576
http://www.state.ma.us/doi

MICHIGAN

Linda A. Watters
Insurance Commissioner
(Appointed)
P.O. Box 30220
Lansing MI 48909
611 W. Ottawa St., 2nd Fl.
Lansing MI 48933
Commissioner: (517) 373-0220
FAX: (517) 335-4978
WATS: (877) 999-6442
Licensing: (517) 335-2069
Licensing FAX: (517) 335-3157
http://www.michigan.gov/cis

MINNESOTA

Glenn Wilson
Commissioner of Commerce
(Appointed)
85 7th Pl. E., #500
St. Paul MN 55101
Commissioner: (651) 297-7361
FAX: (651) 296-8591
Consumer Hot Line: (800) 657-3978
http://www.commerce.state.mn.us/pages/
InsuranceMain.htm

MISSISSIPPI

George Dale
Commissioner of Insurance
(Elected)
P.O. Box 79
Jackson MS 39205-0079
Woolfolk State Office Bldg., 10th Fl.
501 N. West St.
Jackson MS 39201
Commissioner: (601) 359-3569
FAX: (601) 359-2474
Licensing: (601) 359-3582
Licensing FAX: (601) 359-1951
Consumer Hot Line: (800) 562-2957
http://www.doi.state.ms.us

MISSOURI

Scott B. Lakin
Director of Insurance
(Appointed)
P.O. Box 690
Jefferson City MO 65102
301 W. High St., Rm. 630
Jefferson City MO 65101
Director: (573) 751-4126
FAX: (573) 751-1165
Licensing: (573) 751-3518
Consumer Hot Line: (800) 726-7390
http://www.insurance.state.mo.us

MONTANA

John Morrison
Commissioner of Insurance
(Elected)
P.O. Box 4009
Helena MT 59604
840 Helena Ave.

Helena MT 59601
Commissioner: (406) 444-2040
FAX: (406) 444-3497
Consumer Hot Line: (800) 332-6148
http://sao.state.mt.us/

NEBRASKA

L. Tim Wagner
Director of Insurance
(Appointed)
Terminal Bldg.
941 "O" St., Ste. 400
Lincoln NE 68508
Director: (402) 471-2201
TDD: (800) 833-7352
FAX: (402) 471-4610
Licensing: (402) 471-4913
Licensing FAX: (402) 471-6559
http://www.nol.org/home/NDOI

NEVADA

Alice A. Molasky-Arman, Esq.
Commissioner of Insurance
(Appointed)
788 Fairview Dr., #300
Carson City NV 89701
Commissioner: (775) 687-4270
FAX: (775) 687-3937
2501 East Sahara Ave., Ste. 302
Las Vegas NV 89104
(702) 486-4009
FAX: (702) 486-4007
Consumer Hot Line: (800) 792-0900
http://doi.state.nv.us

NEW HAMPSHIRE

Roger A. Sevigny
Insurance Commissioner
(Appointed)
56 Old Suncook Rd.
Concord NH 03301
Commissioner: (603) 271-2261
FAX: (603) 271-1406
Licensing: (603) 271-0203
Licensing FAX: (603) 271-7029
Consumer Hot Line: (800) 852-3416
http://www.nh.gov/insurance

NEW JERSEY

Holly Bakke
Commissioner of Insurance
(Appointed)
20 W. State St., CN325
Trenton NJ 08625
Commissioner: (609) 292-5360
FAX: (609) 292-3144
Licensing: (609) 292-4337
Licensing FAX: (609) 984-5263
http://state.nj.us/dobi

NEW MEXICO

Eric Serna
Superintendent of Insurance
(Appointed)
PERA Bldg., P.O. Drawer 1269
Santa Fe NM 87504
Commissioner: (505) 827-4601
FAX: (505) 827-4734
Licensing: (505) 827-4637
Licensing FAX: (505) 827-4734
Consumer Hot Line: (800) 947-4722
http://www.nmprc.state.nm.us/insurance/inshm.htm

NEW YORK

Gregory V. Serio
Superintendent of Insurance
(Appointed)
One Commerce Plaza
Albany NY 12257
(518) 474-4567
Licensing: (518) 474-6630
Licensing FAX: (518) 473-4600
http://www.ins.state.ny.us

NORTH CAROLINA

James E. Long
Commissioner of Insurance
(Elected)
P.O. Box 26387
Raleigh NC 27611
Dobbs Bldg.
430 N. Salisbury St.
Raleigh NC 27603
Commissioner: (919) 733-2032
FAX: (919) 733-6495
Consumer Hot Line: (800) JIM-LONG
Licensing: (919) 733-7487
Licensing FAX: (919) 715-3794
http://www.ncdoi.com

NORTH DAKOTA

Jim Poolman
Commissioner of Insurance
(Elected)
600 E Blvd., Dept. 401
Bismarck ND 58505
Commissioner: (701) 328-2440
FAX: (701) 328-4880
Licensing: (701) 328-3548
Licensing FAX: (701) 328-4880
Consumer Hot Line: (800) 247-0560
http://www.state.nd.us/ndins

OHIO

Ann Womer Benjamin
Director
(Appointed)
2100 Stella Ct.
Columbus OH 43215
Commissioner: (614) 644-2658
FAX: (614) 644-3743
Licensing: (614) 644-2665
Licensing FAX: (614) 644-3475
Consumer Hot Line: (800) 686-1526
http://www.ohioinsurance.gov

OKLAHOMA

Carroll Fisher
Insurance Commissioner
(Elected)
P.O. Box 53408
Oklahoma City OK 73152
2401 N.W. 23rd St., Ste. 28
Oklahoma City OK 73107
Commissioner: (405) 521-2828
WATS: (800) 522-0071
FAX: (405) 521-6652
Licensing: (405) 521-3916
Licensing FAX: (405) 522-3642
Consumer Hot Line: (800) 522-0071
http://www.oid.state.ok.us

OREGON

Joel S. Ario
Insurance Administrator
(Appointed)
Labor & Industries Bldg.
350 Winter St. N.E., Rm. 400
Salem OR 97301
Commissioner: (503) 947-7980
FAX: (503) 378-4351
Licensing: (503) 947-7981
http://www.oregoninsurance.org

PENNSYLVANIA

Diane Koken
Insurance Commissioner
(Appointed)
1326 Strawberry Sq., 13th Fl.
Harrisburg PA 17120
Commissioner: (717) 783-0442
FAX: (717) 772-1969
Licensing: (717) 787-3840
Licensing FAX: (717) 787-8553
http://www.ins.state.pa.us

PUERTO RICO

Fermin M. Contreras Gomez
Commissioner of Insurance
(Appointed)
P.O. Box 8330
Fernandez Juncos Station
Santurce PR 00910
1607 Ponce de Leon Ave.
Santurce PR 00909
Commissioner: (787) 722-8686
FAX: (787) 722-4400
Licensing: (787) 722-8686
Licensing FAX: (787) 722-4400
http://www.ocs.gobierno.pr/
Note: the Web Site is in Spanish, only.

RHODE ISLAND

Joseph Torti, III
Superintendent
(Appointed)
233 Richmond St., Ste. 233
Providence RI 02903
Commissioner: (401) 222-2223
FAX: (401) 222-5475
Licensing: (401) 222-2233
Licensing FAX: (401) 751-4887
http://www.dbr.state.ri.us/insurance.html

SOUTH CAROLINA

Ernst Csiszar
Director
(Appointed)
P.O. Box 100105
Columbia SC 29202
300 Arbor Lake Dr., #1200
Columbia SC 29223

Commissioner: (803) 737-6160
FAX: (803) 737-6229
Licensing (803) 737-6095
Licensing FAX: (803) 737-6100
Consumer Hot Line: (800) 768-3467
http://www.doi.state.sc.us

SOUTH DAKOTA

Gary Steuck
Director of Insurance
(Appointed)
Insurance Bldg.
445 E. Capitol Ave.
Pierre SD 57501
Director: (605) 773-3563
FAX: (605) 773-5369
Licensing: (605) 773-3513
Licensing FAX: (605) 773-5369
http://www.state.sd.us/dcr/insurance

TENNESSEE

Paula Flowers
Commissioner of Insurance
(Appointed)
500 James Robertson Pkwy.
Nashville TN 37243-0565
Commissioner: (615) 741-6007
FAX: (615) 532-6934
Licensing: (615) 741-2693
Licensing FAX: (615) 532-2862
http://www.state.tn.us/commerce

TEXAS

Jose Montemayer
Commissioner of Insurance
(Appointed)
Texas Dept. of Insurance
P.O. Box 149104
Austin TX 78714-9104
333 Guadalupe
Austin TX 78701
Commissioner: (512) 463-6464
FAX: (512) 475-2005
Licensing - Agents: (512) 322-3503
Licensing FAX: (512) 475-1819
Consumer Hot Line: (800) 252-3439
http://www.tdi.state.tx.us

UTAH

Merwin U. Stewart
Commissioner of Insurance
(Appointed)
State Office Bldg., Rm. 3110
Salt Lake City UT 84114
Commissioner: (801) 538-3890
TDD: (801) 538-3826
FAX: (801) 538-3829
Licensing: (801) 538-3805
Consumer Hot Line: (800) 439-3805
http://www.insurance.state.ut.us

VERMONT

John Crowley
Commissioner of Insurance
(Appointed)
89 Main St., Drawer 20
Montpelier VT 05620
Commissioner: (802) 828-3301
FAX: (802) 828-3306
Licensing: (802) 828-3303
http://www.bishca.state.vt.us/InsurDiv/
insur_index.htm

VIRGINIA

Alfred W. Gross
Commissioner of Insurance
(Appointed)
P.O. Box 1157
Richmond VA 23218
1300 E. Main St.
Richmond VA 23219
Commissioner: (804) 371-9694
TDD: (804) 371-9206
FAX: (804) 371-9873
Licensing: (804) 371-9631
Consumer Hot Line: (877) 310-6560
http://www.state.va.us/scc/division/boi

VIRGIN ISLANDS

Vargrave A. Richards
Commissioner of Insurance
(Appointed)
Kongens Gade #18, Charlotte Amelie
St. Thomas VI 00802
Commissioner: (340) 774-7166
FAX: (340) 774-6953
Licensing: (340) 774-7166
Licensing FAX: (340) 774-9458

WASHINGTON

Mike Kreidler
Insurance Commissioner
(Elected)
P.O. Box 40255
Olympia WA 98504
Commissioner: (360) 725-7000
Licensing: (360) 725-7144
Consumer Hot Line: (800) 562-6900
http://www.insurance.wa.gov

WEST VIRGINIA

Jane Cline
Commissioner of Insurance
(Appointed)
1124 Smith St.
Charleston WV 25301
Commissioner: (304) 558-3354
FAX: (304) 558-0412
Licensing: (304) 558-0610
Licensing FAX: (304) 558-4966
Consumer Hot Line: (800) 642-9004
http://www.state.wv.us/insurance

WISCONSIN

Jorge Gomez
Commissioner of Insurance
(Appointed)
125 S. Webster St.
Madison WI 53702
Commissioner: (608) 266-3585
TDD: (608) 266-3586
FAX: (608) 266-9935
Licensing: (608) 266-8699
Consumer Hot Line: (800) 236-8517
http://www.wisconsin.gov/state/home

WYOMING

Ken Vines
Commissioner of Insurance
(Appointed)
Herschler Bldg.
122 W. 25th St., 3rd Fl. E.
Cheyenne WY 82002
Commissioner: (307) 777-7401
Inside Wyoming: (800) 438-5768
FAX: (307) 777-5895
Licensing: (307) 777-7319
Licensing FAX: (307) 777-5895
Consumer Hot Line: (800) 438-5768
http://insurance.state.wy.us

CANADA

Canadian Council of Insurance Regulators

5160 Yonge Street, Box 85
Toronto ON M2N 6L9
(416) 590-7275
FAX: (416) 590-7070
http://www.ccir-ccrra.org/index.htm

National Regulator

Tony Maxwell
Managing Director
International Liason Div.
Office of Financial Institutions
255 Albert St., 16th Fl.
Ottawa ON K1A 0H2
(613) 990-7788
FAX: (613) 993-8466
http://www.osfi-bsif.gc.ca

Alberta

Patricia Nelson
Minister of Finance
Alberta Finance
402 Terrace Bldg.
9515 - 107 St.
Edmonton AB T5K 2C3
(780) 422-1592
FAX: (780) 422-0752
http://www.finance.gov.ab.ca

British Columbia

Michael Grist
Deputy Superintendent of Insurance
1050 West Pender St., Ste. 1900
Vancouver BC V6E 3S7
(604) 660-2947
FAX: (604) 660-3170
http://www.fic.gov.bc.ca/

Manitoba

Greg Selinger
Minister of Finance
1115-405 Broadway Ave.
Winnipeg MB R3C 3L6
(204) 945-2542;
FAX: (204) 948-4261
http://www.gov.mb.ca/finance/cca/firb/

New Brunswick

Janet Cameron
Superintendent of Insurance
Department of Justice
Kings Place

Room 635, Floor 6
440 King St.
Fredericton NB E3B 5H8
(506) 453-2541
FAX: (506) 453-7435
http://www.gnb.ca/0062//

Newfoundland

Winston Morris
Superintendent of Insurance
Department of Government Services and Lands
Confederation Bldg., West Block, 2nd Fl.
P.O. Box 8700
St. John's NF A1B 4J6
(709) 729-2571
FAX: (709) 729-4151
http://www.gov.nf.ca/gsl/

Northwest Territories and Nunavut

Douglas Doak
Minister of Finance
Department of Finance
Division of Taxation and Assessment
4922 48th St.
Yellowknife NT X1A 3S3
(867) 873-7308
FAX: (867) 873-0169
http://www.fin.gov.nt.ca/

Nova Scotia

Catherine Smith
Superintendent of Insurance
Environment and Labour
Financial Institutions
5151 Terminal Rd., 7th Flr.
Halifax NS B3J 1A1
(902) 424-6331
FAX: (902) 424-1298
http://www.gov.ns.ca/enla/fin/

Ontario

Bryan P. Davies
Superintendent of Financial Services
Financial Services Commission of Ontario
5160 Yonge St., 17th Fl.
P.O. Box 85
North York ON M2N 6L9
(416) 250-7250
FAX: (416) 590-7070
http://www.fsco.gov.on.ca/

Prince Edward Island

Edison Shea
Superintendent of Insurance
Office of the Attorney General
P.O. Box 2000
105 Rochford St.
Charlottetown PE C1A 7N8
(902) 368-4564
FAX: (902) 368-5283
http://www.gov.pe.ca/oag/

Quebec

Jacques Henrichon
Deputy Inspector General of
Financial Institutions
800 Place d'Youville, 9th Fl.
Quebec City QC G1R 4Y5
(418) 528-9140
FAX: (418) 528-0835
http://www.gouv.qc.ca/

Saskatchewan

Jim Hall
Superintendent of Insurance
Saskatchewan Financial Services Comm.
1919 Saskatchewan Dr., 6th Flr.
Regina SK S4P 3V7
(306) 787-6700
FAX: (306) 787-9006
http://www.sfsc.gov.sk.ca/

Yukon Territory

Cynthia Tucker
Superintendent of Insurance
Department of Community Services
P.O. Box 2703 (C-5)
Whitehorse YT Y1A 2C6
(867) 667-5111
FAX: (867) 667-3609
http://www.gov.yk.ca/

GLOSSARY

"A" (or judgment) rates: Rates that are based on the judgment of the underwriter on an individual risk basis and not supported by loss experience.

abandonment: A term that applies to property and signifies both a relinquishing of it and the letting go of all legal rights to it, as well, with the intent to claim a total loss. Abandonment of property to an insurance company is something insureds are expressly prohibited from doing in most property polices.

abandonment clause: A property policy provision that stipulates that the insurer need not accept any damaged property that the insured chooses to relinquish.

absolute liability: The performance of an act so dangerous as to be sufficient to trigger liability regardless of the degree of negligence. Triggering explosives is often used as an example. Sending workers aloft for construction or repair at elevated heights is another. Strict liability is another term that is sometimes used.

accelerated death benefit: An option in a life insurance policy that will pay all or part of the policy face amount prior to death. This benefit can pay the cost associated with catastrophic medical conditions that can include the need for nursing home confinement.

accident: An unforeseen, unintended, and unexpected event, which occurs suddenly and at a definite place. See *occurrence*.

accident frequency: The rate of occurrence of accidents. Along with accident severity, it is taken into account in ratemaking.

accident severity: The measure of the seriousness of a claim, measured in, for example, dollars. Along with frequency, it is taken into account in ratemaking.

accident year experience: Measures premiums and losses relating to accidents that occurred during a 12-month period.

accidental death & dismemberment (AD&D): Coverage, often provided as an optional benefit to a disability policy, which pays scheduled amounts in the event of an accidental death or dismemberment.

account current: A monthly statement provided by an insurer detailing an agent's premiums, commissions, cancellations, and endorsements.

account selling: Trying to handle all of a client's insurance needs, rather than providing for only a portion of those needs.

accounts receivable insurance: Pays for the cost of reconstructing accounts receivable records that have been damaged or destroyed by a covered peril. Even more importantly, it covers any payments that cannot be collected because records cannot be reconstructed.

ACORD: An organization that develops insurance forms used as a standard by many within the property & casualty insurance industry. The Acord certificate, application, and loss form are common means of exchanging information. ACORD stands for Agency Company Operations Research and Development.

acquired immune deficiency syndrome (AIDS): An illness which effectively shuts down an individual's immune systems. This disease has precipitated widespread blood testing for disability income cases with monthly benefits of $2,000 to $3,000 and higher.

act of God: Acts of nature – the term was once widely used to distinguish between manmade events, such as fire and collision and nature's rampages in wind and flood.

activities of daily living: Functional routines that relate to one's ability to live independently. These activities consist of bathing, dressing, feeding, toileting, continence, and mobility.

actual authority: Authority that an insurer intentionally gives to the agent. See *express authority* and *implied authority*.

actual cash value (ACV): A method for placing value on property as of the time of its loss or damage. ACV may be determined as replacement cost less depreciation. The market value of an item may be used to help determine actual cash value. Contrast with *replacement cost*.

actuary: A person highly trained in mathematics and statistics who calculates rates and dividends and provides other statistical information for an insurance company.

additional insured: One who qualifies as insured under the terms of a policy even though not named as insured. Officers of a corporation may be included as insureds under the terms of a policy written in the name of the corporation.

additional living expense insurance: This coverage, found in homeowners forms, provides payment for extra expenses made necessary by the insured's inability to reside in the insured dwelling because of a covered loss – for example, restaurant meals and hotel bills. The amount payable is the difference between normal household expenses and the increase.

additions and alterations: Coverage that protects any additions, alterations, and improvements a condo owner makes to his unit, for up to 10% of the contents limit. This coverage can be increased.

adequate: A criterion of insurance rate regulation that stipulates that an insurer's premium rates must be adequate to cover the insurer's cost of doing business, claims payments, and a reasonable profit to the insurer.

adhesion contract: A standardized set of agreements offered by one (usually the stronger) party to another on a take it or leave it basis. An insurance policy is an example of such a contract. The insurer offers a policy, for example, that an individual may adhere to (or not) but in any case the individual may not change any of its terms. Because it has the stronger position, the insurance company has the burden to spell out its terms precisely. Such contracts are interpreted strictly against the author of the contract. Not to be confused with *aleatory contract*.

adjuster: A person who may act either on behalf of the property & casualty insurance company or the insured in the settling a claim. Employee adjusters work for an insurer, while independent adjusters represent the insurance company on a fee basis; and public adjusters represent the insured on a fee basis.

adjustment bureau: Organization for adjusting property & casualty insurance claims that is supported by insurers using the bureau's services.

administrator: A person legally vested with the right of administration of an estate.

admitted assets: The highly liquid assets of an insurer permitted by the state to be taken into account when reporting financial condition.

admitted company: An insurance company that is licensed (admitted) to conduct business within a given state.

admitted market: The range of insurance available through admitted companies.

adult congregate living facility: Residential or apartment housing, which can include a minimum amount of assistance with the activities of daily living.

adult day care facility: An institution designated to provide custodial and/or minimum health care assistance to individuals unable to remain alone, usually during working hours when the caregiver is employed.

adult day care: Services provided to individuals who cannot remain alone, including health and custodial care and other related support. This care is rendered in specified centers on a less than 24 hour basis.

advance premium: Also called *deposit premium*, an advance premium is a downpayment on what will be the final premium, in policies where the final premium is subject to audit.

adverse selection: The tendency of poorer than average risks to buy and maintain insurance. Adverse selection occurs when insureds select only those coverages that are most likely to have losses.

adverse underwriting decision: Any decision made by an underwriter that is not favorable to the insured. Such decisions involve termination, declination, higher rates, or reduction in coverage. Another example is the placing of a risk in a residual market or with an unauthorized insurer.

advertising injury: Claim arising out of slander, libel, copyright infringement, or misappropriation of advertising ideas. Coverage is provided as part of coverage B of the commercial general liability policy.

agency company: An insurance company that produces business through an agency network. See *direct writer*.

agency contract: The legal agreement between an insurance agency and the insurer detailing the terms of representation.

agency plant: The total force of agents representing an insurer.

agent: One who solicits, negotiates or effects contracts of insurance on behalf of an insurer. His right to exercise various functions, his authority, and his obligations and the obligations of the insurer to the agent are subject to the terms of the agency contract with the insurer, to statutory law, and to common law.

agent of record: The agent indicated on and for each insurance policy, binder or acceptance. The agent on a particular policy or bond.

agent's appointment: The act by an insurer that grants an agent the authority to act as an agent for the insurer. In most states, agents must be licensed and appointed prior to being allowed to sell insurance.

agent's authority: The authority of an insurance agent to act on behalf of the insurer he or she represents. There are several types including express authority (authority to act on specific instructions only), implied authority (actions taken in accordance with prevailing custom), or apparent authority (actions based on appearances created by the agent and acquiesced to by the principal).

agent's license: A certificate of authority from the state that permits the agent to conduct business.

aggregate deductible: A deductible provision in some property insurance contracts where all covered losses during a year are figured together and an insurer pays only when the aggregate deductible amount is exceeded.

aggregate excess reinsurance: A type of excess reinsurance treaty that sometimes is called stop loss or excess of loss ratio reinsurance. The retention in this type of agreement is calculated based on all losses over the period of time that is stated in the treaty. The reinsurer is responsible for the amount of losses between the retention and the limit on the treaty.

aggregate limit: The maximum amount an insurer will pay under a property & casualty policy in any one policy period.

agreed value clause: Though rare, some policies cover for a value agreed upon at the time of writing; if the property is lost because of an insured peril, the amount stated in the policy will be paid. Fine arts insured under a personal articles floater or homeowners scheduled personal property endorsement are examples.

aleatory contract: A contract in which the number of dollars to be given up by each party is not equal. Insurance contracts are of this type, as the policyholder pays a premium and may collect nothing from the insurer or may collect a great deal more than the amount of the premium if a loss occurs. Not to be confused with contract of adhesion.

allied lines: Lines of insurance that cover for perils other than fire, that are usually sold with fire insurance, for example, fire and allied lines.

allocated loss adjustment expenses (ALAE): Expenses directly attributable to specific claims. Includes payments for: defense attorneys, medical evaluation of patients, expert medical reviews and witnesses, investigation, record copying, etc.

alternate plan of care: A long-term care insurance policy feature that allows for substantial flexibility in designing a recovery and / or maintenance program for a claimant, using as many types of long-term care assistance as needed on a reasonable cost basis delivered in an agreed-upon setting.

alternative dispute resolution (ADR): Methods other than lawsuits that are designed to resolve legal disputes. Examples are arbitration and mediation.

alternative markets: Mechanisms used to fund self-insurance. This includes captives, which are insurers owned by one or more non-insurers to provide owners with coverage. Risk-retention groups, formed by members of similar professions or businesses to obtain liability insurance, are also a form of self-insurance.

ambiguity: A standard policy provision that proves to be ambiguous may be interpreted in the light most favorable to the insured.

ambulatory care: Medical services provided on an outpatient basis. Services may include diagnosis, treatment, surgery and rehabilitation.

American Association of Insurance Services (AAIS): An association of insurance companies providing filing and various technical services on behalf of its member companies.

American College, The: An educational institute conferring the Chartered Life Underwriter (CLU) designation.

American Lloyds: Unincorporated associations of individual underwriters who assume specified portions of liability under each policy issued. There is no connection with Lloyd's of London.

amount subject: The maximum amount that underwriters estimate can possibly be lost under the most unfavorable circumstances in any given loss, such as a fire or tornado. Contrast with Probable Maximum Loss.

anniversary date: The anniversary of the original date of issue of a policy as shown in the declarations.

annual aggregate deductible: A deductible applied annually to the total amount paid in claims during a policy period. Claims are generally subject to a per-occurrence deductible; the aggregate is the limit beyond which no further deductibles are applied.

annual statement: Summary of an insurer's or reinsurer's financial operations for a particular year, including a balance sheet. It is filed with the state insurance department of each jurisdiction in which the company is licensed to conduct business.

anti-rebating laws: Laws found in all but two states that prohibit an agent's refunding part of a commission to an applicant as an inducement for placing insurance through the agent. California and Florida allow rebating of comissions on a limited basis.

apparent authority: The *perceived* ability of an agent to bind an insurance contract to an insurance company. If an agent or agency holds themselves out as representing a particular company it is reasonable for the public to assume that such authority is established contractually, even if it is not.

apportionment: The method of dividing a loss between multiple insurers that cover the same loss.

appraisal: A determination of the value of property for the purposes of determining the proper amount of insurance to be bought or in adjusting a loss.

appraised value: Value of an object or location as determined by independent appraiser. This value could be market value, replacement cost value, or utility value.

appurtenant structure: Another structure on the same premises as the principal structure. A detached garage on a dwelling premises is appurtenant to the dwelling. Older homeowners forms refer to the other structures protected under the HO Coverage B as appurtenant structures.

arbitration clause: The clause in an insurance policy that spells out how disagreements over a claim are settled.

arson: The intentional setting afire of property.

asset spend-down: Procedure where an individual's income and assets are diminished in order to attain the minimum required levels of the various states' eligibility requirements for Medicaid assistance.

assigned risk: A risk not generally acceptable to any insurance company but for which the law says that insurance must be acquired. Personal auto liability is one such necessary coverage. Insurance companies do-

ing personal auto business in a state can be required to accept assignment of a portion of the state's unacceptable drivers as insureds.

assigned risk plan: See *auto insurance plan*.

assignment: The transfer by a policyholder of his/her legal right or interest in a policy contract to a third party.

assisted living facility: Residence for long-term care patients that is generally less expensive than a nursing home. Residents can also receive some long-term care services in this type of facility.

assumed liability: Liability assumed under contract or agreement. More commonly known as contractual liability.

assumed premium: Consideration or payment an insurance company receives for providing reinsurance for another company.

assumption of risk doctrine: Defense against a negligence claim that bars recovery for damages if a person understands and recognizes the danger inherent in a particular activity or occupation.

attending physician statement: A report, completed by the proposed insured's (or, in a claim situation, the insured's) physician that documents current and prior health history used in the evaluation process of approving an application (or a claim).

attractive nuisance: Condition that can attract and injure children. The occupants of land on which such a condition exists are liable for injuries to children. Examples of attractive nuisance include swimming pools, earth moving equipment, and playground equipment.

audit: Some policies (such as workers compensation) are written subject to an audit. Since workers compensation premium is based on the insured's payroll, the insurer is entitled to audit the insured's records at the end of the policy to verify that it has collected an adequate premium for the amount of payroll to which it was exposed.

authorized insurer: An insurer granted permission by a state to sell specific lines of insurance within that state.

auto insurance plan: Program set up by various states to ensure that everyone with a valid driver's license will be able to purchase auto insurance. All auto insurers operating within a state are assigned insureds in proportion to the amount of auto premium written.

auto physical damage insurance: Insurance on the vehicle. This coverage usually is broken down into collision and other than collision coverages.

automatic increase benefit: A policy provision that increases, annually, the policy monthly benefit by either a stated percentage or the latest Consumer Price Index measure, without evidence of either medical or financial insurability.

automobile liability insurance: Insurance in which the insurer agrees to pay all sums for which the insured is legally obligated because of bodily injury or property damage arising from the ownership, maintenance, or use of an auto.

automobile medical payments: Insurance applying to the medical, hospital, or funeral expenses of anyone injured while on or in an insured automobile. The coverage is not dependent on liability, being triggered simply by an accident. It may be included in either the Business Auto Policy or the Personal Auto Policy. See also *premises medical payments*.

automobile reinsurance facility: One of several types of "shared market" mechanisms used to make automobile insurance available to persons who are unable to obtain such insurance in the regular market.

automobile shared market: A program in which all automobile insurers in each state make coverage available to car owners who are unable to obtain auto insurance in the voluntary market.

avocation: Extracurricular activity engaged in by the proposed insured, such as hang gliding or scuba diving, which may affect the insurability of the individual due to increased risk exposure.

avoidance of risk: Taking steps to remove a hazard, engage in an alternative activity, or otherwise end a specific exposure.

bad faith: Accusations by policyholders that insurers took steps to deliberately delay, underpay, or deny a claim.

bailment: The act of delivering property in trust to another for a limited time and specific purpose.

bare: Without adequate insurance, especially for a business.

bare walls: This term describes a property policy that insures just the common elements and provides no coverage for the interiors or contents of a unit.

basic causes of loss: The perils of fire, lightning, and removal of property from premises endangered by those perils as shown in the standard 1943 New York fire policy.

basic named perils: Covered perils in a property insurance contract: fire, lightning, windstorm, civil commotion, smoke, hail, aircraft, vehicles, explosion, and riot.

beach plans: Sometimes known as windstorm plans or pools, these are plans devised by coastal states to insure the windstorm exposure of coastal properties. The plans operate in a manner similar to a joint underwriting association with participation by all insurers operating within a state.

benefit period: The length of time for which benefits under a disability or long-term care insurance contract will be paid.

bereavement counseling: A support service designed to assist family members of terminally ill patients to cope with their grief. This service is often available under a hospice care program and a benefit may be payable under a long-term care insurance policy.

Best's rating: A rating given to insurance companies by the A.M. Best Company, independent analysts of the insurance industry. The ratings range from A++ (Superior) down to D (below minimum standards). Also, ratings of E and F are given to companies under state supervision or in liquidation. The ratings reflect A.M. Best's evaluation of an insurance company's financial strength and operating performance relative to the norms of the property/casualty insurance industry.

betterment: A term used to express the difference in the value of property before loss and after restoration. If a 20-year roof is damaged by an insured peril and it has to be replaced in its 15th year and the restoration renews the 20-year life expectancy, the owner has obtained a 15-year betterment in the roof. Without replacement cost insurance on the roof, the owner is expected to reimburse the insurance company for the betterment entailed in the restoration. Also see *improvements and betterments*.

BI: A shorthand expression for bodily injury.

bill of lading: A document issued by a carrier that is a receipt for the merchandise or other property to be transported, and that outlines just what the carrier agrees to do and his responsibilities for the property.

binder: An insurer's agreement, by way of an agent, to provide nonlife insurance on the spot, pending issuance of the policy contract.

binding authority: The authority extended to an agent by an insurer to provide insurance, usually on a temporary basis, until a policy can be written.

blanket bond: An employee dishonesty or fidelity bond covering all persons of a group or class, as opposed to bonds naming specific individuals (name schedule) or positions (position schedule).

blanket coverage: A means of insuring various items of property under one limit of liability.

blanket crime policy: An individual policy covering several crime perils on a single amount rather than on individual limits.

blanket insurance: Insurance covering multiple items of property as a group. Covered property may be at one location or several.

blanket position bonds: Bonds that guarantee the honesty of each of the employees of an entity stated on the bond to the stated amount of the bond.

block policy: A block policy provides a form of inland marine insurance. It covers loss to the property of a merchant, wholesaler, or manufacturer including property of others in the insured's care, custody, or control; property on consignment; property sold but not delivered. A block policy covers loss caused by most perils (including transportation), subject to certain limitations as specified in the policy exclusions. Common block policies are jeweler's block and furrier's block policies.

blood profile: A test that is required on applications with benefit levels of $2,000 to $3,000 and above, that provides the underwriter with a number of clinical values.

bodily injury: A term that refers to physical injury, sickness, or disease, or death resulting therefrom. In some jurisdictions bodily injury includes emotional injury.

bodily injury liability: Legal obligation that flows from the injury or death of another person. This insurance is commonly limited to bodily injury liability derived by way of negligence, but coverage of liability by way of contract (holding another harmless) is also possible.

boiler & machinery insurance: Fired vessels, steam generators, mechanical and electrical objects and turbines, are all examples of objects that might be listed for coverage under a boiler and machinery policy. Coverage is for damage to covered property caused by an accident to an object identified in the policy's schedule. Coverage includes extra expense, automatic 90-day coverage at new locations, defense against liability claims, and supplementary payments like those provided under public liability policies.

bond: A document for expressing surety. A bond engages three entities: the surety (bonding company) sells the bond to the principal for the purpose of paying the amount the principal will owe to the obligee upon failure of the principal to perform some act or provide some service under agreed terms.

bond, fidelity: A bond that guarantees the principal's honesty.

bond, surety: The financial assumption of responsibility by one or more persons for fulfilling another's obligations.

book of business: The accounts written by an agent or company. It can be expressed in a number of ways such as total book of business, book of auto business, homeowners business, etc.

BOP (businessowners policy): See *businessowners policy*.

Boston plan: This is a plan under which insurers agree that they will not reject property coverage on residential buildings in a run-down part of town. Instead, they will accept the coverage until there has been an inspection and the owner has had an opportunity to correct any faults. Boston was the first city to originate such a plan, and many other cities have followed, including New York, Oakland, Cleveland, and Buffalo.

boycott: Another practice defined as unfair under most states' codes. Such a practice occurs when someone in the insurance business refuses to do business with someone else until that person complies with certain conditions or concessions.

broad form perils: A property insurance designation for coverage that extends beyond the basic named perils.

broad form property damage endorsement: A commercial general liability endorsement that removes the care, custody, or control exclusion relating to the property of others and replaces it with a less stringent one.

broker: One who represents the insured in arranging insurance. A broker may also serve as the agent of an insurance company. Typically, a broker does not have binding authority.

burglary: Unlawful removal of property from premises involving visible forcible entry.

burning ratio: The ratio of losses to the amount insured.

business auto policy (BAP): A standardized contract for writing liability and property coverage on commercial autos.

business income coverage: Insurance protecting the income derived from an insured's business activities when curtailed by a covered peril. Coverage includes reasonable extra expense the insured undertakes to expedite return to business operations.

business income, dependent properties: Covering loss to an insured when the operations of a key supplier, customer, or leader property on which the insured's operations are dependent, are shut down by a covered peril. Also referred to as contingent business income.

business overhead expense: A policy that reimburses the insured business owner, during a disability for covered business expenses that are incurred in the day to day operation of the business.

business personal property: A term relating to contents of a commercial enterprise. It may include furniture, fixtures, machinery and equipment as well as stock, all other chattels owned by the insured, and even use interest in building improvements and betterments.

businessowners policy (BOP): A package of property and liability insurance for small and medium size businesses, the BOP owes its origin to the success of the homeowners policy.

buy-back deductible: A deductible that may be eliminated for an additional premium in order to provide first-dollar coverage.

buy-sell (or buy-out): A policy that pays to a corporation or co-owner either a lump-sum or installment payments on disability of an insured owner to provide the necessary funds to buy-out the business interest of the disabled owner.

cafeteria plan: An employee benefit arrangement under Internal Revenue Code Section 125 whereby an individual is allowed to select among certain employee benefits on a pretax rather than an after-tax basis. Disability income is one of those employee benefits.

cancellation; flat, pro rata, or short rate: With respect to property & liability insurance, in a flat cancellation the full premium is returned to the insured; a pro rata cancellation means the insurer has charged for the time the coverage was in force; and short rate cancellation entails a penalty in excess of pro rata for early termination.

capacity: An insurer's (or reinsurer's) top limit on the amount of coverage it has available. The term may also refer to the total available in the respective insurance or reinsurance market.

capital and surplus: The sum of paid up capital, gross paid in and contributed surplus and unassigned surplus.

capitation: Method of payment for health services in which a physician or hospital is paid a fixed amount for each enrolled plan member regardless of the actual number or nature of services provided to each person. Dollars are usually expressed in units of Per Member Per Month (PMPM).

captive agent: A representative of a single insurer. In the case of captive agents, the insurer owns and controls expiration dates and policy records. A captive agent is a member of what may be called an exclusive agency system.

captive insurer: An enterprise with all the authority to perform as an insurance company but organized by a parent company for the express purpose of providing the parent company's insurance.

care coordinator: A person designated by an insurer to organize a plan of care at claim time between the insured, medical providers, and family members.

care, custody, or control: An expression common to liability insurance contracts. It refers to an exclusion in the policy eliminating coverage for damage to property of others that is in the insured's care, custody, or control. The insured has a bailee relationship to the property – in other words, making the insured liable for the care of the property beyond damage caused by negligence. A bailees floater is often used to cover the insured's obligation for the care of such property.

caregiver: A person providing assistance to a dependent person due to medical reasons or the inability to conduct routine activities of daily living.

carry-over account: In a Business Overhead Expense policy, this is the fund that accumulates unused benefits to be paid out to the insured at a later date.

case management: Planned approach to manage service or treatment to an individual with a serious medical problem. Its dual goal is to contain costs and promote more effective intervention to meet patient needs.

cash sickness benefits: A state disability income program in New York, New Jersey, Rhode Island, California, and Hawaii that provides a small benefit on a short-term basis to help replace lost earnings for a worker's "off the job" disability.

cash value rider: Also called Equity Builder, this form of a return of premium begins building values equal to an ever-increasing percentage of premiums paid for a disability policy. Initial values usually appear in the third policy year and build to 100% at age 65, which can be returned to the insured at that time, less any claims.

cash-flow underwriting: Name given to an insurer's practice of nonselectively writing business in order to generate greater amounts of cash for investment purposes.

casualty actuarial society (CAS): A professional society for actuaries in areas of insurance work other than Life Insurance. This society grants the designation of Associate and Fellow of the Casualty Actuarial Society (ACAS and FCAS).

casualty insurance: The type of insurance concerned with legal liability for losses caused by bodily injury to others or physical damage to property of others.

catastrophe (excess) cover: Another term for catastrophe reinsurance, wherein the ceding company is indemnified by the reinsurer after a specified loss amount is reached for losses caused by catastrophes.

causes of loss forms: The reference is commonly to property insurance contracts and the form in question details those perils to which the coverage will respond. Though any property insurance contract must name the perils it intends to cover, for example, crop hail, earthquake, or perils of transit, and so on, the most commonly used general forms are the basic and broad named perils forms and the special form. In contrast to the named perils forms, that list specific perils for coverage, the special form contract covers simply risk of direct physical loss and relies on exclusions to delimit and define the coverage.

cedant: A ceding insurer or reinsurer. See *cede.*

cede: The transfer of all or part of a risk written by an insurer to a reinsurer.

ceding commission: The cedant's acquisition costs and overhead expenses, taxes, licenses and fees, plus a fee representing a share of expected profits, which often is expressed as a percentage of the gross reinsurance premium.

Centers for Medicare and Medicaid Services: The federal agency that administers Medicare, Medicaid, and other federal programs.

certificate of insurance: A written description of insurance in effect as of the date and time of the certificate. The certificate does not ordinarily confer any rights on the holder – that is, the issuing insurer does not promise to inform the holder of change in or cancellation of coverage.

certified copy: Reproduction of a document that the authority having custody of original signs and attests as a true, genuine and authentic copy.

CFP: A designation – Certified Financial Planner. A title conveyed by the International Board of Standards and Practices for Certified Financial Planners. A Certified Financial Planner must pass a series of exams and enroll in ongoing education classes. Knowledge of estate planning, tax preparation, insurance, and investing is required.

CGL (Commercial General Liability): See *commercial general liability.*

ChFC: A designation – Chartered Financial Consultant. A financial planning designation for the insurance industry awarded by the American College of Bryn Mawr. ChFCs must meet experience requirements and pass exams covering finance and investing. They must have at least three years of experience in the financial industry, and have studied and passed an examination on the fundamentals of financial planning, including income tax, insurance, investment, and estate planning.

chronically ill: This is the definition under which an individual qualifies for favorable tax treatment for long-term care expenses, whether self-insured or reimbursed by an insurance company. To be chronically ill, the person must be either unable to perform two of six activities of daily living for at least 90 days or suffer a severe cognitive impairment.

CIC: A designation – Certified Insurance Counselor.

civil commotion: One of the extended coverage perils, paired with the peril riot, that refers to a less widespread or generalized event than riot might be thought to encompass.

claim expense: The expense of adjusting a claim, such as investigation and attorneys' fees. It does not include the cost of the claim itself.

claims-made coverage: A type of public liability insurance that responds only to claims for injury or damage that are brought (to the insurer) during the policy period (or during a designated extended reporting period beyond expiration). This development was in response to long tail claims, such as those related to asbestosis injury, carrying over many years and multiple layers of coverage limits. However, most public liability policies are written on an occurrence basis, covering injury or damage occurring during the policy period even if a claim is brought months or even years later.

clash cover: A type of catastrophe reinsurance for casualty insurance. The retention is equal to the highest limit of any one insurance policy covered by the agreement. Clash cover is written to cover all losses from one source, such as a construction site.

class rates: When property or people share a certain number of characteristics relevant to the cost of providing them with insurance (such as a male driver under the age of 25 without an accident), underwriters can develop insurance rates that reflect the exposures represented by the class and offer insurance based on a class rate rather than by computing individual rates for each member.

classification: The systematic arrangement of properties, persons, or business operations into groups or categories according to certain criteria. Such classification creates a basis for establishing statistical experience and determining rates, and to avoid *unfair* discrimination.

classification code: The identifying number for an occupational classification. It is a four-digit numeric code – based on the nature of the business of the employer – assigned by NCCI or other workers compensation rating bureaus.

clause: A provision or condition affecting the terms of a contract. Coinsurance, cancellation, and subrogation clauses are typical insurance contract clauses.

clear space clause: A clause requiring that insured property, such as stacks of lumber, be stored at some particular distance from each other or from other property.

closed panel HMO: A managed care plan that contracts with physicians on an exclusive basis for services and does not allow those physicians to see patients for another managed care organization. Examples include both staff and group model HMOs.

CLU: A designation – Chartered Life Underwriter – conferred upon successful completers of a series of studies of life insurance and related disciplines designed by the American College.

COBRA: A federal law that allows an employee who leaves a company to continue to be covered under the company's health plan, for a certain time period and under certain conditions. The name results from the fact that the program was created under the Consolidated Omnibus Reconciliation Act. The system is designed to prevent employees who are between jobs from experiencing a lapse in coverage.

coercion: Another act defined by most states as an unfair trade practice. Coercion occurs when someone in the insurance business uses physical or mental force to persuade another to transact insurance.

cognitive impairment: One of the measurements used to determine eligibility for long-term care benefits in a policy, it is the deterioration or loss of one's intellectual capacity, confirmed by clinical evidence and standardized tests, in the areas of: (1) short and long term memory; (2) orientation as to person, place and time; and (3) deductive or abstract reasoning.

coinsurance clause: Coinsurance refers to the bargain between commercial property owners and the insurance industry. This clause in property policies encourages the property owner to gauge coverage needs by possible, not probable, maximum loss. With $1 million at risk but a probable maximum loss of $100,000, for example, the property owner would probably buy $100,000 insurance and bank on avoiding the larger disaster. The bargain offered by the insurance industry is a reduced rate per $100 of coverage if the owner agrees to buy coverage at a specified relation (80% commonly) to value (to possible maximum loss in other words). If the insured accepts the bargain but events prove the amount of insurance is inadequate to the stated coinsurance percentage, the insured becomes coinsurer in the same ratio as the amount of insurance bears to the amount that should have been carried.

collapse: A property insurance peril, subject to its own specific agreement in property policies, that otherwise insure on an open perils basis.

collision damage waiver: When paired with an auto rental agreement, the rental car company agrees to waive the renter's responsibility for any physical damage to the rental car in exchange for an additional payment. Sometimes called a loss damage waiver.

collision insurance: A type of physical damage insurance available for automobiles. Coverage is triggered when damage is caused by striking against another object.

collusion: A secret agreement between persons to defraud another, e.g., an insured driver of an automobile and his passenger may misrepresent the facts of an accident in order to have monies paid to the passenger under the insured's automobile insurance policy.

combined ratio: The sum of an insurance company's loss ratio and expense ratio; used as an indicator of profitability for insurance companies.

combined single limit (CSL): Liability policies commonly offer separate limits that apply to bodily injury claims and to claims for property damage. 50/100/25 is shorthand under such a policy for $50,000 per person/ $100,000 per accident for bodily injury claims and $25,000 for property damage. A combined single limits policy might cover for $100,000 per covered occurrence whether bodily injury or property damage, one person or many.

commercial blanket bond: A bond that covers the named insured against employee dishonesty. A single coverage amount applies to any one loss, regardless of the number of employees involved.

commercial general liability (CGL): The CGL policy is an ISO form, widely used to provide commercial enterprises with premises and operations liability coverage, products and completed operations insurance and personal injury coverage. Premises medical payments coverage is often included as well.

commercial lines: A distinction marking property and liability coverage written for business or entrepreneurial interests as opposed to personal lines.

commissioner of insurance: The official in a state (or territory) responsible for administering insurance regulation; sometimes called the superintendent or director of insurance.

common area: The part of a building or premises either owned by or used by all tenants or tenant-owners of the building (e.g. the swimming pool at a condominium).

community-rated: A rating method required of federally-qualified HMOs that must charge the same amount of premium from each plan member. There is some variability allowed – by age, sex and mix. Some states have further guidelines or restrictions regarding this method of rate calculation.

comparative negligence: A variation of *contributory negligence*, in which the comparative degree of negligence for each party to an accident is taken into account when awarding damages.

compensatory damages: The award, usually monetary, that is intended to compensate the claimant for injury sustained.

competitive state fund: A facility established by a state to sell workers compensation in competition with private insurers.

completed operations insurance: See *products and completed operations*.

completion bond: A bond that guarantees a lending institution or other mortgagee that a building or other construction that they have lent money on will be completed on time so it can used as collateral on the loan.

comprehensive benefits: A long-term care insurance plan that offers a wide variety of coverage for long-term care insurance services. These plans are modeled after the NAIC model policy of 1988. These policies could be both tax-qualified and non-qualified plans.

comprehensive personal liability insurance: Provides individuals and family members with protection from legal liability for most accidents caused by them in their personal lives. Note that any legal liability claims submitted while in the course of business activities are not covered.

comprehensive physical damage (automobile): Traditional name for physical damage coverage for losses by fire, theft, vandalism, falling objects, and various other perils. On personal auto policies, this is now called other than collision coverage. On commercial forms, it continues to be called comprehensive coverage.

compulsory auto insurance: The minimum amount of auto liability insurance that meets a state law. Financial responsibility laws in every state require all automobile drivers to show proof, after an accident, of their ability to pay damages up to the state minimum. In compulsory liability states this proof, which is usually in the form of an insurance policy, is required before you can legally drive a car.

computer fraud coverage: Covers loss if money, securities, or other property is stolen or transferred through computer fraud.

computer insurance: Covers computer equipment and peripherals beyond the normal coverage provided in homeowner's insurance policies, typically between $1,000 and $3,000. Some policies are also designed to cover damage and/or theft of portable equipment, such as laptop computers, and even the costs of data recovery.

concurrent causation: When two perils contribute concurrently to a property loss, one excluded and the other not, the effect of the exclusion tends to be voided in a policy covering on an open perils basis. A concurrent causation exclusion is found in current forms.

condition: One of the obligations of either the insured or the insurer imposed in the insurance contract.

conditionally renewable: Under this policy provision, an insurance company agrees to renewal of a disability income policy providing the insured meets certain qualifications, such as full-time employment.

condominium: Type of dwelling where the structure is owned jointly while spaces within the structure are owned individually. Special property and liability forms cover the interests of the condominium association and of unitowners.

condominium association coverage: A policy that provides coverage for the building, elements of the building, and liability needs for those who collectively own a piece of property.

condominium unit owners form: A policy that provides coverage for the personal property, owned elements of a unit, and liability for the individual unit owner.

consequential loss: An indirect consequence of direct loss to property. Business income may be lost when a store burns down, or frozen goods may spoil when windstorm causes an interruption of power. Consequential or indirect loss is not generally insured by policies covering direct damage (i.e., by fire or wind as in these examples), but insurance is readily obtainable separately for most such consequential exposures – business income coverage being among the most common coverage.

consideration clause: Stipulation that states the basis on which an insurer issues an insurance contract.

constructive total loss: This condition is said to exist when the cost of repairs exceeds the actual cash value of damaged property.

contingent business income: See *business income, dependent properties*.

contingent liability: Liability imposed on a business entity (individual, partnership, or corporation) for acts of a third party for which the business entity is responsible.

contingent nonforfeiture: This long-term care policy feature is included in policies conforming to the NAIC's Rate Stability amendments. It provides a choice of paid-up and other policy scenarios that the insured can choose from if the insurer exceeds the limits of cumulative future rate increases.

contingent workforce: This is a growing portion of the labor market consisting of part-time, temporary, and leased employees, the self-employed and independent contractors. These individuals do not conform to the traditional employer-employee relationship.

continuing care retirement communities: This campus-type environment offers houses, apartments, communal dining facilities, a nursing facility, recreation, a library, and other services. An entry fee and a stipulated monthly payment are required.

contract of adhesion: See *adhesion contract*.

contractual liability: Liability that does not arise by way of negligence but by assumption under contract. For example, in certain leases, a tenant may assume a landlord's liability to others for unsafe conditions on the premises. Some such assumptions are covered automatically under the Commercial General Liability form.

contributing location: A location upon which the insured depends as a source of materials or services. One of the four types of dependent properties for which Business Income coverage may be written.

contributory negligence: A defense to a negligence action in which it is asserted that the claimant failed to meet the standard required for his or her own protection, which contributed to the loss.

controlled business: The amount of insurance countersigned, issued or sold by a producer covering that producer's interests, immediate family, or employees. Many states limit the amount of controlled business that may be written, by placing a maximum percentage of all business that may be controlled.

convention (or statement) blank: The uniform annual financial statement that must be filed by all insurers as prescribed by the National Association of Insurance Commissioners. The convention blank must be filed annually in an insurer's home state and every state in which it is licensed to do business.

conversion: A policy feature common in Business Overhead Expense and Disability Buy-Out plans that provides that the insured can convert to an individual disability policy if the need to have the business disability policy changes.

co-payments: That portion of a claim or medical expense that an insured must pay out of pocket. This is usually a fixed amount in a managed care plan, such as $5 per doctor visit.

corporation: A business whose articles of incorporation have been approved in some state. For insurance purposes, the type of business structure helps to determine who is insured on the policy.

cost of living rider: An optional benefit that increases the disability benefit by a percentage or the latest Consumer Price Index measure.

countersignature: An authorized signature of agent or company representative on an insurance policy. Usually pertains to policies sold by an agent of the insurer located in another state.

coverage trigger: In liability insurance, the trigger is the event that brings coverage into play. It may be either an occurrence of bodily injury or property damage; or, in a form with a claims-made trigger, the formal making of a claim.

covered expenses: In a Business Overhead Expense policy, a listing of typical business expenses that are eligible to be reimbursed during an insured's disability. Examples: rent or mortgage payments, electricity, employee salaries.

covered loss: An accident, including accidental damage by forces of nature, that brings a contract of insurance into play.

CPCU: A designation – Chartered Property Casualty Underwriter – conferred upon successful completion of a series of 10 exams on insurance and related disciplines designed by the American Institute of Chartered Property Casualty Underwriters.

credit insurance: Optional coverage that pays off the balance of an outstanding loan in the event one become disabled, unemployed or dies. Exact coverage depends on the particular policy. Variations include credit life (pays if debtor dies), credit health or disability (pays if debtor gets sick or becomes disabled), and credit unemployment insurance (pays if debtor involuntarily loses job). Usually offered with credit cards, auto loans, and mortgages.

credit score: The number produced by an analysis of an individual's credit history. Studies have shown that credit history provides an indicator of the likelihood of an auto insurance loss. Some companies use insurance scores as an insurance underwriting and rating tool.

crime insurance: A broad category covering loss of property through criminal activity – from employee dishonesty to burglary and robbery, computer fraud, and forgery.

crop insurance: Insurance covering growing crops against hail, wind, and fire. Protection against a broader range of perils can often be arranged as well.

cross liability coverage: In the event of claim by one insured for which another insured covered by the same policy may be held liable, this endorsement covers the insured against whom the claim is made in the same manner as if separate policies had been issued. However, it does not operate to increase the insurance company's overall limit of liability.

cross-purchase agreement: In a disability buy-sell situation, this arrangement has the owners themselves as owner and beneficiary of the policy proceeds. Generally used only where two owners are involved.

custodial care facility: A facility that is licensed by the state to provide custodial care, including assistance with activities of daily living and a nursing staff to oversee the administering of medication.

custodial care: The most common type of long-term care service rendered, it provides assistance with activities of daily living and is generally performed by a trained aide in a variety of settings, most often in the home.

daily: The document – now more commonly found in electronic than in paper form – that provides a property or liability insurer and agent with a quick reference to all pertinent information relative to a contract of insurance such as insured's identification, location, coverage, term, or premium. Sometimes referred to as a daily report.

daily benefit amount: The specified amount of benefit payable for long-term care services. The dollar amount may vary by service such as $100 a day payable for a nursing home confinement and $75 a day payable for home health care, or $130 a day for nursing home and $195/day for home health care.

data processing insurance: Coverage for electronic media, computers, and other electronic data processing equipment.

declarations page: That part of a property or liability insurance policy that discloses information pertinent to the coverage promised including names, addresses, limits, locations, term, premium, and forms. The same information, perhaps in a shorthand version, is contained as well in the daily.

deductible: The part of the loss that is to be borne by the insured.

defense costs: These are that portion of the CGL policy that applies whether or not the claim is legitimate and well founded. These costs may be part of the total stated policy limits ("defense inside limits") or may be in addition to the stated policy limits ("defense outside limits"). Auxiliary charges may be included with defense costs.

demutualization: The conversion of an insurance company from a mutual insurance company to a stock insurance company

dependent properties: See *business income, dependent properties.*

deposit premium: When the price of insurance is tied to fluctuating values or costs that cannot be known until the end of the policy period, inventory or payroll are two common examples, a deposit or provisional premium or estimated premium may be charged at the outset of a policy with final adjustment to come at the end of the term.

depreciation: As property ages and becomes worn it often loses value. That loss of value must be taken into account in any adjustment of property insurance that covers loss of actual cash value.

detached signs: Signs located away from the designated premises. They may or may not be part of the Covered Property.

difference in conditions (DIC): Property insurance obtained through the excess and surplus lines market to supplement and expand on the property coverage available through admitted markets. DIC has been called the property umbrella policy.

diminution of value: The idea that a vehicle loses value after it has been damaged in an accident and repaired.

direct billing: A system for the collection of premiums whereby the insurance company "directly bills" the insured for the premium in lieu of the conventional collection of premiums by the agent or broker. The insurer sends a statement to the agent, usually monthly, recording the premiums collected directly, and credits the agent with the commission on those items.

direct damage: Physical damage caused to property by a peril such as fire or lightning.

direct loss: The immediate consequence of the action of an insured peril. A fire damaged structure is a direct loss by fire. In contrast, see *consequential loss.*

direct premiums: Premiums collected from policyholders before premiums for reinsurance are paid.

direct writer: An insurer that sells coverage directly via its own employees. Contrast with *Independent agent.*

directors and officers liability insurance (D&O): A form of errors and omissions insurance covering the directors and officers of corporations against suits alleging they committed wrongful act(s).

disability income: A monthly benefit paid to an individual in the event of an accident or sickness, to help replace earnings lost.

disappearing deductible: Deductible in an insurance contract that provides for a decreasing deductible amount as the size of the loss increases, so that small claims are not paid but large losses are paid in full.

disclosure: The duty of an applicant and his broker to tell the underwriter every material circumstance before acceptance of risk.

discovery period: The period of time, commonly one year, after the termination of a surety bond during which covered loss may be discovered, reported, and covered.

dishonesty, disappearance, and destruction (3-D) policy: The name once applied to a form used for comprehensive crime coverage. Now known as ISO Form C.

divisible contract clause: A clause providing that a violation of the conditions of the policy at one insured location will not void the coverage at other locations.

dollar threshold: In no-fault auto insurance states with the dollar threshold, it prevents individuals from suing in tort to recover for pain and suffering unless their medical expenses exceed a certain dollar amount.

domestic insurance company: Term used by a state to refer to any company incorporated there.

domiciled: Refers to the state in which an insurance company receives a license to operate. The company is then regulated by that state's Department of Insurance.

drive other car (DOC) endorsement: A business auto or garage policy endorsement providing coverage for named individuals while driving nonowned autos in situations unrelated to the business of the insured.

driver training credit: To encourage driver education courses at schools and colleges, many insurers grant premium rebates to applicants for private passenger automobile insurance who have successfully completed an approved training program.

druggists liability insurance: A form of professional liability insurance for druggists.

duty to defend: Part of the insuring agreement of many policies. The insurer has the duty to defend the insured in event of a covered loss.

dwelling forms: Forms for coverage of dwellings and personal property that are not eligible for homeowners coverage. Tenant occupied rental properties are commonly insured under these forms.

early warning system: A system of measuring insurers' financial stability set up by insurance industry regulators. An example is the Insurance Regulatory Information System (IRIS), which uses financial ratios to identify insurers in need of regulatory attention.

earned premium: Portion of a premium for which protection has already been provided by the insurer.

earnings insurance: A simplified form of insurance covering business income loss, limited to a set percentage of the policy's total amount for recovery of proved loss for each 30-day period.

earth movement: Subject to an exclusion in property policies, this peril includes earthquake, landslide, and mudflow.

easement: An interest in land owned by another that entitles its holder to specific uses.

e-business: The transaction of business by way of electronic media, such as telephones, fax machines, computers, and video-teleconferencing equipment. This generally is broader than e-commerce although some may view e-business and e-commerce as interchangeable terms.

e-commerce: The buying and selling of goods by way of electronic media, such as telephones, fax machines, computers, and video-teleconferencing equipment.

economic damages: Out-of-pocket damages, such as incurred medical expenses, lost wages, etc.

effective date: The date shown in the declarations of a policy upon which coverage is to take effect.

elements of a negligent act: Four elements an injured person must show to prove negligence: existence of a legal duty to use reasonable care, failure to perform that duty, damages or injury to the claimant, and proximate cause relationship between the negligent act and the infliction of damages.

elimination period: In a disability or long-term care insurance policy, this is a period of time during which no benefits are payable and is sometimes referred to as a deductible.

embezzlement: The fraudulent use of money or property which has been entrusted to one's care.

employee benefits plan liability coverage: Protects the insured employer against claims by employees or former employees resulting from negligent acts or omissions in the administration of the insured's employee benefits programs.

employee dishonesty coverage: Insurance protecting employers from loss due to theft by their employees.

Employee Retirement Income Security Act of 1974 (ERISA): Federal law that affects pension and profit-sharing plans. Among other provisions, this law specifies a published summary plan must be distributed to participants within 120 days after adoption of the plan and within 90 days after an employee becomes a participant. The law requires that a summary plan description be issued every 5 years.

employer-paid limits: A table used by an underwriter and agent to determine the maximum amount of monthly benefit the insured can purchase when the employer is paying the premium. This limit is higher than the ordinary issue limit because of the taxation on benefits when received due to the employer's deducting the premium paid as an ordinary business expense.

employers liability insurance: A feature of standard workers compensation policies, this coverage applies to liability that may be imposed on an employer outside the provisions of a workers compensation law.

employers nonownership liability: Employers who buy commercial auto coverage on a basis other than any auto have this exposure whenever an employee uses his or her own auto on the employer's behalf.

employment practices liability insurance: Coverage against allegations of illegal or discriminatory hiring and firing practices, sexual harassment of employees, and so on.

encumbrance: Mortgage, lien or other charge against a property.

endorsement: An amendment to a policy form.

enterprise-wide risk management: An effort to categorize, measure, and treat all types of risk that may adversely affect a business. It includes both traditional hazard risks and other business risks, such as risks posed by competitors, by economic developments, by natural conditions the business cannot control, and by general operations.

entity purchase agreement: In a disability buy-sell situation, this arrangement has the corporation as owner and beneficiary of the policy proceeds. Generally used in situations where there are more than two owners.

ERISA: An acronym standing for the 1974 Employee Retirement Income Security Act, which regulates certain employee benefit plans. See also *Employee Retirement Income Security Act of 1974*.

errors and omissions coverage (E&O): A type of professional liability insurance protecting the insured against claims alleging bodily injury or property damage caused by the professional or technical incompetence of the insured.

estimated premium: See *deposit premium*.

estoppel: The legal doctrine that a party may be precluded from denying that certain rights exist if, by behavior or implication that such rights did, in fact, exist, another party has acted upon this information to his or her detriment.

ex gratia payment: A payment by an insurer to an insured for which there is no contractual liability. Such payments are sometimes made as a goodwill gesture if there is the possibility of a misunderstanding or a mistake.

examination under oath: Found in the conditions section of many insurance policies, the insurer's right to examine an insured under oath following a loss.

excess insurance: Coverage that applies on top of underlying insurance that is primary – insurance that pays until its coverage limit is exhausted at which point the excess coverage takes over.

excess or surplus lines market: The range of insurance available through nonadmitted insurers – insurance companies that are not licensed in a particular state or territory. Specific provisions of state or territorial law control placements.

exclusion rider: Attached to and made a part of the policy, this document, which the insured generally must sign, indicates a condition(s) which is specifically not going to be covered under this insured's policy. Example: any disease or disorder of the lungs. This rider is placed as a result of the individual evaluation of the insured's history.

exclusions: A policy provision that indicates what will not be covered under the disability income policy. Example: disability as a result of war or an act of war, declared or not.

exclusive agency system: See *captive agent*.

executive bonus: A premium paying arrangement for which a deduction is allowable under Section 162 of the Internal Revenue Code for a salary bonus to the insured with which to pay the disability policy premium.

expediting expenses: In business interruption and boiler & machinery policies, expenses to speed up repair or replacement.

expense incurred: A method under which daily benefit amounts are paid based on the actual expenses incurred for the necessary long-term care service.

expense ratio: The dollar amount that represents acquisition and service costs, expressed as a percentage of written premium.

experience: A record of losses.

experience modification: The raising or lowering of premiums under terms of an experience rating plan.

experience rating: A method of rating that uses past experience to establish current rates.

experience-rated: The method of setting premium rates for a group risk based on the actual health care utilization history of that group.

explosion: An extended coverage peril and currently a covered peril in nearly every policy of property insurance. The peril remains distinct from steam boiler explosion, which is covered by boiler & machinery insurance.

exposure: Degree of hazard threatening a risk because of external or internal physical conditions.

express authority: Authority that is distinctly, plainly expressed, orally or in writing. The express authority of an insurance agent is given to the agent by the insurer in the contract they each sign. See *actual authority* and *implied authority*.

extended nonowner liability: A personal auto policy endorsement that provides broader liability coverage for specifically named individuals. When attached, it covers nonowned autos furnished for the regular use of an insured, use of vehicles to carry persons or property for a fee, broader coverage for business use of vehicles.

extended period of indemnity: A time for recovery of proved business income loss after physical property is restored and business reopened. The 30-day extension included in many business income forms may be extended by endorsement.

extra expense insurance: Depending on an insured's requirements, this coverage may be purchased as a supplement to business income insurance, applying to expediting expenses that aid in quickly restoring the insured's operations after a covered loss, or it can be the primary coverage sustaining the extra cost of continuing doing business for those insureds who would find it extremely damaging to fail to meet customer commitments, such as newspapers and dairies.

face of policy: The front of the policy on which normally the name of the insurance company, the name of the insured, the amount of insurance and the type of insurance appear among many other items.

facility: A pooling mechanism for insureds not able to obtain insurance in the voluntary market. Insurers write and issue policies but cede premium and losses on those policies to a central pool in which all insurers share.

factory mutual: A mutual insurance company insuring only properties that meet high underwriting standards. The typical risk is fire-resistive construction with a central station alarm.

facultative reinsurance: A separate reinsurance agreement that is negotiated for a particular risk or insurance policy.

Fair Credit Reporting Act: Public Law 91-508 requires that an insurer tell an applicant if a consumer report may be requested. The applicant must also be told the scope of the possible investigation. Should the application be declined because of information contained in that report, the applicant must be given the name and address of the reporting agency. The insurer may not reveal the contents of the report. Only the agency that compiled the report may release its contents.

fair market value: Price at which a buyer and seller, under no compulsion to buy or sell, will trade.

FAIR plan: An acronym for Fair Access to Insurance Requirements, these plans have been established in many states to make fire and extended coverage (and homeowners in some states) available in areas otherwise not addressed by the voluntary market.

fair rental value: An amount payable to an insured homeowner for loss of rental income due to damage that makes the premises uninhabitable.

farmowners-ranchowners policy: A homeowners type package policy adapted to include farm and ranch exposures.

federal crop insurance: A comprehensive coverage at rates subsidized by the federal government for unavoidable crop losses.

Federal Emergency Management Agency (FEMA): This agency administers the National Flood Insurance

Program, providing disaster relief in floods, earthquakes, etc.

fee simple basis: A form of ownership in which the owner has full rights to dispose of the property held. Common within homeowner associations.

fee-for-service: The traditional way to pay for medical care. Patients see any doctor and use any hospital. Providers are reimbursed based on the fees they charge. Insured pays a deductible and co-payment and insurer pays the balance.

fellow employee coverage: Extends Bodily Injury coverage to one employee when caused by another.

fidelity bond: See *employee dishonesty coverage.*

fiduciary: A generic term for persons or legal entities such as executors, trustees, and guardians appointed by the court, under a will, or by a trust to manage, control, or dispose of the property of others.

fiduciary bonds: Bonds that guarantee an honest accounting and faithful performance of duties by administrators, trustees, guardians, executors, and other fiduciaries. Fiduciary bonds, in some cases referred to as probate bonds, are required by statutes, courts, or legal documents for the protection of those on whose behalf a fiduciary acts. They are needed under a variety of circumstances, including the administration of an estate and the management of affairs of a trust or a ward. See *judicial bonds.*

fiduciary liability insurance: This insurance covers claims arising from a breach of the responsibilities or duties imposed on a benefit plan administrator; or a negligent act, error, or omission of the administrator.

field underwriting: The process by which an agent conducts his own evaluation of the prospect through the thorough completion of an application for insurance on the prospect's behalf.

file and use rating laws: State laws that permit the use of new rates by an insurance company without first obtaining the approval of that state's insurance department.

financial responsibility clause: The clause in an auto policy stating that, when the policy is certified as future proof of financial responsibility, the policy will comply with the financial responsibility laws to the extent required.

financial responsibility law: When applied to automobile operations, this term signifies the minimum statutory limits of an operator's responsibility for bodily injury and property damage caused by negligent operation of the vehicle.

financial underwriting: A method of evaluating data relevant to earned income, unearned income, net worth, fringe benefits, and other components of compensation to determine the proper amount of monthly benefit for which the insured qualifies.

fire: Combustion evidenced by a flame or glow. Insurance distinguishes between a hostile fire (one out of bounds) and friendly fire (such as that contained within the fire box of a stove).

fire department service charge: A fee that may be imposed by a fire department for responding to a call. Most fire coverage agreements include indemnification provisions for such eventualities.

fire legal liability: Public liability policies routinely exclude coverage for damage to property in an insured's care, custody, or control. This leaves a big gap in a tenant's coverage, a gap partially filled by an exception in the commercial general liability policy that restores limited coverage for fire damage to the landlord's building. Perhaps the best benefit of the exception is to call attention to the exposure so arrangements can be made for broader coverage at appropriate limits.

first named insured: An insurance policy may have more than one party named as insured. In such cases, the first named insured attends to policy housekeeping, that is, pays premiums, initiates (or receive notice of) cancellation, or calls for interim changes in the contract. This is spelled out in commercial policies in the common policy conditions.

fixtures: Generally, something tangible that is fixed or attached, as to a building, so that it becomes an appendage or structural part.

flesch test: A method to determine the degree of ease or difficulty for reading material. It counts not only the number of words in a sentence, but also the number of syllables in each word. Some states require that insurance contracts be written so that they have a certain readability level (often, 8th grade).

flexible benefits: Under a Cafeteria Plan, these are the qualifying selected benefits that the insured may choose among on a pretax basis. Disability income is a qualifying flexible benefit.

flood: A general and temporary condition of partial or complete inundation of dry land caused by the overflow of the natural boundaries of a body of water or the unusual and rapid accumulation of surface water runoff. Some insurance policies that include flood as a covered peril only insure against damage caused by overflow of the natural boundaries of a body of water, but other policies also may insure against surface water losses.

flood insurance: Flood insurance, like earthquake coverage, is usually only of interest to those relatively few whose property is exposed. Consequently, losses among this small group will be high and premiums can be prohibitive. However, in 1968 the federal government stepped in to help property owners in designated flood plains with the National Flood Insurance Act of 1968. Coverage is not only available, but may even be required to obtain financing for exposed properties.

flood insurance rate map (FIRM): Provided by FEMA (Federal Emergency Management Agency), this map delineates base flood elevations and flood risk zones, and is used for rating purposes for flood insurance.

floodplain: Any land area susceptible to being inundated by flood waters from any source.

floorplan insurance: A form of insurance covering merchandise held for sale by a retailer which has been used as collateral for a loan. The lending institution, in effect, is insuring its collateral the merchandise "on the floor" of the retailer.

forced place insurance: Insurance purchased by a bank or creditor on an uninsured debtor's behalf so if the property is damaged, funding is available to repair it.

foreign insurance company: Name given to an insurance company based in one state by the other states in which it does business.

forgery or alteration coverage: This type of insurance covers loss sustained through forgery or alteration of outgoing negotiable instruments made or drawn by the insured; drawn on the insured's account(s), or made or drawn by someone acting as the insured's agent. This includes loss caused by any of the following: checks or drafts made or drawn in the insured's name, payable to a fictitious entity; checks or drafts, including payroll checks, executed through forged endorsements; and alteration of the amount of a check or draft.

form: The central document or documents of an insurance contract. Forms may be altered by endorsement.

franchise deductible: Deductible in which the insurer has no liability if the loss is under a certain amount, but once this amount is exceeded, the entire loss is paid in full.

fraud: The intentional perversion of the truth in order to mislead someone into parting with something of value.

free on board (F.O.B.): When goods are shipped F.O.B., the shipper is responsible only until the goods have been placed on board the vessel or freight car or truck or other means of transport. After that the risk belongs to the consignee.

fronting: The practice, in reinsurance, of the ceding company retaining only a small portion of a risk and ceding the remainder to a reinsurer.

full reporting clause: Under this clause, an insured is required to report values periodically. The clause provides for a penalty to the insured if true values are not reported.

functional replacement cost: The cost to repair or replace damaged property with materials that are *functionally* the equivalent of the damaged or destroyed property. For example: replacing a solid mahogany banister with a pine banister.

GAAP accounting: Generally Accepted Accounting Principles as promulgated by the Financial Accounting Standards Board (FASB). See *statutory accounting principles*.

gainful work: As defined under Total Disability, any job for which the insured is reasonably qualified to perform in accordance with education, training and experience and usually with due regard to prior income.

GAP coverage: Guaranteed Auto Protection. Insurance for a lessee designed to cover the difference in selling price between a vehicle's actual cash value, and the payout left on a lease.

garage policy: One of the early package policies, it is written for automobile dealers and may include liability insurance for garage operations, automobile operations, physical damage coverage on garage owned autos, bailees coverage on customers cars, and auto and premises medical payments coverage.

gatekeeper: Role description of the primary care physician who serves to control utilization and referral of plan members.

general liability insurance: See *commercial general liability*.

general partners' liability coverage: A general partner's management and fiduciary responsibilities to a limited partnership closely parallel the director's or officer's to a corporation. Exposure occurs when general partners become the financial managers of a limited partnership. The directors and officers of corporate general partners share this type of exposure.

geriatric case manage:. An individual assigned to handle the various needs of a person unable to do for themselves. This qualified individual can coordinate every aspect of an aging adult's care from interviewing and hiring household help to paying bills, and often serves as the eyes and ears of other family members not located in the immediate area.

glass insurance: Commercial property form that covers plate glass, glass signs, lettering, etc.

good faith: Most ordinary contracts are good faith contracts. Insurance contracts are agreements made in the utmost good faith. This implies a standard of honesty greater than that usually required in most ordinary commercial contracts.

good student discount: The reduction of an automobile premium for a young driver who ranks in the upper percent of their class.

grace period: A period after the premium due date, during which an overdue premium may be paid without penalty. The policy remains in force throughout this period.

grading schedule for cities and towns: A schedule prepared by the National Board of Fire Underwriters for the purpose of determining which of ten grades to assign to a city for fire rating purposes, based on such factors of fire protection as water supply.

graduated driver licenses: Licenses for younger drivers that allow them to improve their skills. Regulations vary by state, but often restrict night time driving. Young drivers receive a learner's permit, followed by a provisional license, before they can receive a standard drivers license.

Gramm-Leach-Bliley Act: Financial services legislation, passed by Congress in 1999, that removed Depression-era prohibitions against the combination of commercial banking and investment-banking activities. It allows insurance companies, banks, and securities firms to engage in each others' activities and own one another.

gross earnings coverage: An outdated term for business income coverage.

gross earnings: Income, before business expenses are deducted and taxes are applied.

gross negligence: The degree of negligence somewhat greater than ordinary negligence. It may be a reckless wanton and willful misconduct causing bodily injury and/or property damage.

group LTD: Disability income coverage issued as a master policy to an employer to provide benefits for employees in the event of a long-term disability. The minimum Elimination Period is usually 90 days with benefits often paid until age 70.

guarantee funds: State mandated funds collected from licensed insurers and maintained as backup protection for policyholders of bankrupt insurers.

guarantee of insurability: An optional benefit in a disability income policy that allows the insured future increases to the policy monthly benefit at specified dates, with a requirement of only financial (and not medical) insurability.

guaranteed renewable: The renewal provision of a disability income or long-term care insurance policy, ensuring that the policy cannot be canceled by the insurer nor can policy provisions be changed without the insured's consent. Policy premiums, however, may be adjusted upward based on the company's experience for an entire class of business.

guaranteed replacement cost: A form of property coverage in which the insurance company agrees to replace damaged property even if the cost to do so exceeds the limit stated in the policy or the underlying rating basis on which the premium is calculated. This extension may be conditional on an approved appraisal and reporting of improvements to the building(s).

guiding principles: Suggested procedures for establishing primacy of coverage in situations involving loss under a variety of coverage forms and, perhaps, more than one interested party. Last promulgated in the 1960s, the spirit of the principles survives because insurers apparently find that the prescribed procedures commonly lead to equitable settlements for all parties.

hacker insurance: A coverage that protects businesses engaged in electronic commerce from losses caused by hackers.

hard market: A condition of the insurance marketplace in which insurance is difficult to obtain and relatively expensive.

hazard: Generally, a condition that increases the possibility of loss.

hazardous waste: Term generally used to refer to pollutants or contaminants that result from industrial processing and must be disposed.

health care surrogate: An individual designated in a medical durable power of attorney to make medical decisions on behalf of another person.

Health Insurance Portability and Accountability Act (HIPAA): This federal legislation, passed in 1996, clarified the tax treatment of long-term care insurance, defining the parameters under which benefits and expenses are received tax-free.

highly protected risk (HPR): A building meeting certain standards of fire protection, which is therefore eligible for a reduced rate.

hired auto: A nonowned auto that may be borrowed as well as rented or leased by the insured. Personal auto policy insureds are covered automatically for hired autos, but business auto policy insureds may not be.

HMO: Organization that provides for a wide range of comprehensive health care services for a specified group of enrollees in exchange for a fixed, periodic pre-payment. There are several different models of HMO varying by consumer choice and cost.

hold back: When a replacement cost policy is triggered due to a loss, most policies pay the actual cash value of the lost or damaged articles immediately and then the full replacement cost once the repair or replacement is done. The differences between these two limits is called a hold back.

hold harmless agreement: A contractual assumption by one party of the liability exposure of another. Lease agreements, for example, commonly require the tenant to hold the landlord harmless for bodily injury or property damage experienced by others on the premises.

home care: This is a type of long-term care service, provided in the home, generally consists of activities of daily living assistance, and is rendered by a trained aide.

home health care agency: An organization providing home health care or home care, state licensed or accredited as required, keeps clinical records of all patients, and is supervised by a qualified physician or registered nurse.

home health care: A program of professional, paraprofessional, and skilled care usually provided through a home health care agency to a person at home. This care is often prescribed by a physician as medically necessary and can include nursing services, physical, speech, respiratory, and occupational therapy.

homeowners insurance: An early and hugely successful example of packaged property and liability insurance. A mid-twentieth century insurance development was introduction of the so-called multi-line era in which insurers became empowered to write both property and liability forms of insurance, making way for the first packaging of these coverages within a single policy.

hospice care: A coordinated program for control of pain and symptoms for the terminally ill, which may also provide support services to family members.

host liquor liability: Part of the CGL, this covers the incidental serving of alcohol by an insured who is not in the business of serving alcohol.

housekeeping: A generalized term that refers to the overall care, cleanliness, and maintenance of an insured's property.

HPR: See *highly protected risk*.

identity fraud: The act of assuming another person's identity in order to gain access to a person's bank accounts or other personal financial information.

impaired property: A liability exclusion relating to the insured's faulty products or work that results in an impairment to the property to which it is attached assuming the insured can salvage the situation by replacing the property or redoing the work.

implied authority: Authority granted to an agent, even though not stated, that lets the agent perform tasks usual and necessary to exercise the agent's express authority. See *actual authority* and *express authority*.

implied warranty: A warranty is a representation by the policyholder that certain conditions exist or will be met. Even if the warranty is not in writing, it may exist as an "implied" warranty, e.g., that a building is not on fire when insured, or that a vessel is seaworthy.

improvements and betterments: Anything that adds to the value of property. Commonly used to describe a tenant's use interest in fixtures added to the landlord's building. May also refer to permanent changes made by a condominium unitowner to his or her unit, such as the addition of new kitchen cabinets.

imputed negligence: Case in which responsibility for damage can be transferred from the negligent party to another person, such as an employer.

incendiary: Malicious setting on fire or preparing, providing and setting the means for fire to start.

incidental medical malpractice: A portion of the CGL policy that is triggered if a covered party or the Association were to be sued because they tried to provide "Good Samaritan" help or other medical first aid type care and were not professionals in the medical field.

increased hazard: Property Insurance policies provide that coverage shall be suspended when the hazard in a risk is increased beyond that contemplated when the insurance was written. If a dwelling owner commences manufacturing dynamite in his home, the hazard is extremely increased, and coverage could be denied by the insurer if there were a loss.

incurred but not reported losses / IBNR: Losses that are not reported to the insurer or reinsurer until years after the policy is sold. Liability claims may be filed long after the event that caused the injury to occur. Asbestos-related diseases, for example, do not show up until decades after the exposure. Also, estimates made about claims already reported but where the full extent of the injury or property damage is not yet known. Insurance companies regularly adjust reserves for such losses as new information becomes available.

incurred losses: The value of claim payments plus reserves.

indemnity: A fundamental concept governing insurance: compensation for loss or injury sustained.

independent adjuster: An individual or member of a firm who contracts with insurers to investigate claims and suggest appropriate settlements. Contrast with *Public adjuster*.

independent agent: A retailer of insurance who, by contractual arrangement with a number of insurance companies, sells and services property and liability insurance. The independent agent owns the policy in-

formation and expiration dates of his client's coverage and thus controls renewals and their placement.

Independent Insurance Agents of America (IIAA): An association of insurance agents who are independent contractors, and represent one or more insurers. Sometimes referred to as the Big I.

Independent Practice Association (IPA): Another HMO model, the organization contracts with networks of independent providers who are paid an annual fixed sum or a per-visit fee for each enrollee. Members are covered only when using HMO doctors and designated hospitals. The providers can maintain a separate practice and see other patients.

indirect damage: Sometimes referred to as indirect loss, this is loss resulting from a peril but not directly caused by that peril. An example is fire damaging a freezer (direct damage), with resultant food spoilage (indirect damage).

inflation guard endorsement: An endorsement attached to an insurance policy whereby the limits of liability on a piece of property are increased on a regular basis by a certain percentage in order to offset increasing building costs associated with inflation.

inflation protection benefit: This optional benefit is designed to help preserve the value of the daily benefit amount. It automatically increases the daily benefit annually on a simple or compounded basis either by a stipulated percentage amount or an index measurement.

inherent vice: A flaw in an item of property that will, in time, reveal itself and show the property as damaged. Property insurance does not normally cover such damage.

inland marine insurance: Property insurance signalling broad coverage of properties exposed to the transportation peril and those subject to being used or kept at a location other than the insured's customary premises. Eligible property is identified in the *Nationwide Definition of Marine Insurance*.

insolvency: Insurer's inability to pay debts. Insurance insolvency standards and the regulatory actions taken vary from state to state, but the last resort in the case of insolvency is liquidation.

insolvency fund: See *guarantee funds*.

installment option: In a Disability Buy-Sell policy, this policy provision offers an alternative payout to a lump-sum settlement by having the insurance company pay out a level benefit in monthly installments for a specified period of time.

institutional property: Schools, churches and many non-profit operations are covered under special policies more cheaply if they qualify.

instrumental activities of daily living (IADLs): These are primarily homemaker services such as preparing meals, shopping, managing money, using the telephone, doing housework, and taking medication.

insurable interest: The potential for financial loss associated with damage or destruction of property.

insurable risk: The exposure to significant, measurable accidental loss from identifiable perils. The exposure, while not catastrophic, must be shared by a sufficient number of potential insureds so that the cost of loss for one can be measured and affordably shared throughout the market.

insurance: A mechanism whereby risk of financial loss is transferred from an individual, company, organization, or other entity to an insurance company.

insurance contract: A legal document defining circumstances under which the insurer will pay, and the amount to be paid. Also see *insurance policy*.

Insurance Crime Prevention Bureau (I.C.P.B.): An organization supported by property and casualty insurers that investigates fraudulent insurance claims and provides a deterrent to such losses. Loss prevention information is maintained by the Bureau for use by member insurers, independent claims adjusters and government authorities across the country.

insurance examiner: The representative of a state insurance department assigned to participate in the official audit and examination of the affairs of an insurance company.

insurance exchange: Term used to describe a facility that exists in a few states to provide a market for reinsurance and for the insurance of large and unusual domestic and foreign risks that are difficult to insure in the normal markets. Examples are the New York Insurance Exchange, the Insurance Exchange of the Americas, and the Illinois Insurance Exchange.

Insurance Institute of America (IIA): An institution offering a variety of insurance diplomas after the successful completion of certain examinations.

insurance policy: The document containing the contract between the insured and the insurer that defines the rights and duties of the contracting parties.

insurance pool: A group of insurance companies that pool assets, enabling them to provide an amount of insurance substantially more than can be provided by individual companies to ensure large risks such as nuclear power stations. Pools may be formed voluntarily or mandated by the state to cover risks that can't obtain coverage in the voluntary market such as coastal properties subject to hurricanes.

Insurance Services Office (ISO): An organization providing statistical information, actuarial analyses, policy language, and related services for the insurance industry.

insurance to value: The concept of purchasing sufficient insurance coverage so as to closely approximate the value of the property being insured.

insured: The party or parties whose interests are covered in a nonlife insurance contract. The less common term *Assured* is sometimes used synonymously.

insuring agreement: In an insurance contract, the insurer's promise to pay.

integrated risk financing: A type of risk financing designed to provide integrated protection against catastrophic losses. It may incorporate both traditional and nontraditional types of exposures, or it may include only traditional property and casualty risks.

intermediate care facility: An institution licensed by the state to provide patient care for those requiring constant availability and support, but very little in the way of skilled care. This facility may also provide custodial care services.

intermediate care: Occasional nursing services, preventive or rehabilitative, performed under the supervision of skilled medical personnel.

internet liability insurance: Coverage designed to protect businesses from liabilities that arise from the conducting of business over the Internet, including copyright infringement, defamation, and violation of privacy.

investment income: Income generated by the investment of assets. Insurers have two sources of income, underwriting (premiums less claims and expenses) and investment income. The latter can offset underwriting operations, which are frequently unprofitable.

jacket: The cover of an insurance policy; it usually contains information such as the name and address of the insurer.

joint and several liability: A legal doctrine whereby a creditor or claimant may demand payment or sue one or more of the parties separately, or all of them together.

joint loss agreement: An endorsement that speeds up payment of insurance proceeds when there are two different carriers for the property and the boiler and machinery coverage and there is a disagreement as to the amount of loss to be paid by each carrier.

joint tenancy: Ownership of property shared equally by two or more parties under which the survivor assumes complete ownership. This is different from a tenancy in common where the heirs of a deceased party to the tenancy inherit his or her share.

Joint Underwriting Association (JUA): These are insurance pools representing all insurers in a state. A few servicing carriers act on behalf of all the insurers, issuing policies, receiving fees, and handling claims. They are reimbursed for losses, and receive fees from the JUA to cover operating costs.

judgment rating: Rate-making method for which each exposure is individually evaluated and the rate is determined largely by the underwriter's judgment.

jumbo risk: A policy of insurance written with exceptionally high limits.

Keeton-O'Connell: See *no fault auto insurance*.

key person policy: A product designed to reimburse the business for financial loss during the key person's disability until recovery or a suitable replacement can be found.

lapse: Termination of a policy because of failure to pay the premium.

larceny: The unlawful taking of personal property of another.

latent defect: A hidden flaw that will, in time, cause property damage that is uninsurable. Such damage is uninsurable because the element of chance is no longer present.

law of large numbers: An underlying principle of insurance; the larger the number of participants in a given arrangement, the more accurate the rate is to the exposure.

leader location: A location that attracts customers to the insured's business. One of the four types of dependent properties for which Business Income coverage may be written.

leased worker: A worker leased from another organization on a long-term basis.

leasehold interest insurance: The insurable interest is that of a tenant who has some years remaining under a favorable lease that is subject to termination upon significant damage to the leased property.

legal expense insurance: Insurance to reimburse policyholders for legal fees incurred for defense from lawsuits involving areas of civil law not covered by standard liability insurance. For example: discrimination, wrongful discharge, contract disputes, and patient disputes.

legal liability: Liability imposed by law, including liability based on negligence, strict liability, or contractual liability.

lessee: The person to whom a lease is granted, commonly called the tenant.

lessor: The person granting a lease, also known as the landlord.

leverage, or capitalization: Measures the exposure of a company's surplus to various operating and financial practices. A highly leveraged, or poorly capitalized, company can show a high return on surplus, but may be exposed to a high risk of instability.

libel: Written defamation of another's reputation.

liberalization clause: A feature of property policies that promises that any future change in the company's form that would broaden coverage with no change in premium will automatically apply under the policy currently in force.

license and permit bonds: Suretyship guaranteeing that the principal will abide by the rules and obligations imposed by licensing laws or ordinances. For example, an electrician may have to post such a bond guaranteeing compliance with building codes before being licensed by a municipality.

lien: A charge upon real or personal property as security for some debt or duty. Also, the security interest created by a mortgage. The conditions of an insurance policy require the disclosure to the insurer of any existing lien on the insured property.

life insurance-based long-term care insurance: This is a form of long-term care coverage where benefits are wrapped inside a life insurance policy. Benefits can be provided for both long-term care insurance and death, with cash values also available for withdrawal.

life settlements: The sale of a life insurance policy for a portion of its face amount value. A terminal illness is not required here, but instead a life expectancy of 10-15 years or less.

like kind and quality: Refers to replacement of damaged, destroyed or lost property with used property of similar type and condition.

limited common element: A portion of the common elements of a condominium association that is restricted to the use of one or several unit owners. Normally such elements become the maintenance responsibility of the unit owner and may become the owner's insurance responsibility too.

limited contition riders: Utilized by the underwriter, a modification of the full exclusion rider is meant to provide some coverage for a medical condition. Example: The policy will not cover any disease or disorder of the right shoulder for the first 90 days of disability.

limited partnership: A form of partnership that consists of one or more general partners, who actively engage in the business, and one of more special partners, who are not liable for the debts of the partnership beyond their initial financial contribution. Commercial insurance policies usually differentiate in the Who Is Insured section between corporations, partnerships, and other business models. Therefore, the type of model being insured is important.

line: A term used to describe a type or class or kind of insurance in relation to the line of insurance appearing in the Annual Statement (inland marine, auto liability, fidelity).

livery use: An exclusion in automobile liability policies applying to the use of autos to carry persons *for hire* as in a taxi service. A share-the-ride car pool is not livery use.

living benefit rider: An optional benefit available to be added to life insurance policies that pays out a portion of the death proceeds in advance due to the insured's catastrophic and/or terminal illness.

Lloyd's of London: An association of individuals, called names, or groups of individuals who write insurance for their own accounts. Lloyd's had its beginning in 17th century London in Edward Lloyd's coffeehouse.

Lloyds syndicate: A group of underwriters at London Lloyds who entrust the underwriting of their business to one underwriter.

loading and unloading exclusion: A feature of commercial general liability (CGL) policies intended to separate that coverage from the automobile exposure. The CGL coverage ends at the point where an item is picked up for loading onto an auto and resumes at the point where the item is deposited upon unloading.

long distance caregiving: A difficult position in caring for a family member while located in another area and not available for day to day assistance.

long tail: Refers to liability under policies written on an occurrence basis. Claims stemming from injury or damage occurring years earlier can be presented for coverage long after the policy has expired. Contrast with *Claims-made*.

long-term care insurance: A specific type of insurance policy designed to offer financial support in paying for necessary long-term care services rendered in a variety of settings.

long-term care rider: This is an optional benefit that can be added to a life insurance, annuity, or disability income policy to provide benefits for long-term care.

loss: An unintentional decline or disappearance in value arising from an event.

loss adjustment expenses: Payments by an insurer for the investigation and settling of claims. They include the cost of defending a lawsuit in court.

loss assessment coverage: Insurance responding to property or liability losses of a property owners association that are not covered by the association's master policy.

loss avoidance: A risk management technique whereby a situation or activity that may result in a loss for a firm is avoided or abandoned.

loss control: Actions to reduce the frequency or severity of losses. Installing locks, burglar or fire alarms, and sprinkler systems are loss control techniques.

loss control representative: Insurance company employees who perform loss control surveys or inspections, and prepare written loss control reports outlining their findings. Also referred to as safety engineers.

loss costs: Loss data that has been modified by insurance advisory organizations by necessary loss development, trending, and credibility processes in order to arrive at the statistical cost of losses to be used in establishing a premium rate.

loss development: An actuarial method to detect and correct for consistent errors in estimating the amount of future loss payments <u>or</u> the procedure for adjusting incurred losses to reflect their future development and ultimate value. Loss development factors are developed actuarially and applied to current losses in order to predict what the ultimate cost of losses will be when the claims are closed.

loss expectancy: The underwriter's calculation of probable maximum loss.

loss experience: What the loss history has been on a particular line or book of business.

loss exposure: A set of circumstances presenting the possibility of loss, whether or not the loss actually occurs.

loss frequency: How often a loss occurs over a given space of time.

loss limit: Commonly used in financial institution bonds, a loss limit is the aggregate amount that will be paid out under the coverage during the policy term. Loss limits also may be used when insuring large property risks where the exposures are spread out geographically. In this type of situation, it is unlikely that all property would be damaged by a single occurrence. Therefore, the amount of insurance may be set at a loss limit per each covered occurrence.

loss of maintenance fees coverage: This coverage protects a condominium association against the loss of maintenance fees when occupancies have been interrupted or impaired by the occurrence of any insured peril. This is a form of business interruption insurance for the association. It assures continuous income while the building is untenantable.

loss payable clause: A property policy provision that, at the request of the named insured, stipulates that claims tied to losses of certain property will be paid to both the named insured and the party named in the subject clause.

loss payout pattern: Losses often are paid over a period of years, especially in casualty lines of insurance. The payout pattern illustrates the way that claims are paid out from the time they are filed until they are closed.

loss prevention: Refers to engineering or inspection activities carried out to prevent losses in the workplace.

loss ratio: The ratio of incurred losses including loss adjustment expenses to earned premiums.

loss reserves: The company's best estimate of what it will pay for claims, which is periodically readjusted. They represent a liability on the insurer's balance sheet.

loss runs: A company produced statement of what losses have been filed for a particular insurance policy during a particular time period. Such information may or may not include information on reserves and loss adjustment costs. Typically provision of such information is mandated by State Law.

loss trending: A method to modify developed losses for changes that will occur in the future. Trend factors are used by rate makers to adjust past losses to more accurately reflect the loss experience expected to develop while the rates are being used.

loss triangle: Used to show how losses develop, a loss triangle is a chart that lists losses by line and by year. It shows the value of each set of annual losses at the end of subsequent 12-month periods.

lost policy release: A means whereby an insured may cancel a policy by signing a statement to the effect that, since his or her policy has been lost, he cannot return it to the insurer to effect cancellation, but still wishes to cancel the policy.

lump-sum payment: In a Disability Buy-Sell policy, benefits are usually payable in a lump-sum at the trigger (or effective) date of the buy-sell. The trigger date is the day following expiration of the elimination period.

managed care: A type of claims management system for long-term care insurance policies using pre-selected providers who have agreed to treat insurance company claimants on a reduced cost basis.

managing general agent (MGA): An agent standing between an insurer and other agents. The MGA sells to retail agents, who then sell to the consumer. MGA's often are said to have the pen because they are given the authority to accept, underwrite, and price submissions received from retail agents.

mandated benefits: Benefits that a health plan is required to provide by law. These are generally benefits that are above and beyond the routine insured provisions in a health plan. These benefits vary by state to state. Common examples include in-vitro fertilization, chiropractic care, and mental and nervous disorder in- and out-patient care. The number of mandated benefits can dictate the price of the policy.

manuscript policy: An insurance policy covering property or liability exposures (or both) that is uniquely assembled from standard or specially created forms to suit the needs of an insured.

market value: The price at which insured property could have been sold just prior to its loss or damage. Along with cost new minus use deprecation, market value is but another gauge used to determine the loss settlement to which an insured is entitled. The insured may choose the gauge that produces the most favorable outcome.

market value appraisal: An appraisal to determine the market value of a building and related personal property.

mass merchandising: Plan for insuring individual members of a group, such as employees of firms or members of labor unions, under a single program of insurance at reduced premiums. Property and liability insurance is sold to individual members using group insurance marketing methods.

material circumstances: Any circumstances that would influence the judgment of a prudent underwriter in determining whether to accept a risk and the amount of premium to change.

material representation: A statement made to the underwriter before acceptance of risk that is material to the decision in accepting and rating the risk.

McCarran-Ferguson Act: Passed by Congress in 1945, this act states that regulation and taxation of insurance by the states is in the public interest, and that congressional silence should not be construed as a barrier to state regulation.

medicaid: The joint federal and state welfare program administered by the states to provide payment for health care services, including long-term care, for those meeting minimum asset and income requirements.

medical loss ratio: The difference between the cost to deliver medical care and the amount of money taken in by the plan. This can dictate future premium costs of the health plan.

medical malpractice: Type of insurance protecting physicians, surgeons, nurses, and other medical practitioners against claims alleging failure to perform.

medical payments insurance: A coverage found in auto and liability policies that pays medical expenses to injured persons without regard to liability.

medical underwriting: The process of evaluating a disability income application for approval by reviewing the potential insured's individual health history.

medicare: Federal program organized under the Health Insurance for the Aged Act, Title XVIII of the Social Security Amendments of 1965, it provides hospital and medical expense benefits, including long-term care services, for those individuals over age 65 or those meeting specific disability standards.

mercantile risk: A term most often used in Property Insurance meaning a retail or wholesale risk as contrasted with a service risk, a manufacturing risk, or a habitational risk.

merit rating: A form of auto rating in which an insured's past experience as well as anticipated experience is taken into account when arriving at a rate.

minimum premium: An insurer's lowest charge for an insurance policy.

minimum residual benefit: During the first six months of a claim under the residual disability provision, this benefit stipulates that the minimum benefit payable to the insured will be no less than 50% of the total disability benefit. Note: Some carriers are applying this benefit for longer than the first six months.

misrepresentation: Generally, misstatement of facts made on an application for insurance. May also be misstatement of coverage made by an agent to an insured.

mobile equipment: Included for coverage under the commercial general liability form, this term relates to land vehicles used in ways that take them out of an explicit automobile liability exposure (e.g., vehicles used only on the insured premises, to carry certain permanently attached equipment, that are not required to be registered, or are designed for solely for off-road use).

model bill: A bill drawn up for insurance regulatory purposes by the National Association of Insurance Commissioners with the recommendation that it be implemented by the states.

money and securities (broad form) rider: A broad form of policy protecting against loss of money or securities. There is no coverage for losses caused by, among other things, employee infidelity.

monoline policy: An insurance policy covering one subject of insurance, as opposed to a combination or multiline policy.

monopolistic state fund: Five states have their own system for providing reparations to injured employees eligible under the state's workers compensation act. Private insurance companies may not compete. The states are North Dakota, Ohio, Washington, West Virginia, and Wyoming.

moral hazard: As physical hazard relates to susceptibility to fire or wind, the term moral hazard relates to susceptibility to loss through moral lapse of the owner (e.g., burn the house down and collect from the insurance company before losing it in a foreclosure to the finance company.).

mortgage holders clause: A standard property policy provision that creates elements of a separate contract between a mortgage company and an insurance company. Any loss to building or structures will be paid to the mortgage company and insured jointly and any act of the insured voiding coverage will not affect the mortgage holder without it first being given an opportunity to comply with the insurer's needs.

motor vehicle record (MVR): An official record of a driver's accidents and traffic violations kept by the licensing state(s). Often used to determine eligibility and/or premiums for auto insurance.

mutual insurance company: A cooperative insurance company organized and owned by its insureds.

mysterious disappearance: A named peril in some forms. Either theft or unexplained disappearance of covered property from a known location may activate coverage.

NAIC model policy: Recommended minimum long-term care policy standards as designated by the insurance industry watchdog, the National Association of Insurance Commissioners (NAIC), originally established in 1988 and amended thereafter. States have the choice to adopt part, all, or none of the standards for their own regulation. HIPAA legislation, passed by Congress in 1996, re-defined some of the provisions of the model policy.

NAIC suitability. This amendment to the NAIC Model Policy requires insurers and agents to seek the most appropriate buyers for long-term care insurance by requiring applicants to complete a Personal Worksheet on finances and, among other requirements, to disclose the company's rate increase history.

named insured: The party or parties specifically named as insured in the insurance contract. Others may have claim on the coverage of a policy by way of internal provisions, but any such right is by way of the agreement between the named insured and the insurance company.

named nonowner policy: Issued to someone who does not own an automobile but who drives borrowed or rented autos.

named perils: A formal and specific listing of perils covered in a policy providing property insurance. A policy covering for damage by fire is said to cover for the named peril of fire.

named schedule bond: A fidelity bond that covers persons listed or scheduled on the bond.

National Association of Independent Insurers (NAII): An advisory organization and statistical agent for insurers, with a membership including hundreds of casualty and surety companies of all types throughout the U.S.

National Association of Insurance Commissioners (NAIC): An association of insurance commissioners and superintendents formed to share information and develop common laws and procedures for insurance regulatory purposes.

National Association of Insurance Women (NAIW): An international association of women (and men) in the insurance industry. NAIW offers the designations of Certified Professional Insurance Woman (CPIW) or Man (CPIM).

National Association of Professional Surplus Lines Offices (NAPSLO): Trade association of and providing services to surplus and excess lines agents and brokers.

National Flood Insurance Program (NFIP): A federal program through which persons with property located in predefined flood plains can obtain flood coverage. See *flood insurance*.

negligence: Action or failure to act that is outside the realm of what would be considered appropriate by ordinary, reasonably prudent persons.

net income: The total after-tax earnings generated from operations and realized capital gains as reported in the company's NAIC annual statement page 4, line 16.

net loss: The amount of a loss, after deductions for salvage, other insurance, and any subrogation, that an insurer is responsible for.

net premium: Premium less expense, such as commission.

net worth: The total nonbusiness related assets of an insured used in the financial evaluation of the disability insurance application. For disability buy-sell policies, net worth is that of the business and is used in the calculation of the value of the owner's interest.

network model HMO: A type of HMO that contracts with a variety of medical groups to serve some geographic location – a multiple provider arrangement.

New York standard fire policy: Once the benchmark of property policies, it was adopted for use in all but a handful of states. The familiar provisions of its 165-numbered-lines–cancellation, mortgagee, appraisal clauses, etc., survive in Insurance Service Office property policies as well as in independently produced forms.

no-fault auto insurance: A few states have laws that partially exempt drivers from legal liability for auto accidents. In these no fault states, car owners buy insurance to protect themselves and their passengers from the economic and medical effects of auto accidents in addition to liability insurance at whatever limit the statute decrees. Professors Robert Keeton and Jeffrey O'Connell gave the no fault notion impetus with the 1967 publication of their study After Cars Crash.

nonadmitted assets: Assets that are not included on the balance sheet, including furniture, fixtures, past-due accounts receivable, and agents' debt balances. (See *assets*.)

nonadmitted insurers: See *excess or surplus lines market*.

noncancelable: The renewal provision of a disability income policy which states that the insurance company cannot change any policy provisions or increase premiums after the policy has been issued as long as the insured makes timely payments of premium.

noneconomic damages: Pain, suffering, inconvenience, loss of consortium, physical impairment, disfigurement, and other nonpecuniary damages.

nonforfeiture benefits: This long-term care insurance policy feature enables the insured to continue long-term care coverage in some form after the insured has ceased making premium payments. A cash return, a paid-up policy, or an extended term feature are typical nonforfeiture benefits.

nonmedical limits: The amount of monthly benefit, at or under which no medical exam is routinely required to apply for disability income coverage. In these circumstances, the proposed insured would answer only the medical questions on the application.

nonowned auto: This term signifies an auto that is neither owned, hired, nor borrowed by the insured under a commercial auto policy. Employees' cars used in company business are commonly classified this way. The employer's auto liability cover for use of nonowned autos is covered by entry of symbol 1 (any auto) or symbol 9 (nonowned autos) on the declarations page.

non-qualified plans: This term refers to all long-term care insurance policies that do not meet the required definitions under HIPAA federal legislation. There could be adverse tax consequences for these plans sold from January 1, 1997 forward.

nonrenewal clause: Provision in a policy that states the circumstances under which an insurer may elect not to renew someone's policy.

nonresident agent: An agent who does not reside in the state in which he or she is licensed.

nonwaiver: An agreement between an insured and an insurer that a claim defense is being undertaken but without agreement that coverage is due. Usually the insured gives up some rights in exchange for the insurer undertaking the defense.

nose coverage: This is the opposite of *Tail coverage*, although it fulfills the same need. Nose coverage most commonly provides prior acts coverage for insureds who are moving from a claims-made coverage form to an occurrence coverage form. It is provided by the replacement policy.

notice of loss: Notice the insured provides to the insurer that a loss has occurred.

nuisance value: The amount for which an insurance company will settle a claim - not because it is a valid claim but because the company considers it worth that amount to dispose of it.

nullification: The act of declaring an insurance contract invalid from its inception so that, from a legal standpoint, the insurance contract never existed.

occupancy: In general, a condition affecting the desirability of property policies.

occupation class: A category of insureds based on specific job duties that dictates the premium and contractual grouping under which the insured would be placed.

occurrence: In general, an event that triggers coverage under any policy. Specifically, an event that triggers coverage under an occurrence-based liability policy. Such a policy covers injury or damage that occurs during the policy period even if claim is brought months or even years after the policy has expired - see *Claims-made* for the alternate arrangement. Also see *accident*.

off premises cover: Commercial property policies commonly establish a small coverage limit that applies to property temporarily away from the insured's place of business.

omnibus clause: An agreement in most automobile liability policies and some others that extends the definition to include others without the needing to name them. An example would be a policy that covers the named insured and those residing with him.

open panel HMO: A type of HMO that contracts directly or indirectly with private physicians to deliver care in their own offices. An IPA would be an example of an open panel HMO.

open perils: Property coverage that applies to risks of loss on a general basis, in contrast with policies that cover for specifically identified perils – see *named perils*. The old term for open perils was all risks.

open rating: A state rating system that allows the insurer to use rates without prior approval. Also referred to as open competition.

operating ratio: The sum of the combined ratio plus investment income.

optional benefit: Coverage in addition to the basic policy, this extra protection assists in the individual design of a disability income program to meet the insured's needs. Examples: cost of living rider, guarantee of insurability benefit.

ordinance or law coverage: This insurance responds to property loss or damage necessitating repair, demolition, or rebuilding in accordance with current building codes.

ordinary payroll: Payroll allotted to employees whose services could be curtailed in event of a long term shutdown of a business without a harmful effect on reopening. This figure is important in calculating business income insurance exposures.

other insurance: When two or more policies cover the same interests for the same exposures, each policy is said to represent other insurance to the other. Most insurance policies contain clauses that specify how or if claims will be paid if other insurance exists for the same exposures.

other than collision insurance (automobile): See *comprehensive physical damage* (automobile).

outline of coverage: A simplified benefit summary of a disability policy provided by the insurance company and required by law in many states to be delivered to the individual insured either at the time of the sales presentation or policy delivery.

out-of-network care: Medical services obtained by managed care plan members from unaffiliated or noncontracted health care providers. In many plans, such care will not be reimbursed unless previous authorization for such care is obtained.

overhead maximum: The total possible benefit payout under the Business Overhead Expense policy, this amount is calculated by multiplying the monthly benefit by the number of months in the selected benefit period. Example: $3,000 monthly benefit, 18 month benefit period would provide an overhead maximum of $54,000 ($3,000 x 18).

own occupation: A term that defines the most liberal wording of the total disability contractual provision, it applies only one test, that of the ability to perform the duties of one's own occupation, in determining disability for purposes of paying a policy benefit.

ownership of expirations: Refers to the ability of an independent agent to place a risk with any of the companies that he or she represents. Unless that customer goes to another agent, the current agent owns the policy and the right to place it as he or she sees fit.

package policy: Any combination of insuring agreements that combines property and casualty coverages. Homeowners, businessowners, and garage policies are examples.

paid losses: The losses that have been paid for a claim.

pair and set clause: Clause that stipulates that partial loss to a pair or set of items will be valued in terms of the lost item, not on the basis of reduced value of the pair or set.

partial disability: A short-term version of residual disability benefits, this policy provision, which also could be available as a rider, pays a specified percentage of the total disability benefit (usually 50%) if the insured is unable to perform one or more of the duties of his own occupation.

partial loss: A property loss that is less than a total loss. See *constructive total loss*.

particular average: A loss that falls on the particular property insured, as opposed to a "general average," which is a loss for the account of all interests. See also *average* and *general average*.

partnership: A business model in which two or more individuals join together to conduct business and share profit and losses. Commercial insurance policies usually differentiate in the Who Is Insured section among corporations, partnerships, and other business models. Therefore, the type of model being insured is important.

pay-at-the-pump: A device for making sure all motorists are insured; the theory being that premiums for basic liability coverage could be collected through taxes at the gasoline pump in a relatively painless manner, thus eliminating the uninsured motorist.

payroll audit: An examination of the insured's payroll records by a representative of the insurer to determine the premium due on a policy for which payroll is the basis.

PD: A shorthand expression for property damage.

per diem business interruption: A type of Business Interruption policy that provides a stated amount to be paid for each day that the business is interrupted due to an insured peril.

per diem: A method for paying the daily benefit amount in a long-term care insurance policy that is based on an elected amount and not on the actual expenses incurred.

per occurrence/per loss excess reinsurance treaty: An agreement under which losses above a certain dollar amount are ceded to the reinsurer, who is responsible for all losses from any one exposure above this amount up to the reinsurance limit. The retention is expressed as an amount incurred per occurrence. An occurrence may be one hurricane, one flood, or one accident that results in injuries to multiple people.

per risk excess reinsurance treaty: Similar to a per occurrence/per loss excess treaty except in the matter of the retention. The retention applies separately to each subject of insurance.

peril: A potential cause of loss.

period of restoration: The period of time following a loss that is necessary to restore a business or organization to a preloss condition.

personal auto policy: The form currently promulgated by Insurance Services Office (ISO) for coverage of personal auto liability and physical damage exposures.

personal effects: The property of an individual covered by the policy in question. Normally refers to items such as clothing, furniture, and jewelry.

personal injury: Distinguished from bodily injury, this term relates to injury inflicted by way of false arrest, invasion of privacy, malicious prosecution, and so on. It is written as Coverage B of the commercial general liability forms and as homeowners Coverage E.

personal injury protection (PIP): The section of an auto policy in a no-fault state that responds to the injuries of the insured such as physical injury, loss of income, etc., of the insured regardless of fault.

personal liability insurance: Insurance for individuals or members of a household offering protection against claims by third parties (outsiders) alleging bodily injury or property damage due to negligence. See also *premises medical payments*.

personal lines: Insurance covering the liability and property damage exposures of private individuals and their households. Contrast with *Commercial lines*.

personal property: Term used in insurance to distinguish chattels from real property.

personal property floater: A broad policy covering all personal property world-wide, including insured's domicile.

personnel replacement expense: An optional benefit that may be added to a Key Person Disability policy, this rider reimburses the business for the costs of searching for and hiring a replacement for the disabled key person.

physical damage: Damage to or loss of the auto resulting from collision, fire, theft or other perils.

physical hazard: A hazard that arises from the material, structural, or operational features of the risk itself apart from the persons owning or managing it.

physician care requirement: This policy provision states one of the eligibility requirements for disability benefits, requiring that the insured be under the regular care and attendance of a physician. Many companies waive this requirement if it can be shown that future treatment would be of no benefit to the insured.

physicians and surgeons professional liability insurance: See *professional liability*.

pilferage: Petty theft, especially theft of articles in less than package lots.

point-of-service plan: A plan where members do not have to choose how to receive services until they need them. This is a hybrid of an HMO and PPO in that it features characteristics of both. There are reimbursement differences depending on how the member elects to receive health care treatment.

policy schedule page: Found in the early pages of a disability income policy, this sheet details all the specific individual policy data such as name, policy number, monthly benefit, and premium.

policy year: Unique to the insurance business, this is a means of cost accumulation in which the aggregate transactions of all policies becoming effective in a given year determine the financial performance of those policies.

Policyholder: See *insured*.

policyholders' surplus: The amount of money available to an insurer to meet its obligations to its policyholders, after subtracting liabilities.

pollution exclusion: Standard general liability policies include an exclusion for loss arising out of pollution. For certain exposures this exclusion may be modified. e.g., "sudden and accidental" pollution arising from a fire.

pollution liability insurance: Coverage for bodily injury or property damage caused by a pollution incident. Insurance Services Office has two forms, one limited to on-site cleanup of pollution spills.

pool: An organization in which insurers cover certain types of risks as a group and share premiums, expenses, and losses. Pools are often used to underwrite larger risks.

pool of money: Under a long-term care insurance program, this is a variation on the typical benefit period. Rather than designate a period of time over which benefits can be payable, this concept creates a lump sum of money to be used as needed during a long-term care claim. The claim ceases when services are no longer needed or the lump sum of money runs out.

portfolio: All of an insurer's in-force policies and outstanding losses, respecting described segments of its business.

power-of-attorney: Commonly used in bonding, this document conveys authority for the individual(s) named on it to execute bonds and other legal documents.

predisability earnings: A policy provision under the residual disability benefit, it defines what constitutes prior income for purposes of calculating the residual benefit. Example: the average monthly earnings for the 12 consecutive months immediately prior to disability.

pre-existing condition: A diagnosed injury or sickness for which medical advice or treatment was sought prior to the effective date of the disability income or long-term care insurance contract.

preferred provider organization: Managed care plan that contracts with independent providers to furnish health care at a discounted rate.

premises: Generally, a piece of land with a building or buildings upon it.

premises and operations liability: Once known as owners, landlords, and tenants legal liability, or as manufacturers and contractors liability, depending on the business's activity, the term refers to the liability exposure of business entities to third parties (customers, guests, and passers by) who may become injured or have property damaged through the negligent acts of the business persons, their agents, or employees. Coverage of this exposure is by way of the commercial general liability policy. Contrast with *Products and completed operations liability*.

premises and operations medical payments: Bodily injury rather than liability is the trigger for this coverage. Sometimes referred to as customer good will insurance, it is a relatively inexpensive addition to the commercial general liability policy and an automatic feature of personal liability protection. Since it responds to injury of customers or guests without regard to fault, it is sometimes effective in heading off a potentially much more serious liability claim against the owner or tenant of the business premises or private residence.

premium: The amount of money the insured pays the insurer to purchase insurance.

premium and dispersion credit: A method of allowing certain credits to large commercial property risks with two or more locations. These credits are based on the fact that there are several locations that are dispersed and, therefore, represent a reduced hazard. Efficiency of management in loss prevention and expense savings in handling large amounts of insurance under one policy are also considered.

premium auditor: A person who examines a liability insurance policyholder's insurance records (sales, payroll, etc.) at the end of the policy term to determine if the basis for the premium charge has either increased or decreased.

premium mode: The particular method of premium payment selected by the insured. The policy can be paid for annually, semi-annually, quarterly or monthly. The choice elected will be indicated in the policy schedule page.

premium tax: A tax, imposed by each state, on the premium income of insurers doing business in the state.

premium to surplus ratio: An insurance company's surplus, the equivalent of capital and retained earnings or net worth for a manufacturing company, is the amount by which assets exceed liabilities. It provides a cushion for absorbing above-average losses. The premium to surplus ratio is designed to measure the adequacy of this cushion or the company's financial strength. The ratio is computed by dividing net premiums written by the surplus. A company that has $2 in net premiums written for every $1 of surplus has a 2-to-1 premium to surplus ratio. The lower the ratio, the greater the company's financial strength. State regulators have es-

tablished as a guideline a premium to surplus ratio no higher than 3 to 1. The average for the property-casualty insurance industry in 1985 was 1.9 to 1.

presumptive total disability: A policy provision that waives the normal total disability eligibility requirements in the event of a catastrophic-type disability such as the loss of sight, hearing, speech, or use of two limbs.

primary insurance: The first policy or coverage to apply. Contrast with *Excess insurance*.

principal: Used in suretyship, it refers to the individual whose performance is guaranteed.

prior approval: Indicates that an insurer must have rate or form changes formally approved by the state insurance department before it can use them

private passenger automobile: A four wheeled motor vehicle, subject to state registration laws, designed to carry passengers (such as a car, station wagon, SUV, or van) on public roads.

pro rata cancellation: See *cancellation*.

probable maximum loss: The maximum amount of loss that one would expect under ordinary circumstances, such as fire departments responding, sprinklers working, etc.

producer: A term identifying the insurance agent, field rep, or other employee who sells insurance.

products and completed operations liability: The liability exposure of the manufacturer whose malfunctioning products may cause injury or property damage or of the contractor whose failed structures or projects may do the same. Coverage of the exposure is a feature of the commercial general liability policy. The insurance does not in any way constitute a guarantee of either the insured's product or work. Contrast with *Premises and operations liability*.

products liability: The liability for bodily injury or property damage incurred by a merchant or manufacturer as a consequence of some defect in the product sold or manufactured or the liability incurred by a contractor after he has completed a job as a result of improperly performed work. The latter described part of products liability is called completed operations.

Professional Insurance Agents (PIA): Trade association of insurance agents.

professional liability: A form of errors and omissions insurance, (sometimes called malpractice coverage for errors alleged against those in the healing and legal professions). Arbitrarily it seems, errors and omissions is the term applied most often to insurance covering liability for mistakes in matters affecting property, for example, coverage for insurance agents E&O, architects E&O – while professional liability is used in reference to coverages such as druggists professional liability, physicians and surgeons professional liability, and lawyers professional liability.

programming: The process of determining how much disability income coverage an individual needs and the sources that will make up this coverage.

promulgate: To develop, file, publish, and put into effect insurance rates or forms.

proof of loss: Following a loss, a formal statement given by an insured to the insurer that includes details of the loss such as the original cost of damaged or destroyed property.

property damage coverage: An insurance policy that pays for damage caused to the property of others, including cars, as a result of a motor vehicle accident. Property damage coverage is often mandatory.

property insurance loss register (PILR): A computerized record of all fire losses over $500 established by the American Insurance Association (AIA). The PILR enables companies to determine undisclosed duplicate insurance coverage and patterns of losses on submitted risks.

pro-rata or proportional reinsurance: A certain portion of every risk is ceded under a proportional agreement. The insurer and reinsurer agree to share a portion of all insurance, premium, and losses in the same amount. The insurer is paid a commission for ceding the risk portion and premium to the reinsurer.

prospect: A potential buyer of an insurance policy or program.

protection and indemnity (P&I) insurance: The nautical equivalent of bodily injury and property damage liability.

protection class: The grading of fire protection, determined by the Grading Schedule of Cities and Towns, for a given area. This designation is used for all fire rating except for dwellings, in which case the Dwelling Class is used.

proximate cause: That event that, in an unbroken sequence, results in direct physical loss under an insurance policy. For example, wind is the proximate cause of loss when a windstorm blows out a window that in turn topples a lit candle that sets fire to a structure and burns it down.

public adjuster: An individual or member of a firm who contracts with private parties to aid with the preparation of loss statements and presentation to insurers. Contrast with *Independent adjuster*.

public liability insurance: Any liability coverage for claims brought against the insured by a third party or member of the public.

public official bond: A performance bond for holders of public office.

punitive damages: An award for damages above and beyond the requirements for compensating third parties for injury or damage. As the word implies the award is meant to punish the offender. Most states and territories permit punitive damages awards to be covered by liability insurance.

purchasing group: An entity that offers insurance to groups of similar businesses with similar exposures to risk.

pure risk: The only consideration is the possibility of loss or no loss, but not making a profit. Contrast with *Speculative risk*.

qualification period: Under the residual disability benefit, the number of days at the start of a disability that the insured must be totally disabled before becoming eligible for residual benefits.

quota share reinsurance: A type of pro-rata or proportional reinsurance agreement under which the insurer and reinsurer agree to share a pre-determined portion of all insurance, premium, and losses. The primary insurer's retention in a quota share agreement is expressed as a percentage of the amount insured.

quote: An estimate of the cost of insurance, based on information supplied to the insurance company by the applicant.

rate filing: Documentation filed by an insurer with the state requesting a change in the existing rates.

rate regulation: The process by which states monitor insurance companies' rate changes, done either through prior approval or open competition models.

ratemaking: The statistical process by which insurers determine risks and pricing for the basic classes of insurance.

rating bureau: A private organization that classifies and promulgates manual rates (or loss costs).

rating: An underwriting decision to approve disability income coverage but at a higher than normal premium due to an increased risk that is usually associated with adverse medical history. An extra premium of anywhere from 15 to 100% or more can be applied.

real property: Land, buildings, and other structures (such as a swimming pool or tool shed).

rebate: In insurance, a portion of an agent's commission returned to a customer as an inducement to place the insurance through the agent. This practice is illegal in all but two states as against public policy.

receiving room coverage: As described under Bailee's Coverage and Bailee, this is a form of coverage to protect the insured against claims alleging loss or damage to property belonging to others but temporarily in custody of the insured. Within associations this may be dry cleaning left in a receiving room or a package left with a doorman.

recipient location: A location that accepts the insured's products or services. One of the four types of dependent properties for which Business Income coverage may be written.

reciprocal exchange: A type of insurance managed by an attorney-in-fact in which members pay premiums and share in losses equally. Membership is required for insurance.

recurrent disability: A policy provision that defines when an injury or illness will be considered continuous if there has been a recovery for a short period (usually six months) and then a recurrence of the same or related cause. A condition considered recurrent will not necessitate new satisfaction of the elimination period.

redlining: Unfair discrimination based not on the risk's characteristics but on its location. The term is commonly associated with an insurer's refusal to consider insuring any home or business within a specific area marked by a line drawn on a map.

rehabilitation: A policy provision under which the insurance company agrees to assist in the expenses associated with a rehabilitation program that the insured enters following disability.

reinsurance: The business of insuring insurance companies. By ceding a portion of its business to a reinsurance company, an insurer spreads the risk of exposure to catastrophic loss.

reinsurance broker: An organization that places (brokers) reinsurance through a reinsurance underwriter – not to be confused with insurance broker.

reinsurance facility: An alternative mechanism to service those insureds that cannot obtain insurance in the voluntary market. Premiums and losses for the business that is ceded to the facility are pooled and all insurers share according to their proportion of the voluntary market.

Reinsurer: See *reinsurance.*

relation of earnings to insurance: A policy provision stipulating that money received from all income sources, including insurance, will not be greater than 100% of the insured's prior earnings.

removal: A provision of the New York Standard Fire Policy in which the insurer agreed to cover the cost of removing covered property from the path of a fire. Presently, property policies express the agreement in terms of preservation of property from imminent danger of damage from any covered peril. Not to be confused with *Debris removal.*

renewability: The policy provision that details the conditions upon which the insurance company agrees to continue to insure the disability income policy. Examples: noncancelable, guaranteed renewable, conditionally renewable.

renewal: The extension of the term of coverage of an expired policy, commonly by replacement with another policy effective on the date of expiration of the previous policy.

rent insurance: A form of business income insurance for a landlord. It protects building owners against loss of income when the building cannot be rented because of damage from any of the insured perils. It provides income while an insured's building is untenantable.

rental value insurance: Refers to protection of either a landlord's rental income or an owner-occupant's economic stake in use of the subject structure. Either interested party can obtain coverage by way of an Insurance Services Office business income form.

renters insurance: Term for insurance for the non-owner occupant of a dwelling or apartment.

replacement cost: The cost of replacing property without deduction for depreciation. See *actual cash value.*

replacement cost appraisal: An appraisal that determines the amount required to replace an existing structure and related personal property.

replacement cost insurance: Covers property–both building and contents–on the basis of full replacement cost without deduction for depreciation on any loss sustained, subject to the terms of the co-insurance clause.

reporting form: A device for insuring values subject to extensive fluctuation that keeps the premium in line with the actual exposure. A maximum limit is set at policy inception and the insured is charged a deposit premium. Actual values are then reported, usually on a monthly basis, and earned premium is figured on the basis of those reports and laid off against the deposit premium.

representation: The acceptance or rejection of an insurance risk and the amount of premium that would be required is determined by information submitted by the person applying for such insurance. Statements which would normally lead the company to decline the acceptance of a risk, or to charge a much higher rate, are material to the risk and are commonly considered "warranties." All other statements such as the insured's address, etc. are referred to as mere "representations" to distinguish them from the more important statements considered to be "warranties." The penalty for false information on material facts or "warranties" may be voiding of the policy.

reservation of rights: An arrangement in which an insurer agrees to proceed with the defense of a case without commitment to provide coverage, in the event that the facts disclosed during the trial reveal that the occurrence is not covered.

reserves or reserved losses: The value of losses that have been estimated and set up for future payment.

residence premises: In homeowners insurance, the dwelling, other structures and grounds, or that part of any other building where the named insured lives.

resident agent: A licensed agent who resides in and is licensed in the state in which business is being written.

residual disability benefit: A policy provision or an optional benefit that promises to pay the insured a portion of the total disability benefit after a return to work based on the percentage of income loss suffered due to the disability. This benefit is usually effective until insured's age 65.

residual markets: Insurance markets established outside the normal insurance marketing channels to cover unusually large or poor risks. Such markets include assigned risk plans, aircraft pools, nuclear pools, and certain government insurance programs.

respite care: Services provided for caregivers to permit temporary periods of relief or rest from caring for a person. These services can be provided by a home health care agency or other state licensed facility and may be reimbursable under a long-term care insurance policy.

respondeat superior: A legal term referring to the fact that, under specific circumstances, an employer (or principal) is legally liable for the actions of his or her employees while in the course of their employment.

retention: Usually used in reinsurance, this is the amount of liability retained by an insurer and not ceded to a reinsurer.

retroactive date: The date that defines the extent of coverage in time under claims-made liability policies. Claims resulting from occurrences prior to the policy's stated retroactive date are excluded.

retrocessionnaire: A reinsurer that contractually accepts a portion of the cedant's reinsurance risk. The transfer is called a retrocession.

retrospective rating: A rating arrangement in which the final premium for insurance coverage is not determined until all claims are closed. The final premium is determined by the insured's actual loss experience during the policy period.

return of premium: In a disability income policy, an optional benefit that provides a refund of a specified percentage of the policy premium at specified dates less any claims that have been paid during the specified time period (i.e., 80% return of premium less claims paid after the policy has been in force for 10 years). In a long-term care policy, an optional benefit that provides a return of all or a portion of premiums paid less claims paid, either on a specified policy anniversary, at policy surrender, or death of the insured.

return to work benefit: A provision under the residual bisability benefit that waives some of the eligibility requirements for residual benefits and bases the claim upon earnings loss only. This provision operates for a short specific period of time, usually 3 to 6 months.

reunderwriting: The process by which the company reevaluates policyholders and, as necessary, imposes surcharges, deductibles or nonrenewal in cases where the policyholder's claims history or other experience presents a consistent pattern that creates an undue liability risk.

rider: Another term for an endorsement attached to a policy that modifies the coverage.

riot: One of the extended coverage perils, related to, but broader than, civil commotion.

risk: Uncertainty concerning loss. Sometimes also used to refer to a piece of business or a submission to an insurer.

Risk and Insurance Management Society, Inc. (RIMS): Trade association of risk managers and insurance buyers.

risk management: The process of handling pure risk by way of reduction, elimination, or transfer of risk, with the latter commonly achieved through insurance.

risk manager: The individual in an organization responsible for evaluation of the organizations' exposures and controlling those exposures through such means as avoidance or transference, as to an insurance company.

risk purchasing group (RPG): A group of similarly situated persons or entities that are permitted under federal law to organize across state lines to buy insurance. The carrier that sells insurance to the group must be licensed in at least one state but need not be licensed in every state where a member of the group resides.

risk retention group (RRG): An insurance company chartered under the laws of a state or other U.S. jurisdiction, composed of members whose business activities are similar, and controlled by its members.

risk-based capital: The need for insurance companies to be capitalized according to the inherent riskiness of the type of insurance they sell. Higher-risk types of insurance, liability as opposed to property business, generally necessitate higher levels of capital.

robbery: The felonious taking, either by force or by fear of force, of the personal property of another, commonly known as a "hold-up."

safe driver plan: Merit rating of automobile insurance. In most states, drivers are charged with points for traffic violations and auto accidents. These points translate to surcharges on the drivers' insurance rates.

salary continuation plan: A program, also called a Section 105 plan, under which the employer makes deductible wage payments, in part or in full, to an individual unable to work due to illness or injury.

salvage: When an insurer makes a payment for lost or damaged property, the insurer is entitled to the salvage of that property.

schedule: List of items on a policy declaration, sometimes also showing descriptions and values.

schedule rating: A debit and credit plan that recognizes variations in the hazard-causing features of an individual risk.

scheduled property floater: An inland marine form of policy specifically insuring various individual items. Articles of unusual value, provided they are movable, may normally be written this way and insured against many hazards, often against "all risks."

seasonal risk: A risk that is present only during certain parts of the year. For example seasonal dwellings such as cottages used for vacations.

self-insurance: An insurance-like strategy for handling one's own exposures to loss supported by the financial wherewithal to meet expected losses. Not to be confused with a decision to forego insurance.

self-insured retention (SIR): That portion of pure risk an insured undertakes to handle on his or her own. A deductible is a form of self-insured retention.

selling price clause: Applicable to the value of goods that have been damaged or destroyed by an insured peril. This clause insures the profit that would have been earned if the goods had been sold. It sets the insurable value of the property that has been sold, but not delivered, at the amount at which it was sold, less any charges not incurred.

severability: A provision that insurance applies separately to each insured under the policy.

sewer back-up coverage: An optional part of homeowners insurance that covers damage done by sewer back-up.

shock loss: Name given to any large loss that impacts an otherwise profitable book of business.

short tail: Additional coverage that may be purchased under a claims-made policy that responds to losses that may have occurred during a policy period, but are not reported until after the end of the policy period. Usually available for no longer than a year.

short-term disability: Usually associated with group insurance, this program pays a monthly benefit for total disability after a minimum elimination period for up to 13, 26, 39, or 52 weeks.

sickness: A policy provision defined as illness or disease that first makes itself known to the insured following the policy effective date. Sickness covers both physical and mental illness unless otherwise specified.

SIG: A self-insured group. An SIG is a group of risks, usually sharing common characteristics or exposures, that join together in order to generate enough premium volume to justify self-insuring themselves. Members of an SIG often are jointly and severally liable for the losses of one another.

significant earnings loss: A provision under the residual disability benefit that promises the full total disability benefit if the insured is back to work and suffers a substantial loss of income, usually 75 to 80%.

sine qua non rule: A legal rule stating that a person's conduct cannot be held to be the cause of a loss if the loss would have occurred anyway.

single interest policy: A policy that insures the interest of only one party in property where there are a number of parties having an insurable interest.

sinkhole peril: Risk of loss by collapse of a sinkhole. This is now covered as a basic cause of loss in commercial property policies.

skilled care: A professional type of nursing assistance performed by trained medical personnel under the supervision of a physician or other qualified medical personnel. It is the only type of care eligible for reimbursement in a skilled nursing facility under Medicare.

slander: The oral utterance or spreading of falsehood harmful to another's reputation. Libel is written; slander is spoken.

slip: At Lloyd's of London, a document that identifies which syndicates are participating on a risk and for what percentage.

smoke damage: An *extended coverage* peril.

social security offset rider: An optional benefit that coordinates benefits with any benefits received through Social Security disability (and, often, other public programs) to avoid either underinsurance or overinsurance.

social security: A federal program that provides benefits to all working Americans in the form of disability, retirement, or survivor benefits. Disability is strictly and narrowly defined and benefits begin in the sixth month of a disability that has an expectation of lasting at least 12 months or will result in the individual's death.

Society of Chartered Property & Casualty Underwriters: Professional society of those having attained the CPCU designation. See *CPCU*.

soft market: A term given to a condition in which insurance is relatively inexpensive and easy to obtain.

solicitor: An employee of an insurance agent or agency who is empowered to sell insurance on behalf of a licensed agent, generally using only those insurers that the agency represents. A solicitor usually does not have binding authority, and the business that is generated by a solicitor usually is owned by the agent, not the solicitor.

solvency: Insurers must have sufficient assets (capital, surplus, reserves) in order to satisfy statutory financial requirements (investments, annual reports, examinations) and to meet liabilities.

special agent: An insurer's representative in a territory. He or she serves as a liaison between the insurer and the agent. The special agent is responsible for the volume and quality of the business written in that territory. Some states require a special license of special agents.

special form: In contrast to the named perils forms in property insurance, those forms that list specific perils for coverage, the special form contract covers simply risk of direct physical loss, relying on exclusions to limit and define the protection intended. See *open perils*.

special risk insurance: Coverage for risks or hazards of a special or unusual nature.

specific excess reinsurance: Another term for per occurrence/per loss excess reinsurance.

specific insurance: An insurance policy that covers only property specifically described in the policy, as opposed to blanket insurance which usually covers all property at specified locations.

specific rate: A rate applying to an individual piece of property.

specimen policy forms: Are often requested when non-standard coverage forms are being used. The specimen form may be reviewed to determine the actual policy provisions before coverage is bound.

speculative risk: Risk that entails a chance of gain as well as a chance of loss. Contrast with *Pure risk*.

split limits: As in auto insurance, where rather than one liability amount applying on a per-accident basis, separate amounts apply to bodily injury and property damage liability.

spread of risk: The selling of insurance in multiple areas to multiple policyholders to minimize the danger that all policyholders will have losses at the same time. Companies are more likely to insure perils that offer a good spread of risk. Flood insurance is an example of a poor spread of risk because the people most likely to buy it are the people close to rivers and other bodies of water that flood. (See *adverse selection*).

sprinkler leakage insurance: Insurance that covers damage due to the accidental discharge from an automatic sprinkler system.

sprinklered risk: Property protected against fire by a system of overhead pipes with regularly spaced heads designed to melt at the heat of a fire, thus releasing water for extinguishment.

SR-22: A form from the DMV that shows a driver holds auto insurance. Many states require it for high-risk drivers.

stacking of limits: The application of the limits of one or more insurance policies to a claim or loss.

staff model HMO: A type of HMO that employs providers directly and those providers see members in the HMO's own facilities. A form of a closed panel HMO.

standard fire policy: See *New York standard fire policy*.

standby assistance: An individual is considered unable to perform an activity of daily living if someone must be in close proximity to him to help when he is attempting to perform the activity.

state fund: A fund set up by a state government to provide a specific line or lines of insurance, such as Workers Compensation.

state insurance department: An administrative agency that licenses insurers to do business in that state and implements state insurance laws and supervises (within the scope of these laws) the activities of insurers operating within the state

state of domicile: The state in which the company is incorporated or chartered. The company is also licensed (admitted) under the state's insurance statutes for those lines of business for which it qualifies.

stated amount: Amends the valuation clause on a policy to include an amount that is stated as the value of the item(s) being insured. Usually, these policies pay the lesser of the ACV of the damaged property, the cost of repairing or replacing the property, or the stated amount.

statement of values: The information required when a single rate is to cover more than one item or building. To determine a correct average, the rating bureau requires the policyholder to give the value of each separate risk and its contents.

statutory accounting principles (SAP): Statutorily mandated accounting principles and practices that must be followed when an insurance company submits its annual financial statement to the department of insurance. The principal objective of statutory accounting is to provide a framework for a conservative measurement of an insurer's surplus. In contrast to Generally Accepted Accounting Principles (GAAP), which are followed by most other businesses. See *GAAP accounting*.

step-rate: A method of premium payment under which the insured pays for the disability income policy with a low initial price that increases after a set number of years (usually five) to a higher, level premium.

stock: Merchandise held in storage or for sale, raw materials, and in-process or finished goods, including supplies used in their packing or shipping.

stock insurance company: An insurance company owned by its stockholders who share in profits through earnings distributions and increases in stock value.

stop loss: A provision in an insurance policy that cuts off an insurer's losses at a given point. In effect, a stop loss agreement guarantees the loss ratio of the insurer.

stopgap endorsement: Provides employer liability coverage for work-related injury arising out of incidental operations or exposure in the states that have monopolistic state funds.

strict liability: Liability ascribed to a manufacturer or seller of a defective or dangerous product regardless of any fault or negligence.

subacute care: Assistance provided by nursing homes for health services such as stroke rehabilitation and cardiac care for post-surgery that offers a lower cost alternative to hospital treatment of the same kind.

subrogation: The right of one party who has paid for the loss of a second party to obtain recompense from the third party who is responsible for the loss. For example, an insurance company becomes subrogated to the rights of its insured to the extent of the insurer's payment for collision damage caused by the negligence of the other driver.

subsidence: A form of earth movement, excluded in most property policies.

substandard risk: A risk falling outside normal underwriting standards. If written at all, it is usually with a substantial premium surcharge.

substitute salary expense: An optional benefit available under the Business Overhead Expense policy, it reimburses the insured for expenses incurred in paying a replacement during the insured's disability.

summons: A legal document demanding the presence of the named individual at a court hearing.

superfund: The better-known name for the Comprehensive Environmental Response, Compensation, and Liability Act (CERCLA) passed by Congress in 1980. Under this law, parties found responsible for polluting a site must clean up the contamination or reimburse the EPA for doing so. Liability is strict, retroactive, joint and several.

superintendent of insurance: In some states the Commissioner of Insurance is known as the Superintendent.

supplemental extended reporting period: An optional reporting period that allows coverage for liability claims made after the policy period.

supplemental health statement: A form that is a direct communication from the underwriter to the proposed insured that asks for more details about a specified medical condition(s).

supplemental monthly benefit: This part of the programming puzzle in calculating disability income coverage for the insured is a non-offset payment of additional monthly benefits for the insured with the same elimination period as the base policy and a short benefit period of six to twelve months. Also called additional monthly benefit, among other terms.

supply bonds: Bonds that guarantee performance of a contract to furnish supplies or materials. In the event of a default by the supplier, the surety indemnifies the purchaser of the supplies against the resulting loss.

Surety Association of America (SAA): A voluntary, non-profit, unincorporated association that is licensed as a rating or advisory organization for surety and fidelity insurance in all states, D.C., and Puerto Rico. The SAA handles statistical information, filings, publications, and surety and fidelity bonds.

surety bond: A three-party agreement guaranteeing that a principal will carry out the contractual obligations the principal has agreed to perform or, alternatively, to compensate the other parties to the contract for losses resulting from the principal's failure to perform. Under many surety bonds, the principal is a contractor.

surface water: Commonly known as water on the surface of the ground usually created by rain or snow that is of a casual or vagrant character, following no definite course and having no substantial or permanent existence. Some insurance policies may include surface water as a covered peril but exclude flood when defined as the overflowing of water from its natural boundaries, such as a lake or river.

surplus: The amount by which an insurer's assets exceed its liabilities.

surplus lines: See *excess & surplus lines market.*

surplus share reinsurance: A type of pro-rata or proportional reinsurance agreement under which the insurer and reinsurer agree to share a pre-determined portion of all insurance, premium, and losses. The primary insurer's retention in a surplus share agreement is stated as a dollar amount of the amount insured.

survey: In cargo insurance, an examination of damaged property to determine the cause, extent and value. In hull insurance, an inspection of the ship to help determine its insurability or, after a loss, the cause and extent of damage.

swing beds: Hospital beds that may be designated as either acute care or skilled nursing, changing from one to the other to continue care to the individual without having to switch rooms or facilities.

syndicate: An association of insurers that work together to insure an especially large or hazardous risk. Also see *pool*.

tail coverage: Coverage for claims made after a claims-made liability policy has terminated; the extended reporting or discovery period. See *nose coverage*.

tax-qualified plans: These are long-term care insurance policies that meet the definition required by HIPAA and therefore are eligible for favorable tax treatment.

temporary worker: An employee hired on a short term, often seasonal, basis.

tenancy in common: The form of property ownership in which each owner owns an undivided interest in real property. In a condominium, all owners have tenancy in common interest in common areas.

tenant's policy: A package policy specially designed to meet the normal insurance requirements of a private tenant covering personal belongings and liabilities.

territorial rating: A method of classifying risks by geographic location to set a fair price for coverage. The location of the insured may have a considerable impact on the cost of losses. The chance of an accident or theft is much higher in an urban area than in a rural one, for example.

theft: Any act of stealing. Theft includes larceny, burglary and robbery.

third party: An outsider; a business or personal invitee or a party with absolutely no connection to an insured who may become a claimant under a form of public liability coverage because of injury or property damage alleged to have been caused by the negligence of the insured.

threshold level: The point at which an injured person may bring tort action under a modified no-fault auto plan. Many no-fault plans allow only tort action for pain and suffering after medical bills exceed some figure, like $1,000, or if disfigurement or death occurs.

tight market: See *hard market*.

time element coverage: Insurance in which the element of time has heavy bearing on the extent of loss. Business income insurance covers loss of income for the unknown duration of the insured's business interruption.

title insurance: Insurance that indemnifies the owner of real estate in the event that someone challenges his or her ownership of property, due to the discovery faults in the title.

tort: A wrong for which a civil (as opposed to criminal) action can be brought. Many tort claims arise from negligence.

total disability: Often the key policy provision in the disability income policy, this feature defines the eligibility requirements necessary for an individual to qualify for full monthly benefits. Usually, an inability to perform work is the major requirement in the definition.

total loss: A loss of sufficient size so that it can be said there is nothing left of value. The complete destruction of the property. The term is also used to mean a loss requiring the maximum amount a policy will pay.

TPA: A third party administrator. A TPA is a contractor who adjusts and administers insurance claims.

transfer of risk: A basic underlying principle of insurance, whereby the risk of financial loss is transferred from one party to another.

transit coverage: Coverage of the insured's property while in transit over land from one location to another. Property insurance policies typically provide coverage only at locations identified in the policy.

transplant donor benefit: A policy provision that considers an insured to be disabled under the sickness provision if donating a body organ.

treatment of injuries: A policy provision or an optional benefit, it pays for expenses incurred during treatment by a physician of an injury, and is paid in lieu of any other policy benefits.

treaty reinsurance: An agreement in which the ceding company agrees in advance to cede certain classes of business or types of insurance to a reinsurance company. The reinsurer agrees to accept all risks or losses that fall within the terms of the agreement.

trend: A factor applied to indemnity (medical) loss ratio to adjust for future inflation relative to exposure.

trial applicaiton: A documented request from an individual to an underwriter to review an extensive and/or serious medical history for the purposes of making a conditional offer under which disability income coverage may be written.

triple trigger: This is the designation for the three ways to be eligible for benefits under a long-term care insurance policy including assistance with activities of daily living, cognitive impairment, or medical necessity. This definition is not available in tax-qualified plans.

twisting: The practice of inducing by misrepresentation, or inaccurate or incomplete comparison, a policyholder in one company to lapse, forfeit, or surrender his insurance for the purpose of taking out a policy in another company.

umbrella liability: A liability contract with high limits covering over top of primary liability coverages and, subject to a self-insured retention (deductible), covering exposures otherwise uninsured.

unallocated loss adjustment expenses (ULAE): Claims expenses of a general nature not directly attributable to specific claims. They include the salaries of claims personnel and the other costs of maintaining a claims department.

underinsured motorists coverage: Coverage for the insured and passengers whenever the at-fault driver in an accident has auto liability insurance with lesser limits than the insured's. This coverage lies atop uninsured motorists coverage or atop the at-fault driver's low limit automobile liability insurance and provides the insured and passengers with protection equal (usually) to the insured's own automobile liability cover.

underlying insurance policy: The policy providing initial coverage for a claim until its limit of liability is reached and an umbrella or excess policy's coverage is triggered.

underlying limits: The limits of liability of the policy(ies) underlying an umbrella or excess policy.

underwriter: One who researches and then accepts, rejects, or limits prospective risks for an insurance company.

Underwriters Laboratories, Inc. (UL): Originally begun as a cooperative of western fire insurers to test materials, the UL is now an independent organization testing virtually every fabricated device and material. Items are permitted to bear the UL seal of approval only after they have passed stringent testing for safety.

underwriting income: The insurer's profit on the insurance sale after all expenses and losses have been paid. When premiums are not sufficient to cover claims and expenses, the result is an underwriting loss. Underwriting losses are typically offset by investment income.

underwriting: The confidential process of reviewing and evaluating personal, financial and medical data regarding an individual for the purpose of approving or disapproving the applicant for disability income coverage.

unearned income: Money that will be available to an individual whether or not he is disabled, it affects the amount of disability coverage that may be purchased based on earned income.

unearned premium: That portion of an insurance premium that would have to be returned to the insured if the policy were canceled.

unearned premium reserve: A reserve equal to an amount of net premium written but not yet earned.

unilateral contract: A contract such as an insurance policy in which only one party to the contract, the insurer, makes any enforceable promise. The insured does not make a promise but pays a premium, which constitutes his part of the consideration.

uninsurable risk: An uninsurable risk is one that is literally uninsurable because loss is certain rather than possible.

uninsured motorists coverage: Coverage for the insured and passengers whenever the at-fault driver in an accident has no auto liability insurance. Coverage is usually to the extent of limits required by state auto financial responsibility laws.

unit owners excess coverage: This type of insurance expands a condo unit-owner's insurance coverage to include damage or loss to alterations, fixtures, and improvements within individual units owned by the unit owner, caused by the insured perils. This includes damage to air conditioners, clothes washers, clothes dryers, cooking ovens, cooking ranges, dishwashers, floor coverings, countertops, kitchen cabinets, refrigerators, and freezers. This coverage applies only as excess insurance over any other valid and collectible insurance that would apply in the absence of this policy.

unlimited liability: requirement that the owner or owners assume full responsibility for all losses or debts of a business.

unoccupied: Where the premises contain contents but no human beings, such persons being temporarily away from the premises, on vacation for example, the premises are said to be unoccupied. This is distinguishable from Vacant in that in vacancy, the contents have been moved out leaving nothing but the building.

unprotected: A property located in an area not regularly serviced by a fire department.

unsatisfied judgment fund (UJF): In some states a person who is injured in an automobile accident and who cannot collect from the person responsible, may collect from a special fund.

utilization: How much and how often patients use medical services that are covered benefits. This is carefully monitored in a managed care plan for appropriateness, cost and treatment effectiveness.

utmost good faith: A basic principle of insurance. Mutual trust in negotiating an insurance contract. The insured and the broker must disclose and truly represent every material circumstance to the underwriter before acceptance of the risk. A breach of good faith entitles the underwriter to avoid the contract.

vacant property: Once defined as devoid of occupants or contents, a stricter definition is being applied as more and more communities find older buildings of three and four stories that are only one quarter occupied. Property policies impose limitations on coverage of vacant buildings so the (changing) definition of vacant property is quite important.

valuable papers coverage: Provides all risk coverage on valuable papers, such as: written, printed, or otherwise inscribed documents and records, including books, maps, films, drawings, abstracts, deeds, mortgages, and manuscripts. It covers the cost of research to reconstruct damaged records, as well as the cost of new paper and transcription.

valuation: To estimate the value of a piece of property usually by considering its replacement cost or its actual cash value. Factored into the estimate is any depreciation or wear & tear.

value reporting form: Commercial form designed for businesses that have fluctuating merchandise values during the year. As values are reported (monthly, quarterly or annually) the amount of insurance is adjusted. Reporting forms help eliminate problems of over-insurance and under-insurance, as well as the need to continually endorse a policy.

valued policy laws: Laws existing in some states that apply primarily to buildings. The laws differ but, in general, they state that in case of a total loss the amount of insurance is the agreed amount of loss.

valued policy: See *agreed amount clause*.

vandalism and malicious mischief: Once treated as a separate peril to be added to a property policy or not, current property forms routinely include the protection.

verbal threshold: Term in no-fault auto insurance, applicable in some states, that says that victims are allowed to sue in tort only if their injuries meet certain verbal descriptions of the types of injuries that render one eligible to recover for pain and suffering.

vested commissions: Commissions on renewal business that are paid to the agent whether or not he or she still works for the insurance company with which the business is placed.

viatical settlements: The purchase, on a reduced basis, of a life insurance policy owned by a terminally ill person.

vicarious liability: The condition arising where one person is responsible for the actions of another, as a parent is often held responsible for the vandalism damage a minor child does to a school.

waiver form: Utilized in the solicitation of disability income insurance, an individual signs this paper documenting that coverage was proposed but not accepted by the insured.

waiver of premium: A policy provision in a disability income or long-term care policy that specifies the exemption of the insured from making premium payments following a specified number of days of disability or a specified period of time during which the insured is receiving long-term care policy benefits, until the insured recovers.

waiver of subrogation: An insurer has the right of subrogation; however, it may waive that right through this method.

war risk: Special coverage on cargo in overseas ships against the risk of being confiscated by a government in wartime. It is excluded from standard ocean marine insurance and can be purchased separately. It often excludes cargo awaiting shipment on a wharf or on ships after 15 days of arrival in port.

wear and tear exclusion: A common heading for an all risks exclusion relating to a group of events that do not represent risk at all. Property will become worn out and torn; it will rust, settle, become rotted, infested, marred, or scratched. It is easy to distinguish however between the marring that occurs over time (excluded) and marring that occurs when a concrete block is dropped onto a fine wooden table.

weather insurance: A type of business interruption insurance that compensates for financial losses caused by adverse weather conditions.

whole dollar premium: The practice of many insurers to round premiums to the nearest dollar, rather than carrying them out to the nearest cent. An amount of 51 cents or more is usually rounded up to the next dollar, and any cents amount less than that is dropped.

workers compensation: A system administered by each individual state that provides benefits if a worker is hurt or contracts an illness on the job.

workers compensation insurance: Coverage that conforms to the workers compensation laws of the states in which it written. See also *employers liability insurance*.

workers compensation self-insurers bond: Workers Compensation laws, at the state and federal level, require employers to compensate employees injured on the job. An employer may comply with these laws by purchasing insurance or self insuring by posting a workers' compensation bond to guarantee payment of benefits to employees. This is a hazardous class of commercial surety bond because of its long-tail exposure and potential cumulative liability.

written premiums: The entire amount in premiums due in a year for all policies issued by an insurance company.

wrongful acts: This is the basic covered injury or damage in a D&O policy. Such acts include unintentional negligent acts, omissions or breaches of duty, or errors relating to the operation of the community association. What is a wrongful act varies from policy to policy. Some D&O policies add advertising injury and personal injury to wrongful act coverage.

XCU: Short for explosion, collapse, and underground, this acronym is used to denote that certain construction projects carry this hazard.

zone system: Developed by the NAIC for the triennial examination of insurers. Under the system, teams of examiners are formed from the staffs of several states in each of the geographical zones. The results of their examinations are then accepted by all states in which an insurer is licensed, without the necessity of each state having to conduct its own examinations.

END OF CHAPTER REVIEW

Chapter 1:
General Principles of
Risk and Insurance

1. False
2. True
3. False
4. False
5. False
6. True

Chapter 2:
Legal Aspects of Insurance
and Risk Management

1. False
2. False
3. False
4. True
5. True
6. True
7. False
8. False

Chapter 3:
Insurance Policy Selection

1. True
2. False
3. False
4. True
5. True
6. False
7. False
8. True
9. False

Chapter 4:
Insurance Company Selection

1. False
2. False
3. False
4. True
5. True
6. False

7. False
8. True
9. True
10. True
11. True
12. False

Chapter 5:
Overview of Property
Insurance

1. False
2. False
3. True
4. True
5. False

Chapter 6:
Commercial Property
Insurance

1. False
2. True
3. False
4. False
5. True
6. False
7. False
8. True
9. True
10. False

Chapter 7:
Automobile and Recreational
Vehicle Insurance

1. False
2. False
3. True
4. True
5. False
6. True
7. False
8. True
9. False

Chapter 8:
Business and Business
Activity Insurance

1. True
2. False
3. False
4. True
5. False
6. True
7. True
8. False

Chapter 9:
Personal Property Insurance

1. True
2. False
3. True
4. False
5. True
6. True
7. False
8. True
9. False
10. True

Chapter 10:
Personal Umbrella Coverage

1. True
2. False
3. True
4. True
5. True
6. False
7. True
8. True

Chapter 11:
Overview of Business Liability

1. False
2. True
3. True
4. False
5. True
6. False
7. True
8. True
9. True

Chapter 12:
Professional Liability Insurance

1. True
2. False
3. True
4. True
5. True
6. True
7. False
8. False
9. False

Chapter 13:
Directors and Officers Liability Insurance

1. False
2. False
3. False
4. True
5. True
6. True
7. False
8. False
9. True
10. True

Chapter 14:
Product/Completed Operations Liability Insurance

1. False
2. True
3. True
4. False
5. True
6. False
7. False
8. True

Chapter 15:
Overview of Health-Related Insurance

1. True
2. True
3. False
4. True
5. True
6. False
7. True
8. True

Chapter 16:
Types of Individual Health Insurance Coverage

1. True
2. False
3. True
4. False
5. True
6. True
7. False
8. True
9. False
10. False

Chapter 17:
Taxation of Individual Health Insurance Coverage

1. True
2. True
3. False
4. False
5. False
6. True
7. True
8. True
9. True
10. True

Chapter 18:
Standard Provisions of Individual Disability Income Insurance

1. True
2. False
3. False
4. True
5. True
6. False
7. False
8. True
9. True
10. True

Chapter 19:
Taxation of Individual Disability Income Insurance

1. False
2. True
3. True
4. False

5. True
6. True
7. True
8. False
9. True
10. True

Chapter 20:
Long-Term Care Policy Coverage and Selection

1. True
2. False
3. True
4. True
5. True
6. True
7. True
8. True
9. False
10. True

Chapter 21:
Standard Provisions of Long-Term Care Insurance

1. False
2. True
3. True
4. False
5. True
6. True
7. False
8. True
9. True
10. True

Chapter 22:
Taxation of Long-Term Care Insurance

1. True
2. True
3. False
4. False
5. True
6. True
7. True
8. True
9. False
10. True

INDEX

Please send me the following : *(please indicate quantity)*

The Tools & Techniques of Life Insurance Planning _____Book (#2700003) $74.95
The Tools & Techniques of Estate Planning _____Book (#2850013) $74.95
The Tools & Techniques of Practice Management _____Book (#2690000) $74.95
The Tools & Techniques of Investment Planning _____Book (#2730000) $74.95
The Tools & Techniques of Income Tax Planning _____Book (#2740000) $74.95
The Tools & Techniques of Employee Benefit and Retirement Planning _____Book (#2710008) $52.95
The Tools & Techniques of Financial Planning _____Book (#2770007) $74.95
The Tools & Techniques of Charitable Planning _____Book (#2500000) $52.95
The Tools & Techniques Online Library _____1 Year Subscription(TTLIB) $195.00

❑ Check enclosed*   Charge My ❑AMEX ❑MC ❑VISA (check one) ❑Bill me

*Make check payable to The National Underwriter Company. Please include the appropriate shipping & handling and any applicable sales tax.

**For Visa/MC, the three-digit CVV# is usually printed on the back of the card. For American Express, the four-digit CVV# is usually on the front of the card.

Card #_____ CVV#**_____ Exp. Date _____
Signature_____
Name_____Title_____
Company_____
Address_____
City_____State_____Zip+4_____
Business Phone (_____)_____
E-mail _____

BB

The **National Underwriter** Company
A Unit of Highline Media LLC

Please send me the following : *(please indicate quantity)*

The Tools & Techniques of Life Insurance Planning _____Book (#2700003) $74.95
The Tools & Techniques of Estate Planning _____Book (#2850013) $74.95
The Tools & Techniques of Practice Management _____Book (#2690000) $74.95
The Tools & Techniques of Investment Planning _____Book (#2730000) $74.95
The Tools & Techniques of Income Tax Planning _____Book (#2740000) $74.95
The Tools & Techniques of Employee Benefit and Retirement Planning _____Book (#2710008) $52.95
The Tools & Techniques of Financial Planning _____Book (#2770007) $74.95
The Tools & Techniques of Charitable Planning _____Book (#2500000) $52.95
The Tools & Techniques Online Library _____1 Year Subscription(TTLIB) $195.00

❑ Check enclosed*   Charge My ❑AMEX ❑MC ❑VISA (check one) ❑Bill me

*Make check payable to The National Underwriter Company. Please include the appropriate shipping & handling and any applicable sales tax.

**For Visa/MC, the three-digit CVV# is usually printed on the back of the card. For American Express, the four-digit CVV# is usually on the front of the card.

Card #_____ CVV#**_____ Exp. Date _____
Signature_____
Name_____Title_____
Company_____
Address_____
City_____State_____Zip+4_____
Business Phone (_____)_____
E-mail _____

BB

The **National Underwriter** Company
A Unit of Highline Media LLC

Order the *Tools & Techniques Series* and other titles by The National Underwriter Company.

Save 5% Instantly when you order online at www.**NationalUnderwriterStore**.com. **Include code BB at checkout.**

The **National Underwriter** Company
A Unit of Highline Media LLC

ORDERS DEPARTMENT
THE NATIONAL UNDERWRITER COMPANY
PO BOX 14448
CINCINNATI OH 45250-9786

ORDERS DEPARTMENT
THE NATIONAL UNDERWRITER COMPANY
PO BOX 14448
CINCINNATI OH 45250-9786